INCA TRAILS

Journey Through The Bolivian and Peruvian Andes

by

Martin Li

authorHOUSE®

To Gabriela
Many thanks for all your help with the book.
Best wishes!

AuthorHouse™ UK Ltd.
500 Avebury Boulevard
Central Milton Keynes, MK9 2BE
www.authorhouse.co.uk
Phone: 08001974150

First published by AuthorHouse 11/20/2007

ISBN: 978-1-4343-1710-0 (sc)

Printed in the United States of America
Bloomington, Indiana

This book is printed on acid-free paper.

INCA TRAILS

MARTIN LI studied physics at Cambridge. A keen skier, horserider and trekker, he has a passion for exploring the adventure and culture of the world's great mountain regions, especially the Himalayas, Alps and, above all, the Andean countries of South America. In 2000, he spent four months writing for *The Bolivian Times* in La Paz, covering diverse subjects ranging from privatisation and the Bolivian stockmarket to cock fighting.

Martin won the 2005 Wilderness Award for this expedition, and has subsequently given several lectures on the journey. More lightheartedly, he was a member of the triumphant "Explorers" team which won the "Test the Nation – Know Your Planet" show broadcast on BBC1 in May 2006.

Martin's other adventures have included riding a horse across the Namib Desert, trekking to Bhutan's most sacred summit, close encounters with black bears in Alaska and rafting the thundering rapids of Panama's Rio Chiriqui. Martin is the author of *Adventure Guide to Scotland* and contributed to *V!VA List Latin America*. He lives in London and is a Fellow of the Royal Geographical Society.

CONTENTS

ACKNOWLEDGEMENTS

The journey, not to mention this book, would not have been possible without the generous and enthusiastic help and support of a great many people.

I would like to thank Journey Latin America and Wilderness Lectures, our generous main sponsors. I am also indebted to Wilderness Lectures for allowing me to share my many unforgettable memories of this expedition through an illustrated lecture. Many thanks also go to Diageo for the crate of Talisker that helped ease the chill of many an Andean night, and helped break the ice with many local people during the journey.

I would like to thank my lovely La Paz friends Alix Shand, Abdul Aspiazu and Judith Hoffmann for their wonderful company and generosity, and for giving me so much encouragement and valuable background information.

José Camarlinghi of Andean Summits in La Paz, Louis Demers of the Residencial Sorata and Juan Carlos Gómez, Director of ANMIN Apolobamba, provided invaluable help with logistics and route planning through Bolivia, as did John Leivers in planning the journey through Vilcabamba.

I am indebted to Ambassador Gonzalo Montenegro of the Embassy of Bolivia in London and Ambassador Luis Solari Tudela of the Embassy of Peru in London for providing introductions that smoothed several administrative situations during the journey.

I was blessed to be able to stay in two fabulous hotels that resonate intensely with the spirit of the Incas: the Posada del Inca on the Island of the Sun in Lake Titicaca and the Hotel Monasterio in Cuzco. For this, I have to thank Darius Morgan of Crillon Tours in La Paz and Orient-Express Hotels.

Dr. Gabriela Ramos of Cambridge University provided much invaluable assistance in my efforts to understand what really happened to the Incas. Without her help, it would have been almost impossible for me to unravel fact from the many distorted accounts of the rise and fall of the Inca empire.

PREFACE

I have long been fascinated by the incomparable landscapes, poignant history and captivating cultures of South America, in particular the Andes and Altiplano regions.

This expedition evolved from a personal quest to undertake an "ultimate journey" through the Andes and Altiplano – in no small part to try to purge a South American travel craving that was stubbornly showing no signs of subsiding. For a journey to have any hope of doing this, it needed to have meaning, and be able to encapsulate – without stage management – the many wondrous highlights of the region.

Whilst scouring for possible routes, I learned that Lake Titicaca was the birthplace of the Incas. I read about the Spanish Conquest of Peru and learned how the surviving Incas made their last stand against the Conquistadores in the wilds of Vilcabamba. Although the Inca empire stretched across vast thousands of kilometres, its birthplace and the scene of its demise lay within the span of a single, substantial expedition. When I discovered that the Apolobamba mountains – a region I had long wanted to explore – lay between Lake Titicaca and Vilcabamba, the expedition route virtually determined itself.

The resulting journey traces the history of one of the most captivating and enduring of all ancient empires. Moreover, it bursts with evocative destinations and indelible sights and sounds, many instantly recognisable even to people who have never visited South America. Who could fail to be stirred by Machu Picchu perched incredibly atop a precipitous Andean peak at the edge of dense rainforest, the azure-coloured serenity of Lake Titicaca, the unexplored Apolobamba and Vilcabamba mountains, condors soaring over lonely Andean peaks, and bowler-hatted cholita women clad in brightly coloured textiles, with haunting panpipe music and the chatter of Quechua for background?

This culturally packed journey also offered glimpses into the lives of remote communities descended from the Incas, who for centuries have preserved ancient lifestyles away from outside influence. Undertaking as much of the expedition as practicable riding mules and horses let us cover the necessary distances without relying on motorised transport and, more importantly, allowed the greatest possible interaction with indigenous people.

In setting out the history of the Incas and the expedition route, I have not undertaken any original research. Instead, I have relied on the accounts of acknowledged Inca authorities, including Hemming and D'Altroy, whose scholarship makes great reading for anyone similarly afflicted with South American fervour.

The expedition succeeded to an extent in controlling my South American habit. However, as with all good addictions, the longing to explore South America hasn't gone away entirely – it probably never will.

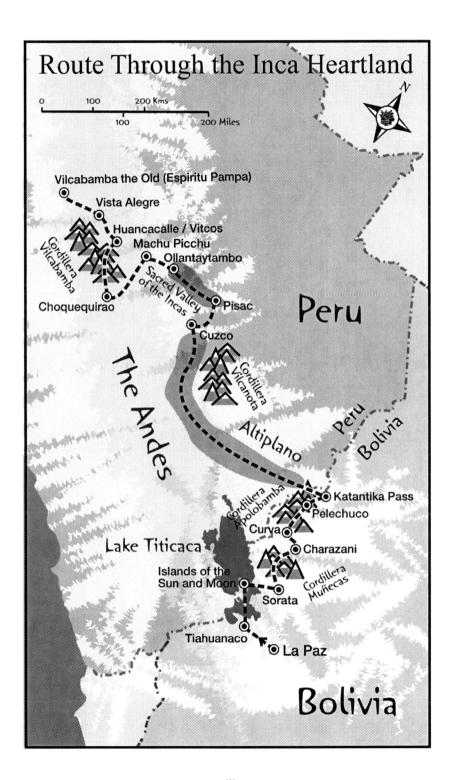

Route Through the Inca Heartland

0   100   200 Kms
100   200 Miles

N

Vilcabamba the Old (Espiritu Pampa)

Vista Alegre

Cordillera Vilcabamba

Huancacalle / Vitcos

Machu Picchu

Ollantaytambo

Sacred Valley of the Incas

Choquequirao

Pisac

Peru

Cuzco

The Andes

Cordillera Vilcanota

Altiplano

Peru

Bolivia

Katantika Pass

Cordillera Apolobamba

Pelechuco

Curva

Charazani

Lake Titicaca

Islands of the Sun and Moon

Cordillera Muñecas

Sorata

Tiahuanaco

La Paz

Bolivia

CHAPTER ONE

LA PAZ

I have been told that playing dead is worth trying as a last resort when faced with a rampaging grizzly bear desperate for a meal. As I collapsed on my bed perfectly still, I wondered if the same tactic might also deter a rampaging Bolivian desperate for a party. It didn't. And to make matters worse, I crushed my last two cigarettes in the charade.

Bolivians don't trifle with social drinking. Not for them a couple of beers or quiet bottle of wine with a meal. In fact, many of my Bolivian friends decline to take a drink with me over dinner, preferring non-alcoholic drinks instead. However, when they drink, they drink by the crate load. And they don't like drinking alone!

I had scarcely walked through the door and hadn't even been able to take off my coat when Doña Celia, my landlady's mother and matriarch of the house, grabbed me firmly by the arm and decisively thrust a large tumbler into my hand. Through glazed eyes, she scanned the room for the nearest of several opened beer bottles. In the course of her unsteady attempts to fill my glass, the señora was now plying Pachamama, the ever-grateful god of the earth, with at least as much beer as was splashing into my glass.

What were we celebrating? I had no idea. I had just arrived in La Paz at the start of an expedition to trace the rise and fall of the Inca empire through a journey across the Bolivian and Peruvian Andes. Here I was at the heart of an Aymaran drinking spree whose joviality grew with every ring of the doorbell, which was inevitably soon followed by the death rattle of another beer crate being brought in.

Not even the Incas could subdue the irrepressible Aymaran spirit. What hope had I? Next time, I think I'll try hiding in the wardrobe.

*****

Several hours earlier, as my plane descended towards the vast, hazy expanse of the Bolivian Altiplano and the flickering lights of La Paz, I pondered that during the height of the Inca empire, everything I could survey, and much more besides that now lay obscured by the curvature of the earth, fell under the power of the all-conquering Incas.

The Incas were the last of the great pre-Columbian civilisations to evolve in South America. They have also been the most enduring. Half a millennium after their conquest and overthrow, the Incas still retain such a timeless mystique and fascination that their spirit, if not presence, to this day permeates most journeys to the Andes and Altiplano.

Settling in the Cuzco region of the Peruvian Andes, the Incas believed they had been chosen by the Sun God to bring civilisation to a chaotic and barbarous world. The Incas believed that their ruler was a living god, a direct descendant of the Sun, who interceded with other gods on behalf of his earthly subjects. Combining military might with skilful diplomacy and masterly administration, the Incas forged a vast empire that spanned the length of the Andes.

The Incas believed they had conquered the whole of the civilised world within their empire. They called their empire "Tawantinsuyo", meaning the "Four Quarters of the Earth together", with Cuzco at its heart. At their height, the four quarters stretched for nearly five thousand kilometres down the rugged spine of western South America: from southern Colombia in the north to central Chile in the south; and several hundred kilometres across: from the Pacific Ocean in the west to the impenetrable barrier of Amazonia in the east. Ruling over more than 10 million inhabitants, the Inca empire was the grandest ever witnessed in South America, and possibly the largest in all the pre-Hispanic Americas.

The achievements of the Incas are particularly astonishing given they were accomplished in only three generations. Most of the conquests of the Incas have been credited to Pachacuti Inca and his successor Topa Inca Yupanqui, with Pachacuti's grandson Huayna Capac credited with consolidation of the empire and the final phases of expansion.

The Inca empire evolved uniquely from thousands of years of development in the high Andes, isolated from outside influences – a Bronze Age society surviving into the Renaissance. As the Romans had done centuries before them, the Incas founded their empire on the achievements of earlier civilisations. They didn't destroy the creations of earlier civilisations but built beside them. Thus, the Incas incorporated into their culture the accumulated wisdom of more than 4,000 years of Andean development.

The Incas upheld a state religion and state-prescribed core beliefs that justified their supremacy, and directed and gave purpose to their lives. They also manipulated history where it suited their purposes politically, for instance to assert their supremacy or that of one kindred line or another.

One of the greatest achievements of the empire was the system of efficient administration it developed, particularly recognising that the Inca aristocracy ruled over a vast domain that comprised diverse subjects who outnumbered them by a hundred to one. The Incas governed the heart of their empire directly. In remoter corners of the empire, they oversaw a hierarchy of caciques (local leaders).

Living in the hostile environment of the high Andes, the Incas demonstrated extraordinary genius in overcoming the natural challenges of their environment. They carved beautiful and elaborate agricultural terraces to enable them to grow crops on incredibly steep terrain that otherwise wouldn't have yielded any harvests. They devised systems of irrigation channels and ditches to husband limited water resources to where they were most needed. They filled storehouses throughout the empire with food and clothing to maintain marching imperial armies and local subjects alike. They used transmigration to plant loyal subjects in areas far removed from their power base, or in parts of the empire where there were risks of uprisings.

My quest in South America was to trace the rise and fall of the Inca empire by way of a journey across the imperial heartland of the Bolivian and Peruvian Andes. From the Incas' birthplace in Lake Titicaca, I planned to travel through the remote Apolobamba range of the Andes to the empire's magnificent pinnacle at Cuzco and Machu Picchu, and beyond to the poignant scene of the Incas' final stand against the Spanish Conquistadores in the densely forested mountains of Vilcabamba, in which hide several Inca "lost cities".

As my plane approached the massive La Paz airstrip (at such high altitude, the air is so thin aircraft need a long runway to take off and land) over the grid-structured, low-level city of El Alto, I was struck by the inordinate number of churches jutting from the sprawl. These churches were often separated from each other by only a couple of streets of bleak adobe housing. I later learned that these churches mostly resulted from the largesse of one man: a German friar named Padre Obermeier. Equally striking was an alarming profusion of ancient aircraft rotting beside the runway, which I hoped there would never be a need to coax back into service.

I landed in La Paz early one April morning. At 3,600 metres above sea level, La Paz is the world's highest capital (although Sucre is Bolivia's official capital, La Paz is the seat of government and commercial centre). The airport at El Alto lies another 500 metres higher into the thin air. Spanish Conquistadores founded La Paz in 1548 on the site of a busy Aymaran village, and more importantly on the strategic trade route between the Bolivian silver mines and the Pacific ports.

I was pleasantly relieved to find on stepping off the plane that I could still breathe quite normally. Following advice to refrain from drinking alcohol and overeating during the flight had paid off. The "Sala de Oxigenoterapia" (Oxygen Therapy Room) next to the luggage carousel confirmed that arriving at such high altitude isn't always this straightforward. Inside, as if to emphasise the point, the man who had sat two rows ahead of me on the plane now lay stretched out on his back, keenly clutching an oxygen mask to his face.

Next door in the Immigration Office, a young Chinese man, who I think (from disjointed scraps of broken conversation) had been deported from France for a crime I couldn't translate, was trying to clear immigration without the benefit of sharing a common language with any of the documents, officials or other passengers now surrounding him. I tried my best to help communications, but the immigration officers eventually ushered me away and closed the door on what would undoubtedly be a lengthy morning.

The drive from the airport to the city centre was unforgettable. We bumped along poor roads, passing slums and scattered street markets until, rounding a corner, the ground suddenly fell away on one side and the great bowl of La Paz unfolded below us in one of the most dramatic skylines I have seen anywhere in the world. Modern skyscrapers soared from the pit of the bowl (the heart of the city centre), lining a single main avenue running along the base of the huge canyon. From the city centre, a carpet of squat adobe dwellings clawed its way steeply up the walls of the canyon towards the lip, which stretches nearly five kilometres rim to rim. Mount Illimani's triple snow-covered peaks dominated the horizon majestically whilst all around, the Altiplano and other snow-crowned Andean summits stood out in razor sharp clarity against the cloudless, deep blue sky.

Unlike most cities, the poorer districts of La Paz lie higher up and the wealthier districts lower down. The shanty adobe jumble of El Alto, the impoverished satellite district (where the airport is situated) that now challenges the city in the bowl for size, sprawls high above central La Paz from the edge of the lip across the Altiplano. In contrast, the Zona Sur region that lies in the bowl at a lower level than the city centre is warmer, wealthier and altogether more comfortable. Not surprisingly, many expatriate families and wealthier Bolivians prefer to live there.

Notwithstanding the comforts of Zona Sur, nowhere comes close to the city centre for capturing the essence of La Paz. Breathlessly steep cobbleways lined with street vendors; pulsating, seemingly endless markets; and a huge population of bowler-hatted cholita women clad in brightly coloured traditional costumes, all set against the backdrop of Illimani and the chatter of Aymara.

As my taxi bumped and rattled its way steeply into the Sopocachi district of central La Paz, I didn't regret my decision to forgo the comforts of Zona Sur to stay in a house in the centre. After all, how could I say I had lived in La Paz until I had experienced the full glory of a traditional "Frankenstein" shower, whereby an electric element heats water as it passes through the shower head, controlled by a dangerous-looking power switch on the wall (hence the name)?

My chatty and inquisitive driver found the street easily enough, and the numbers close to the house we were looking for. However, La Paz residents have a curious habit of not numbering their houses in sequence, and we prowled the area for some time before finally arriving at my base for the next few days.

After recovering from the impromptu merrymaking I had stumbled into on arrival, the first thing that struck me about La Paz was that it is virtually impossible to walk or do anything quickly when first arriving at this altitude. Even locals take their time, particularly climbing the city's many steep streets, when walking at any pace can lead to severe breathlessness.

Fortunately, my inability to do anything very active didn't depress my appetite, and many of my initial explorations of the city were culinary. Often waking early due to jetlag, I took it upon myself to buy the breakfast bread from the expressionless woman who owned the nearest of several small and darkened neighbourhood shops. The rolls were excellent: soft, light and topped with a sprinkling of toasted cheese. Other delicious buys from the vibrant local markets included large, perfectly ripe avocados that spread like butter and sweet, juicy papayas the size of rugby footballs.

One of the local dining treats is the salteña, a mid-morning pastry snack of chicken, meat or vegetables in tasty gravy. Pausing for a couple of salteñas became the highlight of many a La Paz morning, although I struggled to master the peculiar technique of eating them without splashing gravy everywhere. Locals somehow manage to eat and suck at the same time, noisily slurping away all the gravy and leaving plates spotlessly clean, rather than sprayed with gravy as mine invariably were.

At the other end of the day, another Bolivian dining treat is the late night anticucho, a delicious beef heart shish kebab (sounds disgusting, tastes divine) served with peanut sauce and a potato, sold by nocturnal street vendors. I soon learned that the supreme anticucho in La Paz is flame-grilled on a street corner in Zona Sur. Queues of cars form every night in front of the tiny barbecue's leaping flames, with hungry drivers bellowing their orders without even bothering to get out of their vehicles.

The Sopocachi house where I lived was owned by a friendly and very cheerful Bolivian couple, Rina and Ivan, who lived there with Rina's son Sergio and mother Doña Celia. Rina and Ivan were young and hard working. They rented out several rooms in the house to expatriates and maintained an extremely convivial atmosphere (as I had already experienced!). Hosts and guests often congregated together in the family kitchen or sitting room.

The family pet was a less-than-charming parrot with an unnerving habit of clawing its way up people's arms to perch on their shoulders. Happily, the family soon countered this menace by adding a lovable though hyperactive and sharp-toothed husky pup, with soft light-coloured fur and piercing blue eyes. High altitude and the depths of the Andean winter dragged temperatures close to freezing every night. Like most residences in the city, the Sopocachi house was unheated. The pup came in very handy as a makeshift hot water bottle when it finally ran out of energy and could be laid sedately across one's lap.

Under the direction of Don Pancho (Doña Celia's estranged husband), a small team of workers was putting the final touches to an extension to the house. The traditional Andean way to bless any new construction is to hold a challa, whereby offerings of sweets, llama foetuses and alcohol are buried in the ground as offerings to Pachamama, Mother Earth. Such auspicious events are never allowed to pass without the most earnest celebration, and Rina and Doña Celia were hatching plans for a suitable festivity.

As I had already found out when first arriving at the house, Andean people love drinking bouts, particularly those involving much dancing and singing. Drinking sessions celebrating something specific are particularly dangerous. The prospect of the looming challa to bless the new extension was enough to send one of my housemates on four days of tough trekking in preference to a night of Bolivian revelry.

With the help of friends and neighbours, the family prepared a huge feast of Andean specialities including an entire carcass of pig roasted in a communal oven (lechón), a greasy pork soup usually served as a morning after hangover easer (fricasé), raw fish marinated in lemon juice (ceviche) and avocado salad (guacamole).

Much more important than food to the occasion was of course beer – and lots of it. Once again, raucous revellers brought in crate after crate of the La Paz brew, part-drunk bottles of which soon lay scattered all about the house. Music blared from a small player, and dancing and singing erupted spontaneously.

It wouldn't have been too bad if the well-meaning hosts simply handed you your glass and left you alone to drink it. But they don't. Their first tactic is to serve drinks to a gathering using only a single communal glass. The jovial host approaches an unsuspecting guest and pours a large glass of beer. So as not to create a drinking bottleneck, and goaded on by others feigning near-death by thirst, you are obliged to drink up quickly. The second tactic again involves a single glass, with each recipient nominating the next drinker in turn – by motioning the glass in his or her direction accompanied by a cheerful "Contigo!" (With you!) – before they gulp their beer.

Bolivians measure the success of their parties by the size of the wall of empty beer crates stretching across their courtyards the following morning – like miniature versions of the Andes. If the wall of crates doesn't obscure the view and block out the sun entirely, the party cannot be deemed a roaring success. Rina and Ivan needn't have had any concerns there. The next morning, the poor husky pup was clearly confused by the massive new structure that had suddenly sprung up in the courtyard overnight and now required some effort to navigate around. In the sitting room, several comatose revellers lay sprawled out over various sofas, some still clutching half-drunk bottles of beer.

At the same time as my hosts were finishing the new wing of their house, builders were also renovating another property across the street. Late one afternoon, tragedy struck these other workers. Most of the first floor of the house collapsed on top of two of the workers, burying one up to the waist. A few of us heard the roar of sliding masonry and ran over to the accident. We tried our best to help, clawing away as much of the collapsed rubble as we could by hand and giving water to the half-buried man. My limited Spanish prevented me from understanding the full scale of the accident at the time, although I later learned that this man died from his injuries.

Another sombre shadow was also casting its gloom over my first few days in La Paz. Social unrest, most visibly manifested as road blockades, was stretching across much of the country. Blockades have long been accepted as an inescapable part of Bolivian life – the population's standard way of expressing unhappiness over any social, political or other grievance. With a hugely diverse society making disparate claims over the country's meagre resources, not much time passes without one group or another feeling aggrieved enough to demonstrate.

The aggrieved – miners, campesinos, coca growers, students, teachers, etc – march through cities and along trunk roads, bearing banners, chanting their claims and setting off loud explosions as they go. Massive boulder fields appear out of nowhere to form impassable barriers across key roads. Bolivia has very few highways – only three main roads lead out of La Paz – and it doesn't take many protestors to shut down all transport links around the country. After several days of blockades, food inevitably starts to run low in markets and prices rise accordingly.

During the most heated demonstrations, protestors stone and dynamite their fury at the police and even passers-by. Police retaliate with water cannon and tear gas. Desperate presidents have on occasion called in the national army to settle the most passionate disputes, often killing many protestors in the process.

Residents of El Alto, the impoverished district on the Altiplano overlooking La Paz, are particularly prone to protesting, and with good effect. Two of the three main roads leading out of La Paz, including the road to Lake Titicaca, pass through El Alto.

The current dispute concerned a proposed new hydrocarbons law, which would increase taxes on foreign gas companies from 13% to 50%. Although the proposed hike in taxes sounded quite high, it seemed that many Bolivians didn't think the new law went far enough. They wanted the gas industry completely re-nationalised, irrespective of what that might do to frighten off any prospects of much needed foreign investment in the future. These extremists were now noisily protesting their views all around the country.

The blockades were making it very difficult for me to travel out of La Paz, the only positive upshot being the additional acclimatisation this enforced. I also took advantage of these unplanned extra days in La Paz to indulge in eating even more salteñas and anticuchos, and to catch up on background reading on the Incas.

I had already learned that the story of the Incas took place some 500 years ago. Successive Inca rulers applied advanced techniques of distribution, administration and communication to overcome the great geographical challenges of ruling their vast and mountainous domain. The Incas created planned towns and linked them by a huge system of roads, building innovative suspension bridges where necessary to cross chasms over furious rivers. They carved tier upon tier of irrigated terraces to grow crops on precipitous mountain slopes – huge expanses of which still yield plentiful harvests today. To store their food and other valuables, the Incas maintained storehouses brimming with food and other supplies – some so filled to bursting they outlasted the fall of the empire by several decades.

Like many imperial powers before them, the Incas asserted a creation separate from the rest of mankind, to allow them to distinguish their chosen, blessed line from those of their subjects.

The Incas claimed their origins at Lake Titicaca, the vast, high altitude lake that straddles the Bolivia-Peru border. According to legend, the first Inca Manco Capac (the Sun God) and his sister-queen Mama Ocllo (the Moon Goddess) rose from the waters of Lake Titicaca near the Islands of the Sun and Moon. They proclaimed that they had been sent to earth by the Sun, carrying with them a divine mandate to civilise the world and spread the religion of the creator god Viracocha and the Sun god Inti. The Incas began their sacred ministry after Manco Capac buried a gold chain and staff on the Island of the Sun.

During their supremacy, the Incas tried hard to suppress all recognition of their Andean predecessors. However, modern archaeological excavations show that their material and spiritual lives were in fact an amalgam of several thousand years of all the Andean cultures that preceded them.

Having left such a dazzling legacy, it astonished me to discover that the Incas weren't actually around for very long. The height of the Inca empire lasted less than a hundred years.

To begin my journey, and to discover how the Incas evolved from a small hill tribe to become the overlords of the Andes in just a couple of generations, I had to go back much further in time, to around 1500 BC and the evolution around the southern shore of Lake Titicaca of the Tiahuanaco culture.

By some amazing good fortune, I was just at that time learning from my hosts of a possible opportunity to escape the present blockades stalemate. Although protestors resolutely blockaded many roads, the road to Tiahuanaco somehow remained clear. I grabbed this chance to explore the capital of one of the first major cultures to evolve in the Andes.

CHAPTER TWO

TIAHUANACO

The Tiahuanaco culture developed on the vast plain to the south of Lake Titicaca, in present-day northern Bolivia. According to pre-Hispanic myths, Tiahuanaco and Lake Titicaca together gave birth to the Andean people. From their capital, the people of Tiahuanaco prospered into a vast state – the most important ever witnessed in the Andes – that lasted about three millennia and absorbed within it many of the earlier Andean tribes. At its height, the Tiahuanaco empire encompassed present-day western Bolivia, northwest Argentina, northern Chile and southern Peru. In all, Tiahuanaco ruled a domain only slightly smaller than the Inca empire, which extended further north into present-day Colombia and further south into central Chile and Argentina.

Tiahuanaco first rose to religious and pilgrimage prominence, later developed as an important hub for trade and subsequently grew into an imperial power. Sometime in the middle of the first millennium AD, people from Tiahuanaco began to expand from their capital to create the first Altiplano state. By the late fourth century, the site at Tiahuanaco had grown into a large urban centre. Its great capital included many monoliths, temples, a pyramid, Sun and Moon Gates and an extensive residential community.

Centuries later, the Incas would seize the remnants of the by then long defunct Tiahuanaco state and appropriate its structures and mythology as their own, in order to buttress their own beliefs and ideology. The

Incas came to revere Tiahuanaco, in large part because of the role nearby Lake Titicaca played in the Incas' own creation myths, in which the creator god Viracocha, the Sun, the Moon and the first Incas all emerged from the lake.

Having adopted Sun worship as the central pillar of their religion, the Incas incorporated the Sun Gate at Tiahuanaco and several other monoliths from the site into their mythology. They granted Tiahuanaco the prestigious status of a symbolic capital and universal shrine, whose status in the empire ranked only marginally lower than the imperial capital of Cuzco itself. Tiahuanaco was not regarded as highly as the principal shrines of Cuzco, Pachacamac and Copacabana, but was nevertheless venerated because of the size and antiquity of its buildings.

Most of the greatest achievements of the Tiahuanaco culture date from the empire's last millennium, known as the Classical and Expansion Periods. During these periods, we begin to witness many of the feats that would later come to define many of the most impressive accomplishments of the Inca empire itself, including advanced agriculture, irrigation, astronomy, religion, road networks, administration and, most visibly, elegant stonework. The Tiahuanacos imposed a rigid social and political hierarchy that may have spawned the conspicuous elitism of the Inca empire.

On a more practical level, the Tiahuanacos have been credited with the cultivation of yams, sweet potatoes, quinoa and some 300 varieties of potato. They also invented a novel dehydration process for potato conservation. Andean people still use the freeze-drying process masterminded by the Tiahuanacos to turn potatoes into blackened, unappetising to behold, but (unfortunately) ever so long-lasting chuños, a stern challenge to most non-Andean taste buds that has gotten the better of many a foreign visitor.

Like the Incas and other Andean tribes who came after them, the Tiahuanaco people were intensely spiritual. They lived with a profound reverence for nature, a tradition maintained to this day by the homage Andean people still pay to Pachamama (Mother Earth), and their respectful attitude towards the mountains, which they revere as achachilas (protector spirits of ancestors that inhabit the high mountains).

Tiahuanaco was a theocratic state; religion formed an integral part of every human activity. In the ceremonial centre of their capital, the Tiahuanacos constructed huge temples incorporating vast open spaces to allow them to study astronomy and offer worship to their divinities. Dating to the Tiahuanaco culture, and persisting to this day, Andean cosmology has distinguished three dimensions: the "alajpacha" (the spiritual, holy world in which live the sun, moon, stars, lightning and the spirits of their ancestors); the "akapacha" (the material world inhabited by man and nature); and the "mankapacha" (the mysterious underworld of which man has no knowledge).

The remains of Tiahuanaco are located on the bleak Altiplano along the Royal Inca Highway between Cuzco and La Paz. Heading towards the site, my tiny, cramped minibus meandered along an undulating road, surrounded by sparsely populated plains, low hills and pink-brown soil showing beneath thin, scrubby grassland.

Tiahuanaco's Aymara name of Taypicala means "Stone in the Middle", and derives from the local natives who believed this was the centre of the world, from where originated the people who repopulated the earth after a great prehistoric flood. Various legends account for how Tiahuanaco first came into existence, including one version whereby it was a great city built by giants.

The name "Tiahuanaco" derives from an incident when an Inca monarch received a messenger in the town. The messenger had arrived from Cuzco at such high speed that the Inca invited him to "Tiay, guanaco," which means, "Sit down and rest, guanaco," a guanaco being a swift animal related to the llama and alpaca.

It is said that Manco Inca, who led the greatest native rebellions against the Conquistadores, was born in a royal palace at Tiahuanaco. Another royal prince, Paulo, was born to the emperor Huayna Capac as the Inca was returning to Cuzco from an expedition around the empire.

Arriving at the remnants of the Tiahuanaco site, I first came upon what is left of the Akapana Pyramid, once a spectacular stone-faced structure, but now just a massive and forlorn mound potted with archaeological excavations.

Nearby and much more impressive was the Kalasasaya, a huge elevated ritual platform enclosed by imposing walls constructed of massive rectangular blocks – an unmistakeable precursor to the masterly stonework of the Incas.

The walls of the Kalasasaya are made of medium and large sized stone blocks fitted together without mortar. Blocks of red sandstone and other brown or grey-coloured stones were skilfully worked to incredible smoothness and flatness. At intervals, other very large and more irregular stones have been placed vertically like buttresses. The principal gateway consists of just three large and well-worked stones, one placed vertically on each side and a huge slab spanning across the top of the pillars.

The size of some of the individual stone blocks and scale of the overall complex are both very striking and highly suggestive of the timeless Inca masonry that would follow centuries after these stones were laid. What makes the scale of the stonework even more remarkable is that no stones or quarries exist within many miles of the site. Without the aid of wheels, winches or other labour-saving machines, we can only marvel at what human strength and endurance were needed to extract such huge blocks of stone, carve them so precisely, carry and set them here.

Another striking feature of Tiahuanaco is the great antiquity of the complex. These buildings stood here long before the expansion of the Incas. There is even evidence that the Incas remodelled the great edifices of Cuzco on the structures they found at Tiahuanaco.

In one corner of the Kalasasaya compound stands Tiahuanaco's famous Sun Gate, unfortunately no longer in its original position (its movement is blamed on Conquistador hooligans). This intricately sculpted gateway was built from a solid block of andesite, and is believed to have been used for Sun worship and possibly as a calendar.

The central carved figure on the Sun Gate is the image most generally attributed to the creator god Viracocha, who, along with the Sun and Thunder, was considered one of three principal Inca gods. In human form, Viracocha had rays of sun emanating from his head, snakes twisting around his arms and the heads of pumas projecting from his body. According to legend, after creating the people of the world, Viracocha walked out into the ocean off the northern coast of Peru – by coincidence the very same stretch of coast where Pizarro later landed to begin the conquest of the Incas.

Viewed from the Sun Gate's original position on the platform, the sun dawns precisely over two corners of the Kalasasaya on the summer and winter solstices. The Incas might well have used the Sun Gate as the basis of their own system for measuring the seasons by observing the position of the solstice sunrises.

Beside the Kalasasaya stands or rather sinks the Subterranean Temple, a neat rectangular pit in the ground lined by red sandstone blocks from which protrude small, carved stone faces.

Scattered all around the Tiahuanaco site, gigantic monoliths still proudly guard the fallen citadel. Archaeologists believe there may be many more monoliths still to be found below ground, together with great expanses of residential buildings, irrigation canals and more cut stone enclosures. Vast numbers of cut stones, including large, worked slabs are also believed to lie buried at Tiahuanaco.

Excavations, some stretching a considerable distance away from the centre of the complex, have uncovered many such stones, which hint at the potential scale of the grand city. Owing to a shortage of funds, however, only a tiny fraction of the site is ever likely to be excavated in the near future. Even with further excavation, Tiahuanaco is likely to remain an enigmatic mystery, with successive looting of the site having destroyed much of its history.

What archaeologists have managed to discover is that in around 1200, the civilisation suddenly vanished into obscurity, joining the ranks of other "lost" civilisations in the dark night of history.

Nobody knows what caused the end of Tiahuanaco. Ironically, one of the chief suspects in its demise is Lake Titicaca itself, the great lake that originally gave birth to the civilisation. One theory suggests that the Tiahuanaco empire suffered a "pachacuti" event. In the Andes, pachacuti means "overturner of the earth", a concept that would later become highly symbolic for the Incas. In this context, pachacuti described a cataclysm of water – possibly a large storm preceded by earthquakes and volcanoes.

According to this theory, the level of Lake Titicaca rose because of the pachacuti event. Rising water swamped the high plain and flooded Tiahuanaco, covering the city and all the surrounding lands in thick layers of silt and mud. The result was a century of drought that forced the people of Tiahuanaco to migrate away from the lakeshore. This human "big bang" expansion away from the lake created many separate polities that later crystallised through intense warfare into numerous small kingdoms, one of which was the Incas.

After its collapse, Tiahuanaco remained largely neglected until the Incas expanded here from Cuzco and revived interest in the ancient site and its mythology. The Incas found the temples in ruins after hundreds of years of neglect, and adopted Tiahuanaco into their own history and cultural identity.

Linking their identity to that of Tiahuanaco and its origin myths, the Incas were able to extend their own short history much further back through time, and expand their rightful geographical influence across the Andes and Altiplano. This helped them legitimise their claims to rule and conquer.

After overthrowing the Incas, the Spanish Conquistadores looted Tiahuanaco. They tore buildings apart in their insatiable search for gold and treasure, and reduced the site to a mound of tumbled rocks that much of the complex sadly still resembles today.

As the fierce afternoon sun began to set towards the surrounding hills, a faint haze shimmered in the direction of Lake Titicaca. After returning to La Paz to finalise preparations, the next stage of my journey would take me (blockades permitting) to the shores of the great lake, from where I would follow in the footsteps of the first Inca Manco Capac to the imperial capital of Cuzco.

CHAPTER THREE

LAKE TITICACA

The mysterious, gemlike waters of Lake Titicaca have been sacred to many cultures. The lake was the cradle of Andean civilisation and remains enduringly known as the birthplace of the Inca empire. My journey to trace the empire's rise and fall would begin in earnest beside its peaceful shores.

The lake is a four-hour bus journey from La Paz. Although there finally seemed to be a resolution to the hydrocarbons dispute, I was alarmed to learn of continuing threats of road blockades the day before I planned to set off. My La Paz hosts Rina and Ivan were more phlegmatic. "Don't worry," they reassured me, "there won't be any blockades this week, at least not in the mornings since the blockaders don't get up until late." They nevertheless advised me to travel early, just in case.

Setting off on a bright, crisp morning to the Cementerio district of La Paz, from where buses depart for the lakeside town of Copacabana, I asked my taxi driver whether he thought the blockades were likely to materialise. He turned up the radio and a timely news broadcast advised that the threat of blockades had indeed been lifted for a week (so allowing the blockaders to sleep in even later). That should leave enough time to explore the lake and its islands and then get far enough beyond La Paz to escape the worst effects of any blocked roads.

The early morning rush of white-coated schoolchildren (the outer garment of the state school uniform resembles a white lab coat) was in full flow as we climbed towards the huge graveyard. The ever-hopeful calls of the voceadores (youngsters bellowing bus routes from minibus windows for the benefit of non-readers) vied for attention above the racket of screeching tyres, grinding gears and screaming engines. Even by the chaotic standards of Bolivian driving, the calm exterior of my driver hid an unusually intemperate traffic weaver and total disregarder for the rights of other road users. Several times, we pulled out directly in front of beeping minibuses that clearly had right of way. I was amazed we didn't hit anything as we hurried through the squalid, cluttered streets towards Cementerio. Happily, this was relatively low-risk dodgems as nothing was moving fast enough to cause serious damage even had we pranged anything.

Getting out of the taxi at Cementerio, I was immediately approached by a very enthusiastic ticket seller who was incessantly yelling, "Copacabana, Copacabana!" I happily bought a ticket from him before I discovered to my slight annoyance that the bus opposite was leaving half an hour earlier. I wished its ticket seller had been more vociferous. The extra half hour allowed plenty of time for assorted vendors to come on board and offer passengers everything from toilet paper and newspapers to mandarins, biscuits, sweets and other nibbles.

The choking smell of diesel fumes filled the bus as we finally ground our way slowly onto the steep cobbled climb out of the city at what seemed like little more than walking pace. Bolivian buses are aromatic, rattling, groaning triumphs of optimism over mechanics, time over distance. Ancient, creaking buses are one of the slowest ways to travel around a country the size of Bolivia, albeit you do so at a cost as low as the average speed. Colourfully painted bodywork invariably bears religious slogans – "Jesus loves you", "the God of May" – probably in prayer that the vehicle will keep running long enough to reach its destination.

Bolivian buses are invariably crammed full of cholitas and their stuffed aguayos (the brightly striped cloths indigenous women fold into sacks that they carry on their backs to transport everything from onions and potatoes to small children). Hanging from the windscreen and rear view mirror are religious and other feathery figurines and trinkets that sway violently with any movement of the bus. Blasting out over crackly speakers is the ubiquitous beat of Radio Chacaltaya – the local broadcaster of non-stop cumbia dance music. Though often scorned and more often derided, people somehow always know the lyrics to cumbia songs, and their mindlessly catchy rhythm provides the essence of any Bolivian bus journey.

Levelling out on the flat plain of El Alto, we entered a harsh cacophony of hooting horns, groaning diesel engines struggling in the thin air, and screaming street vendors and minibus voceadores. Crowds of people were busy breakfasting, packed around tiny tables at street stalls like islands in a seething mass of indigenous humanity. Street vendors were everywhere, selling salteñas, buñuelos (deep-fried flour pancakes), api (a vibrant non-alcoholic drink made from a purple corn flour base that lends it a distinctive, if alarming, violet shade), and other breakfast favourites. Just beside one of these stalls, an elderly cholita woman was pathetically rummaging through a pile of rubbish spread out before her – much as do the nocturnal La Paz street dogs.

Beyond El Alto, we picked up speed across the flat, treeless, pale green savannah, interspersed at intervals by low, isolated hills. The ice-capped Cordillera Real sparkled beneath a dusting of fresh snow on our eastern horizon. Tiny settlements and isolated farmhouses were scattered across the bleak rolling plains. Small groups of campesinos worked diminutive fields, their small herds of straggly llamas and alpacas grazing on the thin but surprisingly rich pickings. Even at altitudes approaching 4,000 metres above sea level, the Altiplano yields abundant crops of potatoes, quinoa and other indigenous plants, particularly in the prolific microclimate sustained by the huge mass of water in Lake Titicaca.

As we approached the lake, parched, pink-brown soil started to show through beneath the thin covering of vegetation. The landscape was becoming increasingly hilly. Even here, determined highlanders had extorted miniscule patches of cultivation from the harsh and occasionally steeply sloping terrain.

The Copacabana peninsula straddles the Bolivia-Peru border. In order to remain in Bolivian territory, the journey from La Paz to Copacabana requires taking a boat across the narrow (less than a kilometre wide) Strait of Tiquina, spanned by the sleepy villages of San Pablo and San Pedro.

The Strait of Tiquina divides Lake Titicaca into its small and large sections. The small southern section is called Wiñay Marka (Aymara for "Eternal City") and is comparatively shallow, at an average depth of only some five metres. This has sustained the legend of a city lying hidden beneath the lake – a Bolivian Atlantis – and researchers have in recent years recovered human artefacts from the lakebed near here.

Arriving in San Pablo, the passengers jumped into a small motor launch whilst our bus crossed the strait more leisurely aboard a large wooden raft. As our launch motored towards San Pedro, the pristine white headquarters of the "Armada Boliviana Cuarto Distrito Naval Titicaca" gleamed into view before us. Its Bolivian flag flew proudly, albeit at half-mast in defiance that landlocked Bolivia hasn't renounced its claim to the Pacific lands lost in war to Chile. However, there was no sign of any navy boats, let alone an armada. Undeterred, crisply dressed naval cadets milled around the San Pedro dock. Looking back across the strait, in the middle of which our bus was still making its stately progress, a line of trees marshalled on the hill high above San Pablo. I wondered if this might be a practice firing range for the armada. Then again, possibly not.

After being reunited with our bus, we twisted and turned for another hour along a dry and dusty road (beside which still lay a disarray of rocks and boulders from the recent blockades) high above the lake, before we finally descended into the town of Copacabana.

Located by the shore of two inlets, and nestling attractively at the base of two steep hills, the peaceful town of Copacabana occupies a promontory jutting out into Lake Titicaca.

The Bolivian Copacabana long predates its more famous Brazilian counterpart. The emperor Topa Inca Yupanqui (son of the all-conquering Pachacuti Inca) founded Copacabana as a resting place for pilgrims travelling the great Inca pilgrimage to the Island of the Sun. The emperor's grandson carved a wooden image – the Dark Virgin – that sparked off a series of healings when it was installed in the local church. These miracles cemented Copacabana's status as an important pilgrimage site and led to the construction of the great Moorish style cathedral that now dominates the town.

To reach Copacabana, pilgrims first had to pass through the border town of Yunguyo. Lying where the promontory narrows to an isthmus, Yunguyo served as the gateway to the sacred peninsula. The Incas built a wall across the isthmus, stretching from one beach to the other, and guarded it with gates, watchmen and soldiers to control access to the sanctuary and pilgrimage route to the Island of the Sun.

Arriving pilgrims were required to confess their sins at Yunguyo. After a penitence of some blows on the back and abstinence from certain foods, the pilgrims were allowed to progress on to Copacabana. Here, they made another confession so as to arrive with even greater purity on the Island of the Sun.

Resting houses and food stores were set along the road from Yunguyo to Yampupata, the village at the tip of the peninsula that marks the closest point on the lakeshore "mainland" to the Island of the Sun.

The Island of the Sun is one of two islands in southern Lake Titicaca that are uniquely important to Andean prehistory. The Island of the Sun is the largest island in the lake, and is carpeted with thousands of agricultural terraces dating from Inca and pre-Inca times, most of which local people still use to grow food today. The smaller of the two islands is the Island of the Moon (also called Koati).

The Incas incorporated the two islands into their empire in the middle of the 15th century. They revered the islands and dedicated them to the Sun and the Moon.

Along with the Copacabana peninsula, the Islands of the Sun and Moon were among the most sacred sites in the Inca empire. In imperial times, indigenous people across the Andes knew of these two islands, in part due to the central role they played in Inca cosmology, and in part because of their sacred importance to Inca religion.

As befitting the sacred importance of the peninsula and the two islands, the Incas constructed many fine shrines, temples and religious facilities in the area, designated a large number of attendants, priests and confessors to serve there, and made many sacrifices of animal and human blood. The Copacabana peninsula became so famous and venerated that people came here from throughout the empire, converting the area into a great pilgrimage destination – one of the three most sacred destinations in the Inca empire.

The three most important shrines in the Inca religion were first, Coricancha, the Sun temple in Cuzco, second, Pachacamac, a religious shrine on the Pacific coast that held a famous oracle, and third, the Sacred Rock on the Island of the Sun. Of these three shrines, the most important pilgrimage was to the Sacred Rock.

The Sacred Rock lies at the northern tip of the Island of the Sun, near where Inca legends record the rising from the depths of the first Inca Manco Capac and his sister-queen Mama Ocllo.

When the Conquistadores first arrived at Lake Titicaca in the 1530s, local Indians told them that the sun had risen into the sky for the first time from a sacred island in the great lake, and that the island housed a series of ancient temples.

Soon after the Conquest, the Spanish appropriated the sacred nature of the peninsula area for Christianity, although they moved the centre of religious worship from the Islands of the Sun and Moon to the mainland. After Christianity supplanted the Inca religion, locals chose the Virgin of Candelaria as their patron saint, a position she retains and has further enhanced as now patron saint of all Bolivia. To this day, Copacabana remains one of the most important Catholic pilgrimage destinations in South America.

Beyond Copacabana's dazzlingly white cathedral, I climbed up a wide, unrelentingly steep stone staircase past 14 Stations of the Cross (and the stench of stale urine) to the summit of Cerro Calvario, one of the two hills that hem in the town. The summit provided jaw-dropping views across the emerald blue water towards the Islands of the Sun and Moon.

The most devout pilgrims would not only have done penance at each of the Stations of the Cross, but might also have walked here all the way from La Paz, some 160 kilometres away. On the summit of Cerro Calvario, modern day pilgrims burn incense, and buy and wear trinkets of miniature houses, cars and bundles of dollar bills, representing their hearts' desires, in the fervent hope that the Virgin will help draw the reality into their lives.

Copacabana's sacred renown also provides excellent business for beggars and the blind. Followers of the Virgin believe that people so inflicted carry certain powers when they chant over incense – powers that will help ensure the Virgin grants the devout their wishes.

On a more pragmatic level, many Bolivians bring their vehicles to Copacabana for a blessing by the Virgin, which, judging by my earlier taxi journey, is a very sensible precaution. On weekend mornings, drivers gather in front of the cathedral and adorn their cars and minibuses with garlands of flowers, coloured ribbons, flags and model reed boats. They beseech the Virgin's protection and pour ritual offerings of alcohol over the vehicles' tyres and bonnets to consecrate them.

Despite Copacabana's continuing importance as a religious and pilgrimage centre, the town is nowadays a commercial clamour of tourists, artesania shops and many trout restaurants. Fortunately, it still provides the starting point for retracing the greatest of the Inca pilgrimages – from Copacabana to the Incas' Sacred Rock at the northern tip of the Island of the Sun.

This was my quest as I hurried out of Copacabana (after an obligatory fish lunch) towards the village of Yampupata at the top of the peninsula, from where I would take a boat to the Island of the Sun. Little did I suspect that this afternoon's trek would provide an unforgettable way to experience the intense serenity of Lake Titicaca and its islands.

Striding out along the dusty track from Copacabana, I was almost immediately overtaken by several cyclists and minibuses, which I later discovered were all converging on a local football match taking place on a field at the far end of the road.

Just beyond the football pitch, I climbed a slope onto a wooded headland, turned a corner and was at once engulfed by the overwhelming solitude and timelessness that is Lake Titicaca. The thin air was still, the surface of the great lake unruffled. Not a sound interrupted the profound silence.

Lake Titicaca lies at the northern edge of the Altiplano, and at over 3,800 metres is the world's highest navigable lake. Its intensely blue water spreads over a vast area of Bolivia and Peru, and is particularly mesmerising when viewed through the crystal sharp light of the Altiplano. Viewed from the north, the lake's outline resembles the shapes of a puma, fish and man – forms also found in Peru's mystifying Nazca lines.

The lake's original name was Khota Mama (Aymara for "Mother Lake"). The lake was only renamed Titicaca after the Conquest, when Spanish Conquistadores misunderstood what the natives meant when they referred to the "Island of Titi Qala". The Spaniards mistakenly thought the natives were referring to the lake's name when they were in fact referring to a rock (the "Rock of the Titi", a titi being a wild Andean cat) on the Island of the Sun. That rock is now more commonly called the Sacred Rock.

The undulating, twisting coastal path to Yampupata skirted cool woods and steep terraces that fell away sharply to small sandy beaches and the silent expanse of deep blue calmness. I passed occasional trout fisheries and silent bays clogged with characteristic totora reed beds. These giant bulrushes grow plentifully around the lakeshore, often to over three metres in length. Lakeside dwellers centuries ago learned how to lash bundles of these reeds together and turn up the ends to form reed boats that some people still use today for fishing.

A few campesinos were working small fields containing pigs, sheep, llamas and cows. Several families were harvesting oca (a sweet potato), and the shore was dotted with wigwam-shaped piles of dark green haba beanstalks drying in the blindingly bright afternoon sun.

Just beyond Chani, a short, tanned, barrel-chested man with bloodshot eyes rode past me on his bicycle. After exchanging greetings, he dismounted and started walking beside me (unusually at this altitude, at a pace slower than mine). He explained that he was returning from a visit to Copacabana and that he owned a hostel in the village of Sicuani (on the way to Yampupata) that was listed in a well-known guidebook. By coincidence, I happened to have in my pocket some pages from that very guidebook and, yes, there he was, described as the "amenable Mamani family".

The man introduced himself in broken English as José Mamani and shook me vigorously by the hand. As we walked along together, I asked José whether he visited Copacabana often. "Every Saturday and Sunday," he replied. I pointed out that today was Tuesday, but this technicality seemed to make little impression. José went on to explain that he was suffering from a very sore head after some days of heavy drinking during his last visit. Could José have been drinking since the weekend?

By good (or bad?) fortune, José informed me that tomorrow marked the start of the annual three-day festival in his village, which would inevitably involve further unbroken bouts of the heaviest drinking. I feared for José's head. José urged me to stay in Sicuani for the festival. I explained that I had already made arrangements to head across that afternoon to the Island of the Sun. José pointed out that Challa and Challapampa, two settlements on the island, were also due to hold their annual festivals on the same days. So, wherever I was, there would be no escape from yet more heavily partying Bolivians.

José and I shared my water and some fruit as we continued along the meandering path. We reached the Gruta de Lourdes where I climbed up to peer into its small grotto. We then endured a long, hot climb to the top of another headland, at the summit of which José jumped back onto his bike and hurried off downhill to wait for me at his hostel.

I passed through the village of Titicachi where more families were out working small fields. By now, I was starting to receive plenty of offers of boat trips to the island, even more so as I entered nearby Sicuani, where José waited proudly outside his hostel with his 20-year-old son. José offered me a beer but it was now 4:30pm and I reluctantly had to decline his hospitality, as I knew I had to hurry if I was going to reach the island before nightfall.

People I met couldn't understand why I wanted to walk all the way to Yampupata rather than travel to the island much more comfortably in their boats. I pondered the same question myself as the last stage of the trek to Yampupata became an ungainly slog up and around two deceptively sizeable headlands before I finally descended into the scattered houses and beach at Yampupata.

I walked down to the shore and had scarcely put down my pack when I was approached by the smiling Rogelio Paye. Rogelio offered to row me across to the island for 20 Bolivianos. This seemed a reasonable fare, although I had to work hard to rebuff the attempts of a stony-faced cholita woman (who turned out to be the local boat master) to add on various taxes and surcharges.

It was now late afternoon. The hills above Yampupata glowed golden brown in the setting sun as we pushed away from the tiny pier. I sat in the bow while Rogelio rowed, standing, from the back, pushing on the oars. As we reached the middle of the icy lake, the Island of the Moon edged silently into view, beyond which rose the magnificent glinting summits of the Cordillera Real. The temperature dropped noticeably as we rowed into the shadow of the Island of the Sun's southern peak, although the sparkling diamond necklace of the Cordillera Real continued to light up the horizon.

Just as I was congratulating myself on how smoothly the day had gone, I discovered that Rogelio was only planning to drop me at the southernmost tip of the island. This point – called Punku, meaning "Gate" – was where the original pilgrims would have landed after crossing from Yampupata in totora reed boats, although it is some distance from the settlement of Yumani where I would be staying. Although Rogelio complained of the additional distance, I (or rather the offer of some additional money) persuaded him to row me a little further to the ruined palace of Pilko Kaina, where Inca emperors stayed during their annual visits to the island.

Even after forty-five minutes of high-altitude rowing, during which time he was happily chatting to me throughout, Rogelio was not in the slightest bit out of breath and had not one bead of sweat on his forehead when we docked at the deserted pier at the bottom of the Pilko Kaina ruins. Rogelio motioned that Yumani was only half an hour away on the mountain track as he cheerfully started rowing back to Yampupata.

CHAPTER FOUR

ISLAND OF THE SUN

The sun had set completely by the time I climbed up to the ruined two-storey Pilko Kaina palace, beyond which lay the path to Yumani. A locked gate and high fence barred access to the path, and I was forced to clamber back down over large rocks to lake level and then scramble up again breathlessly to reach it.

Yumani, the largest settlement on the Island of the Sun, sits high on a ridge to the south of the island. From its elevated position, it enjoys sweeping panoramic views, particularly east towards the Island of the Moon and the Cordillera Real beyond. Its buildings are scattered around a tiny church and are connected by a network of steep, uneven rocky paths. These village "streets" are not the most clearly marked, particularly in gathering gloom. More than once, I lost the path and found myself wandering across somebody's garden, on one occasion chased off by a justifiably indignant dog.

It was dark by the time I staggered exhausted into my Yumani hotel – the elegant, colonial-style Posada del Inca. By that time, my thoughts and language were far from pilgrim-like, although I reasoned in my defence that Inca pilgrims probably never had to haggle their boat trip across to the island or struggle across barricaded paths.

A thunderstorm early the next morning delayed the start of my walk to the religious complex at the north of the island. The Incas revered the god of thunder as a celestial being who wielded a club and sling. When he cracked his sling, he produced thunder; his slingshots and shining garments produced lightning.

Believing that all precipitation derived from the Thunder God, the Incas worshipped many meteorological phenomena, including rain, hail, thunderbolts, lightning and rainbows. Whenever a rock or stone was found to hold water after rain, this was held as evidence that the Thunder God had sent it as an object of worship. Moreover, the Incas believed that the Thunder God passed across a large heavenly river (the Milky Way) from which he drew rainfall. Even today, the Milky Way is still known as "the River" in many regions of the Andes.

With the rain finally abating, I climbed steeply out of Yumani following a campesino family, and almost at once somehow managed to lose the path along the ridge that runs the length of the island. I had to leap down several agricultural terraces before I regained the correct trail. Fortunately, campesinos on the Island of the Sun are friendly. Understanding farmers pointed me in the right direction and even invited me to clamber down over their stepped plots. I shuddered to think of the reaction such behaviour might have provoked in other parts of the Altiplano.

Although I could see several families at work on the land, once again the feeling was one of intense serenity – almost aloneness. The pungent aroma of koa – a herb with many medicinal benefits – filled the air, as did towering eucalyptus trees planted 300 years earlier by Spanish Conquistadores. I passed colourful bushes of kantuta, Bolivia's national flower, which displays the red, yellow and green of the country's flag.

I soon reached a well-maintained path lined on both sides with irregular boulders. I was walking through a delicate patchwork of steep tiny fields and terraces of different hues of green, yellow and brown, criss-crossed by zigzagging walls tumbling down to pretty sand beaches and the lake's intense blueness. Pigs, sheep, even cattle, crowded inside tiny stone enclosures. Llamas grazed quietly beside the track.

Inca pilgrims would have walked the same path as me to reach the north of the island. Three gates once guarded the northern shrine complex, although these are now difficult to distinguish from the surrounding rocks. Only the highest-ranking Incas and priests would have been allowed to pass through the third gate, called Intipunku (meaning "Sun

Gate"), that guarded the shrine itself. Even the Inca himself would remove his sandals at this point as a mark of respect. Lesser pilgrims would have been allowed no nearer to the sacred complex than the Intipunku, and would have handed over their offerings to the shrine priests at this gate.

After passing deserted bays, silent passes and curious stone structures, I reached the squat Chincana ruins hugging the northern tip of the island. This stone labyrinth is believed to have once been a monastery for Inca priests. Myriad doorways lead to a maze of tiny chambers, small plazas, stairs and twisting passageways, some retaining their original slab stone ceilings. Built of fieldstones once covered with painted mud plaster, the ruins bear the characteristic trapezoidal doors and niches of sacred and high status Inca structures. Trainees progressed by learning and ritual through the series of rooms before emerging as priests by graduating from the upper room.

Virgin nuns from the nearby Island of the Moon weren't always so fortunate. Several virgins from that island's nunnery were brought to this site each year to be sacrificed during the Inca's annual visit.

Beyond the Chincana ruins, the Island of the Sun falls away to an inviting sandy beach, reminiscent of a secluded Mediterranean cove, beyond which plunge some of the lake's deepest waters.

The north of the Island of the Sun is rife with Andean mythology. According to the Inca creation legend, the first Inca Manco Capac and his sister-queen Mama Ocllo rose from the lake near here, under orders from the Sun, and began their ministry to bring civilisation to the world after burying a gold chain and staff on the island.

In another legend, the titi (a wild cat found around the lake that appears in much Andean iconography) lived on the island with the blessing of the Sun and Moon. Knowing that a terrible storm was brewing, the titi leapt up and ate the Sun and Moon to protect them (thus causing an eclipse), after which it landed back on earth on a rock with its eyes smouldering bright red. This rock, the "rock where the cat shone", became known as Titi Qala or Titi Kharka, meaning "Rock of the Titi", from which evolved the lake's name Titicaca.

The terrible storm duly arrived, bringing with it tremendous floods that plunged the earth into a period of darkness and cold that nearly wiped out mankind altogether. Ancient legends told of a long period without light from the heavens, after which local people finally saw the sun rise up one morning with unusual brilliance from a large solid crag, which they consecrated as the Sacred Rock. An alternate legend told how the sun safely hid underneath the crag during the great storm, after which it rose again into the sky and favoured the crag with its first brilliant rays.

In the Inca version of the legend, sometime after the great deluge, the creator god Viracocha rose from the depths of Lake Titicaca. He wished to liberate his children the Sun and Moon. He hurled down a clap of thunder that created the Islands of the Sun and Moon. From the Sacred Rock, Viracocha commanded the Sun, the Moon and the stars to rise into the sky.

Next going to Tiahuanaco, Viracocha fashioned new men and women out of stones and sent them to the four quarters of the earth to begin repopulating the world. In this manner, Tiahuanaco and Lake Titicaca together became the sacred birthplace of all Andean people. Viracocha himself travelled all the way to the northern coast of Peru, calling out the people from the lakes, valleys, caverns and mountaintops as he went. Reaching the coast, he told his servants that his messengers would one day return. He then walked out over the sea and disappeared in the west.

From my sublimely beautiful vantage point at the north of the island, it was easy to appreciate the awe that the brilliantly shining sun and a moon rising over the island must have inspired in people living around the lake.

At dawn on the winter solstice, June 21st, the sun rises directly from the direction of the Sacred Rock. Not having the winter solstice sunrise to help with identification, I wasn't sure which of the nearby large outcrops was the Sacred Rock. With some embarrassment, I had to ask a local man, who refreshingly pointed me in the right direction without offering either guiding services or an outstretched hand in which to receive a tip. He pointed to a massive crag of reddish sandstone with a cavernous opening, in the shadow of which I had been shading from the fierce midday sun. Inca priests would have placed offerings at the foot of the Sacred Rock and worshipped a shrine placed in the cave. Unknowingly, I had sat on its hallowed surface.

The Sacred Rock would have been much simpler to identify in Inca times, when its convex side, which slopes away to the lakeshore, was covered by a curtain of cumbi, the finest and most elaborate imperial cloth. Sheets of gold and silver covered the concave side.

The altar of the Sun was placed inside the cave in the concave face of the rock, which was covered with holes into which the attendants threw the pilgrims' offerings. A round stone containing an orifice was placed in front of the altar, into which priests poured vast quantities of chicha for consumption by the Sun.

The Incas offered frequent and lavish sacrifices at the Sacred Rock, which included much shedding of human blood. After the arrival of the Conquistadores, the Incas buried many of their religious treasures from the Islands of the Sun and Moon, hid them on other islands or even hurled them into the lake to avoid them falling into the hands of the Spanish.

The face of the Sacred Rock that once bore the precious metals shows, by way of natural forms and fractures, the images of two great Andean deities: the bearded creator god Viracocha and a roaring puma, the symbol of energy and intelligence. I peered intently at the rock face but once again, I had to ask for help in identifying the images. The same man picked up some pebbles and rather disrespectfully lobbed them at the features on the rock face until I was finally able to distinguish the sacred figures. Both deities suffered the indignity with fitting poise.

The Sacred Rock defined one side of a ceremonial plaza, another side of which was still visible through the remains of an Inca wall that runs from the rock to a smaller outcrop. Facing the Sacred Rock is the third component of this religious complex – a stone table said to be a site of sacrifice in Inca times. Judging by its contemporary appearance, neat outline and regularly placed stumps set all around at comfortable seating height, it looked suspiciously to me like a modern picnic area set up by enterprising snack vendors.

I returned south along an ancient path that snakes beside the eastern shore of the island. Just south of the sacred complex, I came across the

"Footprints of the Sun", curious, oval-shaped splashes of yellow on the rocky path that resemble the prints left by a giant with rounded feet.

I passed peaceful villages and hamlets by the lakeshore that could easily have been Mediterranean but for the ever-present backdrop of the snow-crowned Cordillera Real. After encountering several pigs foraging by the shore, chickens, and cows in tiny stone enclosures, I reached the village of Challapampa, set around a sweeping sandy peninsula.

The village seemed gripped by keen activity. Colourful costumes were lined up across the school playground, a row of silver-coloured mantles dazzling brightly under the intense sun. Just as José had told me, villagers was preparing for their annual Festival of Ascension. At the entrance to the village, I was approached by a very inebriated-looking man who was supported on either side by his wife and daughter. The wife confirmed that the festival was indeed starting today, albeit not for another two hours!

I was famished after all the walking and searched for somewhere to eat. The surly owner of one closed establishment brusquely pointed me in the direction of a restaurant he said was open. I followed the directions to the open restaurant, which was hidden in a block in the centre of the village. An unpromising farmyard smell and darkened entrance didn't bode well. However, my hunger and the enthusiastic welcome of a man emerging from the gloomy interior overcame my reservations. The man struggled to switch on a dim light in what looked every bit an unfinished building. I was ushered upstairs past two more unfinished landings. To my amazement, I emerged into a bright and unexpectedly finished rooftop dining room, with windows on all sides, where I devoured a very welcome meal of soup and pejerrey (king fish).

One of the festival brass bands struck up as I was working my way through the main course. Shortly afterwards, I could glimpse a procession of brightly costumed dancers parading through the village and along the lakeshore, behind which followed the band. I still had a long way to walk back to Yumani and it was already late afternoon, but I couldn't miss this opportunity to watch the opening stages of the festival.

The parading dancers, musicians and revellers eventually crowded into the main square. There were two bands, each comprising formally dressed men wearing dark suits and sometimes hats. One played outside the open doors of Challapampa's plain stone church; the second lined up along the adjacent wall. The bands took turns to blare out their monotonous, often discordant, brass tunes (although they didn't always wait for the other to finish first!), timed by the regular thump of huge drums and cymbals. At one point, one of the bands attempted an out-of-tune rendition of "Happy Birthday to You", although it wasn't obvious who the gesture was aimed at.

The square was ablaze with the colour of five or six groups of brightly clad dancers. The setting afternoon sun produced a particularly rich riot of reds, yellows and greens. Finely dressed cholita women twirled their shawls and long skirts. Others wore intricately decorated dresses, some yellow and others black, with ornate hats adorned with bunches of tall feathers and streams of long, brightly coloured ribbons. Men swayed and lurched; younger ones leapt and adopted various warrior poses.

Andean people have long been much given to singing and dancing at every available opportunity. They celebrate festivals and happy and sad events alike with copious amounts of singing, dancing and drinking wine, beer and chicha. Although most of the dances don't look particularly complicated, the dancers (the male ones in particular) always seem to consider it necessary to lighten the effort of dancing by drinking to huge excess.

As well as helping to alleviate, or at least numb, the harshness of their existence, excessive drinking also symbolised sharing between people (hence the custom for gatherings to drink from a single glass), and was used to seal relationships or agreements.

The majority of the revellers were dancing the morenada, an ancient dance that celebrates the Aymara, mining and black slave folklore of the local people. The Aymara heartland has traditionally been the area around Lake Titicaca. The male costumes resemble fish, and are covered with tiny mirrors representing scales. These costumes are so heavy and cumbersome that the dancing amounts to little more than lurching from side to side in small steps, all the while trying not to be toppled over by the weight of the costume.

Miners from the great silver-mining town of Potosi in southern Bolivia also adopted the morenada, and many dancers today wore symbolic miner's hats. The Aymaras ridiculed everyone who wasn't Aymaran, including the black slaves brought in from Africa and Brazil after the Conquest. Many dancers wore black facemasks to capture that part of the morenada tradition.

The other dance on display today was the tinku, which celebrates a bellicose tradition originating from settlements in the region to the north of Potosi. People in that area have a long history of fighting as a result of wars between chiefdoms, to make human sacrifices and because the Aymaran religion decrees that the earth needs to be blessed by blood sacrifices. After the Conquest, the Spanish forbade and punished this ritualised fighting and sacrifice, except once a year, after which the locals had to attend a mass of atonement and forgiveness.

The tinku dance celebrates this annual symbolic fighting. Though the fighting here was very much symbolic, I learned that the tinku still takes place very much for real in towns north of Potosi. Fuelled by vast quantities of alcohol, whole villages fight furious battles. The combatants often have to be separated by police using tear gas and people regularly die in the hostility.

It was only late afternoon on the first day of the festival, but drinking formalities were already in full swing. A bowler-hatted man weaved and shimmied his way between dancers to serve beer to performers from a single glass, even making the effort to pour beer down the throats of men whose massive morenada costumes made self-service impossible. Another man entered into the spirit of the occasion by dancing with a half-full crate of beer.

As the festivities raged on, spectators – who were already participating in the drinking – gradually joined in the dancing as well. Before long, the square was a swelling mass of brightly dressed festival dancers interspersed by more dowdily dressed spectators, all resounding to the indefatigable strains of the brass bands. I was watching from what I thought was a safe distance when I felt a tap on my shoulder. I turned around to see a pretty Aymara girl giggling broadly beneath the shade of her angled bowler hat. The girl spoke to me in words I couldn't understand – probably fluent Aymara. When I failed to respond, she motioned me towards the square. When I still hesitated, she pulled me by the arm until I suddenly found myself in the midst of the swaying throng.

Bolivians curiously tend to dance in two long lines facing each other. One such double line now extended diagonally across the square, including the giggling Aymara girl and me somewhere near its cramped middle. After dancing to several "tunes" bumping into neighbours in this format, I pulled the girl through the line so that we now danced at right angles to everybody else. Although we now had much more space, the girl protested indignantly at this breach of protocol and looked positively uncomfortable, even after two of her friends joined this breakaway line, presumably to ease her awkwardness.

I knew I was dicing with darkness again as the festival lurched into full swing. Finally, with the sun disappearing behind the village and lengthy shadows stretching way out into the lake, I hurried up a steep path to rejoin the island ridge and return south. I could still hear the festivities continuing to rage from some distance away, before I eventually dropped into a low-lying area of woodland. I regained the path I had followed in the morning and speeded up. I passed several campesino families returning home after a day working their fields. Accompanying them were several heavily laden donkeys whose bulky loads often slipped and needed to be retied. The nearby hills echoed to the calls of many donkeys and mules.

In my rush to get back before nightfall, I compressed a walk that had taken me two-and-a-half hours in the morning into less than two. It was just as well I hurried. If I had arrived back in Yumani any later, I would have needed a torch to find my hotel. Only minutes after arriving back at the Posada, the dark night sky was already alight with stars.

After handing over their offerings to the attendants at the Sacred Rock, Inca pilgrims would have continued next to the Island of the Moon, the second station of their pilgrimage. Next morning, following in their footsteps, I set out in search of a boat to take me to the Island of the Moon. I edged past a couple of llamas blocking the path outside the Posada and bounded down the Inca Steps.

Although many Andean sites are incorrectly labelled "Inca" when they are in fact much older, this steep flight of over 200 stone steps, and the fountain of natural spring water that cascades beside it, both date from the Inca period. The three-nozzled stone fountain spouts water from the top of the steps. The Incas found these natural springs, which condensed in hollows within the rock, and drilled holes to release the water.

The Spanish regarded the spring as the "fountain of youth" after they observed how drinking water from the spring seemed to revive the energy of the natives. This ancient fountain remains an important water supply for Yumani, whose residents still come daily with their donkeys to carry water back up to the village.

Pilgrims walking to the Sacred Rock would have paused here to receive a blessing at the triple fountain. First, they would have drunk water from the spring to purify their spirit. They would then have received a sprinkled blessing of water from Yumani priests as they pledged obedience to the three sacred tenets of obedience to Viracocha, which are in Quechua: "Amasua" (don't steal); "Amallulla" (don't lie); and "Amakella" (don't be lazy). These three laws were sacrosanct across the Andes. Breaking any of them would have resulted in severe punishment, even death, and they can still be found on the otherwise tacky hatbands sold by pouncing artesania vendors patrolling the Inca Steps.

The only boat sailing to the Island of the Moon that day was doing a circuit that would first take me back to the celebrating village of Challapampa. The village was well into the second day of its festival and I could hear the raucous band music long before we docked at the small pier. I watched the festival celebrations again briefly, before the boat continued to the island of Koati, more commonly known as the Island of the Moon.

The Incas dedicated the island of Koati to the Moon (Koati means "of the Coya", the Coya being the Inca queen) and built on it a magnificent temple containing a statue of a woman that was gold from the waist up and silver from the waist down.

We docked at a small jetty on the southeastern shore of the island, beside which runs a narrow stretch of sandy beach on which a small flock of sheep was grazing peacefully. A small house decorated with vivid red flowers brightened up the arid landscape. Outside the house sat a cheerful cholita woman making small craft items on her lap.

Until a few decades ago, the island was used as a prison for political prisoners. Today, the Island of the Moon has a population of less than 30, including one islander who makes a very tasty cheese (with a slight hint of wine – I had tried some in La Paz) from the milk of only two cows.

A ruined Inca nunnery, Iñak Uyu (Aymara for "Women's Enclosure"), occupies a deserted site above the jetty. I climbed up to the site where I bumped into a man who turned out to be the cheese maker's husband, and who was collecting entrance money for the ruins. The nunnery occupies an artificial terrace set in a natural depression. It was built in an elaborate U shape around three sides of a small plaza, with numerous inner chambers, large exterior niches and a series of terraces. The fourth side was intentionally left open to provide a magnificent view over the lake to the chain of snow-covered peaks of the Cordillera Real.

Although I was the closest I had yet been to the peaks of the Cordillera Real, the range had disappointingly disappeared beneath a duvet of fluffy white clouds. I could only guess at the sublime awe the ancient worshippers of the celestial deities must have experienced when they watched from this sacred site the rising of the sun and moon from behind the snow peaks, and the reflection of those luminous orbs in the lake's shimmering waters.

After the disappointment of the cancelled audience with the cloud-wrapped royal mountain range, our boat continued south past the Island of Suriqui (famous for its reed boat building) towards the floating reed islands of the Uros Iruitos people.

Three tribes of Uros evolved in the Andes, their first traces dating back to 8000-5000 BC. First arrived the Uros Chipayas, who created Pukina – the first mother language of the Andes. Then came the Uros Muratos and finally the Uros Iruitos. Dominated by the more powerful Aymara and Quechua tribes, the Uros sought sanctuary on Lake Titicaca and Lake Poopo (which is connected by river to Lake Titicaca), living on artificial floating islands built of the totora reeds that line much of the lakeshore.

Anchoring our modern boat a safe distance from the islands, we jumped into a smaller wooden craft rowed by an elderly Uros man. Our boatman had a haggard face and was clad in a woollen hat, coarse orange poncho and worn open sandals. He clearly laboured as he rowed us through choppy water towards the cluster of floating islands set amongst totora reed beds.

Walking over the floating reeds felt very peculiar, particularly close to their spongy edges, where I was very mindful of putting a foot straight through the island. Such behaviour would have been most unbecoming of a visitor, besides which I didn't want to fall in, as the dazzlingly bright water was also freezing cold!

Several tiny reed huts were set around the island. Piles of totora lay drying in one corner. Although these islands are over a metre thick, their reed bases disintegrate as lower reeds fall away, and the islands need to be replenished on a regular basis by relaying their top layers.

There now remain only some 30 Uros Iruitos families around the lake. Some, like the family I was visiting, are struggling to preserve their ancient traditions, including the Pukina language. Uros families cultivate fruit and vegetables in small greenhouses fertilised by scurrying guinea pigs and quails. They also fish, mainly at night. An appetising smell emanating from one of the small huts in a corner of the island was revealed to be a simmering soup of karachi, the small fish that forms the staple catch of Uros fishermen. For dessert, I was handed a stripped totora reed, which had a slightly sweet taste and a crisp, refreshing texture. I would have happily stayed on the island longer to eat more reeds, but by now the elderly boatman was waiting to take me off his home.

Another declining tradition around Lake Titicaca is the totora reed boat, although a few such boats still share the lake with the bow waves of sleek motor cruisers and hydrofoils capable of over 30 knots. The lake's most famous reed boat builders come from the Island of Suriqui. I was honoured to meet Demetrio Limachi, one of the celebrated trio of brothers who won a competition to build the adventurer Thor Heyerdahl a 12-metre reed boat, the RA II, in which he successfully sailed across the Atlantic in 1970 (RA I had sunk in an earlier attempt).

Demetrio demonstrated the intricacies of his craft and proudly described the series of boats he had helped build. Although the skill of the boat builder was undeniable, it wasn't hard to see why this tradition is dying when Demetrio explained that reed boats have a working life of less than a year, after which they need to be completely overhauled or replaced altogether.

Clambering back aboard our longer-lived, though much less elegant craft, we motored home to the Island of the Sun. I trudged my way back up the now deserted Inca Steps and beyond to the top of the island ridge. I drank a coffee in a small café set in a wooden shack as I watched the sun slowly set. Small trains of heavily laden llamas and donkeys climbed up to the ridge at the end of their day's labour.

The setting sun lit up the distant Peruvian shore in a warm glow, but when I crossed back to the eastern (Bolivian view) side of the ridge, my jaw dropped. The Cordillera Real and the Island of the Moon (particularly its distinctive red northern headland) glowed radiantly in the rich blaze of the dipping sun. I was again engulfed by the total solitude of my setting, made more immense by the clear sky and endless visibility.

As evening descended over the distant mountains, I set off in search of Emily, a young English teacher at the Yumani school, who I had been recommended to meet. Sheep, donkeys and llamas grazed their way lazily along the uneven, rocky path that led to the school entrance. The school was spread over two adjoining square fields, around which were laid out classrooms and several teachers' houses. A female herder was encouraging a small flock of sheep across the larger of the school courtyards. Some young children were playing a three-a-side game of football on the smaller yard. Radio Yumani – the community broadcast tannoy – blared out public messages at intervals from its nearby headquarters, encouraging villagers to attend English classes and other skills workshops.

I was directed to Emily's classroom, which was set on the larger of the two courtyards. Teaching the only class still in progress at 7pm, Emily was heavily wrapped up in a scarf against the unheated classroom and a recent bout of flu.

Emily divided her students according to profession. Tonight was the class for restaurateurs, as testified by a blackboard full of words like spoon, bowl and plate. Tonight's class comprised three men and two girls. The latter two rushed out when Emily announced that it was time for a test.

The stark and sparsely furnished classroom had only two rows of double desks that barely filled the front half of the room. Students often had to sit on windowsills. The only light in the room came from a single bulb hanging precariously over the door in the corner, which was connected by bare wires to a power source outside a nearby block. The power went off abruptly at one point during the test, causing much rushing around by examinees before the light was restored and the test could continue. Emily explained that these lighting arrangements actually represented an upgrade; she previously taught by the light of her torch. Not surprisingly, she now guarded her bulb and cable preciously and carefully packed them in her bag when we left.

At the end of the test, Emily introduced me to the three examinees, each of whom enthusiastically practised greetings and basic questions in English. One of the restaurateurs invited us to his establishment for dinner, but we declined his offer, as it would have required a torchlit trek across the ridge. We opted to go instead to a cosy candlelit eating shack in central Yumani, which Emily was surprised to find was run by one of her students who should have been at tonight's test. Like his classmates earlier, the amiable but slow man delightedly practised English greetings with me. He also offered us a sharp-tasting tea made from koa to help speed Emily's recovery from flu, while we waited over an hour and a half for our food.

Returning to the Posada by the light of my torch, I gazed out once more over the Island of the Moon, over which a full moon had fittingly risen into a dark sky smeared with stars. The moon's reflection rippled over the calm lake surface, joining the Islands of the Sun and Moon in a shimmering bridge of light. Occasional flashes of lightning danced over the distant peaks of the Cordillera Real, beneath the northernmost of which nestled my next destination – the mountain village of Sorata.

Here I was on a silent, perfectly still night on the Island of the Sun, marvelling at a spectacular display by two of the Incas' most revered deities. Even knowing nothing about Inca beliefs and the mythology of the Islands of the Sun and Moon, this was an intensely awe-inspiring spectacle. With the Inca legends added in, the experience verged on the spiritual.

CHAPTER FIVE

ORIGINS AND EXPANSION

The Incas were no more than a small, insignificant mountain tribe in the Cuzco valley just a century before the Spanish Conquistadores arrived and found them the undisputed overlords of South America.

Early monarchs had led the then small Inca tribe into the Peruvian Andes sometime around 1200 AD. They established their capital at Cuzco and believed themselves to be the chosen people of Inti, the Sun God. They believed that the Inca ruler (the Sapa Inca) was a living deity directly descended from the Sun – the son of the Sun. According to their beliefs, the creator god Viracocha sired the Sun, who in turn sired the Sapa Inca.

Many of the accomplishments of the dazzling but short-lived Inca empire are credited to one man: Pachacuti Inca Yupanqui, the ninth Inca ruler. The name Pachacuti means "Overturner of the Earth" and he is probably the first historical rather than mythical Inca ruler. Above all his numerous accomplishments, Pachacuti transformed a small regional state into one of the greatest empires the world has ever witnessed.

Son of the semi-mythical Viracocha Inca, Pachacuti was a skilful soldier and supreme statesman, who rose to power after defending Cuzco against overwhelming odds. As Inca ruler, Pachacuti established an ordered system of religion, government and city planning, and launched the Incas on an unparalleled series of military conquests. Pachacuti's son Topa Inca and grandson Huayna Capac continued the tradition of religious worship, ordered government and military expansion.

Long before the heroic exploits of Pachacuti Inca Yupanqui, the Incas were already familiar with the concept of "pachacuti" or cataclysmic event, when one historical age ends and another begins. According to their chronicles, the world had already been destroyed four times in ancient times. The arrival of the Incas marked the dawn of the fifth age, an epoch during which the Incas, under direct orders from the Sun, were to fulfil their destiny of bringing civilisation to a chaotic world.

The great Inca empire came very close to never happening at all. Following the collapse of the Tiahuanaco empire sometime around 1200, the Incas were only one of many regional tribes vying for supremacy. By the reign of Viracocha Inca, around two hundred small states occupied the Cuzco region.

Around 1440, the neighbouring rival Chanca tribe attacked Cuzco as part of its own expansion ambitions and almost overwhelmed the unprepared Incas. The reigning Viracocha Inca abandoned his capital and fled with his people to a hilltop stronghold above the town of Calca in the Sacred Valley. Vowing to die rather than flee with his father, Viracocha Inca's son Pachacuti gathered a tiny force and assumed the impossible task of defending the city against the overwhelming might of the Chancas.

On the eve of battle, the creator god Viracocha appeared in a dream to Pachacuti and promised to send warriors that would help the young lord to victory. As the massed ranks of Chancas descended onto the plain above Cuzco, 20 squadrons of warriors duly appeared as if from nowhere and helped Pachacuti to a great and miraculous victory. Several chronicles reported how stones from the fields transformed into these warriors.

The victorious Pachacuti then routed the Chancas beyond the limits of Cuzco. To consolidate his triumph, Pachacuti assembled an army of one hundred thousand warriors and quickly subjugated neighbouring tribes that had allied themselves with the Chancas.

The Incas used to good advantage this illusion of being helped by stones (pururaucas) that would transform into armed human warriors, and they worshipped these stones as shrines. The fear these pururaucas inspired caused many enemies to flee from the Incas almost without putting up a fight.

Among the first chiefdoms that Pachacuti subjugated were those of Vitcos and Vilcabamba, two remote regions isolated in the jungle-choked mountains northwest of Cuzco. Ironically, these scenes of some of the earliest Inca triumphs were later to witness the final days of the crumbling empire, when the remnants of the Inca forces fled into the Vilcabamba forests pursued by Spanish Conquistadores.

Pachacuti's victory over the Chancas launched the Incas on their incomparable course of explosive expansion. Pachacuti ("Overturner of the Earth") is a fitting name for a man whose empire building exploits have been likened to those of Alexander the Great, and who was responsible for a string of great conquests that set the Incas on their way to ruling a domain comparable in size to the Roman Empire. Pachacuti and his sons personally led or directed numerous expeditions to discover, conquer and subjugate any lands they desired, as far as they wished.

Three generations of ruling Incas each combined a voracious appetite for conquest with masterly skills in warfare and administration. Pachacuti, his son Topa Inca Yupanqui and to a lesser extent his grandson Huayna Capac each marched huge Inca armies from one victorious campaign to another. This trail of conquest spurred the dynamic imperialism that unified the diverse and warring peoples and states that occupied the Andes at the time. These rulers were driven partly by the Incas' belief in their destiny and partly by the need for each successive ruler to secure his own wealth.

Together, these three generations of rulers created one of the world's greatest empires, which stretched from southern Colombia to central Chile and Argentina, and from the Pacific Ocean to the Amazon. This vast empire stretched some 5,000 kilometres down the length of the Andean spine and spanned several hundreds of kilometres across. At its height, it encompassed over 10 million subjects.

Despite their undoubted military prowess, the Incas' explosive expansion probably owed just as much to military bluff and their powers of diplomacy and persuasion as it did to brute force. When they began their expansion, the Incas didn't enjoy vast military superiority over their neighbours. Neither did they enjoy any advantages of great wealth or vastly superior manpower. They bolstered their numbers by conscripting the troops of native chiefs and defeated enemies, and offered favourable terms, even gifts and enhanced status, to encourage leaders of areas they wished to annex to surrender without a fight.

Such became their renown and the terror they caused in their opponents that the Incas often conquered areas without even needing to fight. Pachacuti would march his massive army into areas he wished to annex and simply demand that native chiefs subjugate themselves to the "Son of the Sun", who was there to lead them out of their bestial and barbarous lives. Should they refuse, the alternative was that the Inca would soon be drinking blood from their skulls, wearing a necklace strung with their teeth, playing flutes made from their bones and beating drums fashioned from their skins – threats that the Incas weren't afraid to carry out if necessary.

The Incas' primary motivations for going to war were their ambitions to expand the empire, punish rebellions and repress border enemies. Inca preparations for military campaigns invariably involved much divination, feasting, fasting and ritual sacrifices of animals and sometimes children. The Incas marched into battle carrying with them an array of their most important idols, including images of the Sun, the Thunder, the founding Inca Manco Capac and other idols specific to each emperor. The Incas also made a point of seizing the idols of their enemies, which to them symbolised capturing their power. The Incas displayed these captured idols in Cuzco, thus reinforcing their power over their subjects by forcing them to come to Cuzco in order to worship their gods.

The Incas liked to attack or threaten attack by presenting overwhelming force, which if necessary would attack by all rushing forward together with great shouting and clamour.

Long-range weapons used in warfare and hunting included slings, spears and arrows, sometimes fired with poisoned tips. Native Indians were particularly effective with the sling. They could reputedly hurl large stones with enough force and accuracy to kill a horse, and could break a sword in two from a distance of thirty paces.

To catch and bring down an enemy, they threw a bolas: two weighty round stones joined by a thin cord. Thrown low at a victim, the cord would entangle the legs of a man or horse and the stones would swing tight to immobilise him. Indians were so skilled in the use of the bolas they could bring down a running deer in a hunt. For closer range combat, the Incas used lances, halberds, pikes, darts, clubs and battle-axes.

Although the precise size of the Incas' invading forces remains uncertain, what isn't in doubt is that Inca forces never travelled light on manpower. To quash a rebellion in what is today Bolivia and Chile, Topa Inca reputedly gathered an army of one hundred thousand warriors, in addition to which he took five thousand men as personal guards, one thousand noble lords from Cuzco, another four thousand from towns around Cuzco, and his personal friends.

Other reports survive of Huayna Capac travelling into battle with 2,000 concubines (leaving twice that number of wives back home in Cuzco!), which gives some idea of how many the fighting force plus the porters and servants must have numbered in total. When Manco Inca laid siege to Cuzco in 1536, he reputedly assembled a combined army of over 200,000.

The Incas assembled their forces from native chiefs around the empire. They rewarded their armies with various spoils of war, including captured women, gold and silver, valuable garments, livestock and land.

It was an Inca tradition that at the end of victorious campaigns, their generals marched important prisoners of war back to Cuzco at the head of the triumphant army. On reaching Cuzco, the returning general would present to the Inca the captured clothes, weapons and insignias of these important prisoners. The Inca would then trample these items as a symbol of his dominion over the defeated state or region. Prisoners were then thrown into jails containing wild animals (lions, bears and snakes) where many were eaten alive. Those not eaten after three days were released and allowed to swear allegiance to the Inca, Cuzco and the Sun.

In addition to his imperialist conquests, Pachacuti is also credited with the complete reconstruction of the city of Cuzco, and the building (or at least starting the building) of several of the most magnificent Inca citadels: Sacsahuaman, Ollantaytambo, Machu Picchu, Pisac and possibly Vitcos. If all that wasn't enough, Pachacuti also created brilliant systems of government, law and administration, and fashioned the Inca religion.

Pachacuti may also have instigated the creation legend whereby Inca monarchs descended divinely from the Sun (as Sons of the Sun) and their sister-queens (coyas) descended from the Moon. This established the authority of the Inca royalty as absolute and incapable of being challenged. To challenge the Inca would be to challenge God himself, and the reverence demanded by this divine link helped buttress the impregnable right of the Incas to rule.

In addition to the personal dynamism of the great conquering Incas Pachacuti, Topa Inca Yupanqui and Huayna Capac, several other factors contributed to the Incas' meteoric ascent from rural hill tribe to undisputed lords of the Andes in just a few dazzling decades.

First, attack was often the best means of defence during the age of continued conflict that followed the collapse of Tiahuanaco. Subjects naturally looked to military leaders who could deliver security, resources and spoils of war. In this manner, successful military expansion became a requirement of all Inca kings.

Second, Inca ideology, such as their belief in their god-given mission to civilise a chaotic world, and their idealised dynastic histories, further drove their leaders to continued conquest.

Third, individual Inca leaders sought personal wealth. Under the Andean tradition of split inheritance, each successive monarch inherited the throne and state resources but not the deceased ruler's personal wealth, which the dead king's kin group retained so that they could continue to worship him forever. Each new Inca monarch therefore had to accumulate wealth for himself and his kin group.

Over the years, the quest for plunder calmed into the annexation of productive resources, such as the Altiplano for its flocks of alpacas and llamas, the Bolivian mines at Potosi for their silver, the jungles for their gold, and the southern Andes for their minerals.

CHAPTER SIX

SORATA

Leaving behind the tranquillity of Lake Titicaca, the founding Incas Manco Capac and Mama Ocllo travelled north to the city of Cuzco, where they founded their capital and built their civilisation.

Back on the Bolivian "mainland", my aim was to follow in their footsteps, which meant another grinding bus journey across the Altiplano, this time to Sorata. The mountain village of Sorata lies in the foothills of Mount Illampu at the northern extreme of the Cordillera Real. It was in Sorata where I would search for the riding mules I would need for the main part of my expedition north into Peru.

Buses for Sorata leave from a cheerless street corner around which converge several tiny shops and assorted street vendors. Small selections of colourful fruit and vegetables lay wilting in wooden crates in front of the shops. Stony-faced shopkeepers sat in the shade of their darkened doorways. One of the shops was receiving a delivery of flour. Two men were involved in the backbreaking work of carrying the weighty sacks from the back of a truck into the shop. They wrapped their head and shoulders with large cloths, but couldn't avoid getting covered in white powder every time they hauled one of the sacks.

Arriving at the bus station in the late afternoon, I was concerned to find the jovial bus driver still fixing the vehicle minutes before we were due to depart. Two Israelis were asking if they could travel in a smaller bus, but were told that this medium-sized vehicle was the only one available. What did they know that I didn't, but perhaps should? Several local people who didn't have tickets waited in the hope of seats, at least on the floor of the vehicle. From my previous experience of Bolivian bus travel, I doubted that they would be turned away.

Having bagged the front seat next to the driver, I naively thought I would be insulated from the inevitable squeezing in of extra passengers into every inch of available space. Not so. As I suspected, the minor detail that all the seats had been taken didn't prove in any way a hindrance to would-be travellers. What I hadn't expected was that two would squash into the footwell in front of me.

Yet again, we began our journey at a frustratingly pedestrian pace. Bolivian bus drivers tend to drive slowly at the start of journeys to pick up additional passengers (even when buses appear full). The walking pace at which we set off was ridiculous even by these standards. More than once, I felt like shouting at the driver to get a move on. We weren't even picking up many additional passengers, not that there was any space left for them to occupy.

To make matters worse, after plodding in this manner for an hour, we had to endure an impassioned half-hour presentation from a health supplements salesman (who implored passengers to please just take a look, with absolutely no obligation to buy). He then had the audacity to ask if anybody could change a 100 Bolivianos note. This request was met by a deathly silence, after which the salesman sat back down sheepishly at the back of the bus and disembarked soon afterwards with his stock intact.

We navigated around the remnants of more roadblocks in El Alto and reached the massive, 200 kilometre-long flank of the Cordillera Real, at which point the driver finally found a gear higher than second. Unfortunately, he also found the volume switch for the bus's entertainment system, which suddenly blared out crackly cumbia music at ear-bursting decibels. Several passengers seated beside the rear speakers shouted at the driver to turn the volume down, but their cries were no match for the music. They suffered the deafeningly loud music for several kilometres before the driver finally heard their pleas and moderated the noise level.

Crouched in the aisle between the driver and me (behind the two in the footwell) was a formidable cholita ticket collector cum general fixer, one of whose duties was to persuade police officers to ignore the fact that we were obviously travelling considerably overladen with passengers. Arriving at a police checkpoint, the fixer unceremoniously shooed several startled passengers off the bus to walk through the checkpoint and be picked up on the other side. Not even the Bolivian transport police – who aren't noted for high intellect – fell for that one. The cholita's stern expression immediately mellowed into one full of charm and innocence. After repeated pleas and imploring looks, she finally won over the policemen, who allowed us to progress on our over-heavy way.

Since arriving in Bolivia, I had had many opportunities to observe the various traditional costumes worn by cholitas. Most are based on several layers of ample skirts. The outer skirt is plaited and often itself layered, and sometimes finished with a bright satin finish. On top of these skirts, they sometimes wear a simple apron with pockets. Wrapped around their shoulders, they wear a broad, brightly decorated shawl with long tassels, over which they throw their stuffed aguayos (brightly striped cloths folded into universal carrying sacks).

They neatly weave their black hair into one or two long plaits (joined together at the bottom if two), with more tassels at their ends. On their heads, they wear the distinctive, "bowler" hat with a narrow, upturned rim. These vary according to region, but are invariably worn at an angle and appear several sizes too small. How these hats stay on their heads remains an unsolved Andean mystery. The small hat, bright shawl and voluminous skirt give cholitas a brightly coloured cone shape and an overriding impression of an excessively decorated Christmas tree.

Reaching the open road, we passed peak after peak of the glittering Cordillera Real on our right hand horizon. First came Chacaltaya, notable for the sloping tongue of ice that provides some of the highest skiing in the world. Then came Huayna Potosi, one of Bolivia's most popular 6,000-metre climbing peaks. Then loomed the dark form of my favourite – Condoriri. Needing no translation of its name, twin ridges sweep down from either side of its angular summit, giving the mountain the appearance of a huge condor lifting its wings on takeoff.

After two hours, we reached the town of Achacachi, which seemed to comprise little more than a long main street along which ran two shabby rows of rundown brick and adobe hovels. Many of these dwellings had lost entire window frames, and others were even missing parts of their walls. Achacachi is most noted for the belligerence of its inhabitants (who have been the instigators of many a blockade), and as the home of one-time leading activist "Mallku". As we stopped briefly at the far end of the main street, the usual army of cholitas swarmed around the bus, offering through the windows plastic bags of dangerous-looking juice and stomach-threatening cooked savoury snacks.

After a brief pause, and with some vendors still frantically doing trade beside the moving bus, we emerged from the narrow street onto a dry, open plain from where we could see the whole elongated flank of Mount Illampu. We turned in a large sweep towards a stone bridge over a small river. Several people had driven cars and vans into the shallow water and were using the river as a natural car wash.

Leaving Achacachi, we turned off the main road onto a bumpy track heading straight towards the mountains. The bus was still packed with many cholitas carrying brightly coloured sacks bursting with produce. Many disembarked at what seemed like the middle of nowhere. Illampu and her sister Ancohuma loomed ever larger, their glacier-streaked gullies and white snow peaks glistening in the bright sun.

We bumped along on a dusty single-track road for almost three hours. We were repeatedly thrown violently from side to side as we struggled along heavily rutted tracks. Clouds of dust regularly choked all on board and obscured all view from the windows. When we could see through the dust plumes, a window-swamping view swept down from high peaks past isolated hamlets and lush fields into the green and brown chequerboard of the farmed valley far below. Sorata itself was tantalisingly visible in the distance, although we could see that we would need to twist and turn many, many more times along the meandering track before we could even begin to contemplate arrival.

The late afternoon sun was blinding as it sank towards the Altiplano; then darkness descended rapidly. Low clouds drifted over a mountain pass, reflecting back the bus's headlights in an eerie haze. Visibility became very difficult through the muffling mist; fortunately, so bad that we couldn't see any of the awful drop-offs that threaten for much of the high altitude journey.

We passed fields of tall maize with withered brown leaves. We occasionally stopped on the narrow track to let oncoming traffic – including a small herd of cows – pass. Small groups of campesino families were doing their laundry in the energetic though narrow river, their voluminous skirts laid out to dry like large flowers with white petals edged with purple.

Just as we were losing daylight along the single-track road, we ground to a halt at a standoff with the vacant-looking driver of an oncoming bus. The other driver just sat resolutely in his cab and refused to reverse or in fact do anything, despite the protestations of our driver. I didn't fancy the other driver's chances once our cholita fixer started to let fly with her quick-fire tongue, particularly after most of the other passengers from our bus surrounded his cab. After another verbal barrage from our fixer, the other driver duly reversed to a wider part of the road and let us pass. During the stalemate, most of the other passengers from my bus curiously got off and walked down the road, as if not trusting our driver in this manoeuvre. Some passengers shone torches and gesticulated excitedly in an effort to progress proceedings.

As we finally neared Sorata, we descended into a local bus service and stopped increasingly frequently. I became trapped beside a small, dark-skinned man dressed in a charcoal grey suit, sandals and hat, who smelt heavily of coca. The characteristic slow jaw movements, cheek bulge and white sack over the shoulder confirmed my suspicions.

Coca is a leafy bush that grows at the edge of humid forests on the eastern slopes of the Andes. Chewing it releases a tiny quantity of cocaine, which produces a mildly narcotic effect – excellent for dulling the pain of hard labour and harsh climates. Used since the days of Tiahuanaco, coca leaves are sacred to campesinos. The leaves play a major role in all Andean rituals and religious ceremonies, and are drunk in a tea (mate de coca) as a cure for everything from altitude sickness to period pains.

By now, my backside was numb and I wriggled around uncomfortably in my seat as if in the final act of a lengthy opera. I was starting to lose the will to live when we finally lurched into Sorata's medieval looking main square. The darkened square was centred around pretty gardens and planted with towering trees that direct the eye to the glaciated summits of the high mountains beyond.

Snuggling beneath the northern extreme of the Cordillera Real, Sorata lies at an altitude of 2,700 metres in the foothills of Illampu and Ancohuma, whose massive white snow peaks loom large over the village. A network of energetic rivers plunges down the valley all around Sorata, joining downstream to form the Rio San Cristobal, which loops north as the River Beni to Rurrenabaque and eventually Brazil.

I headed straight for the Residencial Sorata, a once impressive, but now fading, colonial-style hotel that commands one corner of the square. The hotel seemed deserted and the receptionist handed me a large key from a long line hanging on the wall. To reach my room, I walked through the hotel's cavernous reception area and warren of courtyards and pretty gardens, and passed open, high-ceilinged public rooms filled with period furniture. Reaching my room, I immediately collapsed on the bed.

Notwithstanding the evocative colonial styling, my overwhelming reason to stay at the Residencial was to meet the manager, Louis Demers, a French Canadian who several Bolivian contacts had told me possessed an encyclopaedic local knowledge. I had spoken to Louis from La Paz and he had suggested I might well find suitable riding mules or horses around Sorata. The signs were already looking positive. Having seldom before seen horses in Bolivia, I had spotted three just outside the village. Just as we arrived, a man was riding an attractive white mount through the main square.

After resting in my room for an hour, I retraced my steps through the courtyards and huge reception area in search of Louis. Louis had just returned from a walk into the nearby hills, which he took every evening. Louis was a pensive, bearded man who had lived in Bolivia for over a decade, despite repeated disenchantment at the local business climate and regular threats to leave. Louis bemoaned that following the disruption of the recent blockades, I was the only guest staying at the hotel that night. "Lying at the end of a long cul-de-sac mountain road on the wrong side of Achacachi, Sorata is always the first town to be blockaded and the last to be un-blockaded," he lamented.

Brightening up, Louis grinned and said, "I think I've found a mule for you," as we walked together into the single-roomed mountain guides office on the opposite side of the alley in front of the hotel. Louis introduced me to Eduardo, one of the local guides, who smiled a lot and told many jokes. More relevantly, Eduardo explained that he knew of a fine looking mule that I could buy to use on the expedition. The animal lived in the hills above Sorata and its owner had gone away on business, but I could go and ride it tomorrow if I wished.

Very encouraged by the news of the mule, I set off into the night in search of somewhere to eat whilst Louis returned to the hotel to sort out some paperwork. Sorata's main square contained a number of small eateries, ranging from basic to very basic, plus a couple of more upmarket Italian-style brasseries. A further number of eateries lined the now quiet cobbled market street leading off the square. I opted for a tiny traditional eating house on the far side of the square from the hotel, where I enjoyed a five-course dinner beside the din of a crackly television.

On my way back across the square, I stopped at one of a couple of dimly lit stalls to buy a couple of chocolate bars and some packets of toasted haba beans. These were the beans I had seen drying in the sun beside Lake Titicaca. I soon found out that these beans are not only tasty and nutritious, but in toasted and salted form, are very difficult – almost impossible – to stop eating, no matter how much you might already have eaten for supper.

Returning to the hotel, I found Louis eating his own supper alone in the antique kitchen of the Residencial. We chatted late into the night and Louis told me many stories about the area and his experiences of Bolivian life. Most fascinating was the tale of Warmi Marka, a legendary village of Amazonian women near Sorata, to which men go but never return! Natives apparently directed Spanish Conquistadores there when they demanded to know where the Indians had hidden their gold and treasure. Locals maintain that gold still lies hidden at Warmi Marca, but that the women will kill any male would-be prospectors!

The next morning, I ate a leisurely breakfast in the Residencial's deserted dining room with just the gentle beat of cumbia music for company. Looking out through the open window shutters, the sun was shining brightly over densely planted gardens of colourful flowers and fruit trees that reached up to the first floor balustrade of the garden courtyard.

After breakfast, Eduardo and I set off to look at the mule. We walked up a steep alley and passed several lanes of houses and small trees ablaze with bright purple flowers. As Sorata started to peter out, the track climbed steeply through a series of dusty switchbacks and levelled out on a ridge, beside which stood a fine looking mule tethered to a small patch of grazing.

Just as Eduardo had said, the mule was a handsome, ebony-coloured animal with a tan and grey muzzle. It was uncommonly tall for a mule (most local mules were the size of donkeys, whereas this one stood as high as a horse), had a sleek, shiny coat and long, fluffy ears.

Eduardo didn't have any riding tack, so I rode on a saddle of blankets. Without stirrups, I had to jump up onto the mule's back from the ground, which wasn't easy onto an animal of this height. In place of reins was a length of rope passed through a ring on the head collar. Not surprisingly, the mule was difficult to control.

As soon as I jumped up onto the mule, it immediately started marching off up the hill. Great, I thought. My principal concern had been of a stereotypical mule digging in its hooves and resolutely refusing to move. At least that seemed unlikely to happen. However, it didn't take long before I realised that none of the usual riding aids – to go, to turn and, most alarmingly, to stop – had any effect on this animal. The mule and I had clearly been brought up in very different schools of equitation!

The narrow path and the mule's tendency to walk without being asked meant that the only problem at this stage was stopping. I tried to teach the mule to stop to "whoa" and pressure on the makeshift reins, but pulling on the head collar rope soon turned into a test of strength I knew I was never going to win. Amazingly, I had some successes, although stopping distances were worryingly long.

The mule at first seemed docile but my attempts to exert some control over our direction of travel seemed to annoy it, to the extent that it tried to buck me off several times. I dismissed this as a temporary rather than irretrievable breakdown in our relationship. On the plus side, at least the mule wasn't constantly diving into every patch of edible vegetation. I decided this animal would do.

The mule, like many animals in the Andes, had no name. I decided to christen it Coco, short for Coconut, on account of its dark brown coat and the great difficulty of cracking it.

Back in his office, Eduardo introduced me to Arturo Lasso, another local man who would act as our arriero (horse/mule handler), while Eduardo would come as guide and cook. Arturo would also bring along two of his own mules to help carry our equipment.

CHAPTER SEVEN

CORDILLERA MUÑECAS

The next morning, leaving Sorata on a long dusty track, Arturo, Eduardo, our three mules and I descended towards the tiny village of San Pedro, whose few houses and school were scattered around a sloping football pitch of parched earth. The village was so quiet I wondered whether anybody actually lived there. A couple of tethered donkeys were grazing on pitifully slim pickings. Only the occasional crowing of a cockerel, clucking of chickens or barking of a lone dog broke the silence. Otherwise, there was just the faint background murmur of birds.

Beyond the village rose the peaks of the Cordillera Muñecas, the relatively tame mountain range sandwiched between the mighty glaciated summits of the Cordilleras Real and Apolobamba.

We re-tied the cargo on our mules outside the very ramshackle school, which had many shattered windows and much rubbish and broken furniture strewn about its classroom. Loads checked and secure, we descended past many cactuses through a steep-sided although not deep canyon towards the Rio San Cristobal.

Arturo explained that the river had unfortunately been denuded of fish by upstream mining contamination. This being the dry season, the river was only a trickle of its summer torrent, as testified by the width of the dry bed we walked over to reach the water's edge. Even so, there was no dry crossing available. We had to take off our boots and socks and wade across the icy melt water after the mules (even Coco was carrying food and equipment so it wasn't possible to ride).

Patches of strikingly red soil and rock peeked through a thin covering of scrubby grass on the mountainside. The glacial ramparts of Illampu provided a constant, dominating backdrop, its snow-burdened summit towering high above the abundant, green valley.

Climbing beyond the river, we topped a rise and could see the canyon stretching into the distance on its westward path. Through the far-off haze, we could see the shadowy, jagged profile of the Cordillera Muñecas.

We passed silent hamlets where nothing (not even the ubiquitous fierce dogs) stirred. Parched maize fields had recently been harvested, and these plots of stubble were now grazed by small numbers of cows and a few sheep with long, thin legs. High up on the mountainside, a shepherd was driving a tiny flock of sheep. Smoke rose from a couple of forest fires on the opposite side of the valley as campesinos prepared soil for next season's planting.

The climb was long and hot, and we passed only tiny tricklets of streams, where we paused to rest and let the mules gorge themselves on piles of dried maize leaves. The animals were surprisingly well behaved, apart from occasional minor squabbling over first watering rights, and on one occasion making a rumbustious beeline for a farmer's stubble field.

We reached a barely acceptable camp at around 2,700 metres on a not quite level patch of rocky terrain just to the side of the path, beside which grew several fruit-bearing avocado trees. While we stuffed ourselves with coffee and biscuits and pondered the many stones we would need to remove from the ground to be able to sleep comfortably, the mules were tethered unsatisfactorily to the steep slope with very limited grazing.

As dusk fell, Arturo and I went in search of mule food. We scrambled up a steep grassy slope to an isolated farmhouse hidden on a balcony above our camp. Passing a sheep pen, barking dog and inquisitive donkey, we reached the farmhouse entrance, where an amiable elderly couple greeted us. Arturo explained the purpose of our visit and the elderly man confirmed that he had plenty of spare food for our mules.

The woman led the way down through the couple's decimated maize field to a corner piled high with dried leaves. We were invited to help ourselves to as much as our mules could eat (or rather, as much as we could carry) for a payment of 5 Bolivianos. Arturo gathered a huge pile of dried leaves, which he then lifted onto his back secured by just a flimsy-looking piece of canvas cloth. Bent double under the mountain of leaves, he then proceeded to skip back down the steep slope carrying the massive load much faster than I could follow. Back at camp, the mules snuffled excitedly as the mountain of maize approached. They munched away contentedly whilst Eduardo started to cook supper.

The flank of Illampu turned golden brown in the warm evening light as we started to eat our supper of vegetable soup with noodles. Gloom chased the golden glow up to and beyond the snowline at a visible rate, replacing it with dull shadow as we watched. Arturo and Eduardo chattered away in Aymara.

I drifted to sleep to the snorting and rhythmic munching of mules enthusiastically working their way through their large mounds of maize leaves (doused with salted water to give them energy) just outside my tent. Several times, one of the mules was so frantic in its attempts to scrape up its food I felt certain that momentum would carry it at any second into my tent. Sleeping opportunities coincided with short breaks between the mules' noisy eating bouts, and were further interrupted by a furiously barking dog in the middle of the night.

Hot coffee and porridge eased the chill of a cold dawn as the morning sun took an age to reach our camp. Rearranging our equipment onto Arturo's two mules and tying the huge mound of remaining maize leaves onto Coco, we climbed gently on a wide path bordered by sloping corn fields. All around, the green mountainside was criss-crossed by a maze of tracks and pathlets. A buzzard hovered above the razor sharp outline of the mountains standing out against the pure blue sky.

We reached Chuchulaya, a quiet village that was just getting going for the day. Adobe houses with corrugated iron roofs clustered around a central sloping maize field grazed by cattle, around which were yet more maize fields – all too steep for the otherwise-obligatory football pitch. We stopped to buy bread, only to find the village shop closed. We continued climbing up a path behind an elderly cholita who used a stick and hurled small rocks to herd some sheep and cattle to higher grazing.

We didn't see another person for several hours, until meeting a cheerful man, his wife, young child and even younger puppy, driving a herd of miniature goats in the opposite direction to us. We chatted briefly on the path before the group hurried on down the trail and all was silent again.

Spiny, red-leafed cactuses, and some of the upright, sentinel variety familiar to watchers of spaghetti westerns, lined the path. Just below us were wispy, pale yellow wheat fields that swayed lightly in the breeze. Every sense suggested total tranquillity.

Our path crossed many side valleys, which had been gouged with such deep indents we zigzagged endlessly. In the process, we lost much hard-earned altitude and covered very little real distance. The village of Chuchulaya, which we had left several hours earlier, still looked discouragingly close.

We eventually reached Carazani village, with its rundown adobe houses, some thatched, and pigs and dogs lazing in the middle of its car-less streets. We paused for lunch beside a small cluster of above ground adobe graves topped with corrugated iron sheets and simple wooden crosses.

We stopped early at 3pm on a terraced balcony of flat grass at around 3,300 metres, beneath the hamlet of Cumlile. A group of campesino shepherds had advised us that the next river was two hours away (or should I interpret that as four given the speed at which locals walk?). We decided to camp at this spot since there was good grazing for the mules, although the "river" by which we camped was no more than the tiniest of trickles. We had to leave a pan to fill slowly beneath the trickle of droplets to collect enough water to cook supper. During the evening, several cows and sheep wandered through our camp to graze and share the precious water.

Examining our surroundings, we discovered that we had camped on a series of disused agricultural terraces. With several levels available over which we could spread out, we cooked on one, set up our tents on another and tethered the mules to a third.

I woke next morning to the sound of lively chatter. Several local shepherds had wandered through our camp. Eduardo was engaging them in earnest conversation that involved much arm waving and pointing in different directions. It turned out that we were on the wrong path and needed to change course.

Eduardo thought he knew a "direct route" to the correct path, but this involved a section he hadn't travelled before – a steep descent through dense woodland to an uncertain river crossing for the mules.

Reaching the point where we would soon start descending towards the trees and river, we thought it best to check our directions. Arturo darted nimbly down the steep path and sped up to an elevated pasture to consult a shepherd tending a small flock of sheep.

Watching the speed at which Arturo raced up the steep slope reminded me of the Inca chasquis I had read about – running relay messengers who carried information along the road network through a combination of spoken messages and quipus (records comprising knots tied on multi-coloured strings). Scholars have estimated that chasquis could cover almost 250 kilometres a day, carrying everything from news of military conquests to fresh sea fish for the Inca's supper. Such was their speed that chasquis could bring the Inca news in Cuzco of what was happening in Quito (some 1,500 kilometres away) in just eight days. Chasqui blood surely coursed through Arturo's veins.

Whilst Arturo hurried off to ask directions from the shepherd, the less energetic Eduardo shouted to another campesino high up on the hillside above the woodland. Both conversations seemed to confirm that both we and the mules should be able to descend the path and that the water level was low enough to allow a safe crossing. The campesino with whom Eduardo had been conducting a long-range conversation walked down the hillside to join us on the path. After some further conversation, he agreed to lead us down to the river. We gave him an apple and 10 Bolivianos for his trouble.

The exasperated mules must have thought we were complete idiots. First, we led them down a difficult, narrow path, and then allowed them to wander back up – munching all available vegetation along the way – whilst we deliberated at length which way to go. Finally, we dragged them down the same path again, and on through dense woodland with barely enough clearance for crouching people, let alone pack-laden animals.

I hadn't expected to need a machete until we reached Peru's wildly overgrown Cordillera Vilcabamba, but one would have been very handy that afternoon to help us fight our way through the stinging thorns and entangled branches. Finally emerging from the darkened woodland, we slipped and slid our way down a steep narrow gravel path to what turned out to be a very tame river crossing.

After re-securing the loads on the mules, we endured a long hot afternoon climb to a horrible camp by the side of a gravel road just outside a hamlet. The camp was improved only by the superb view it offered of the flanks of Illampu and Ancohuma, the hushed radiance of their summits lit up in the glorious evening glow of the setting sun.

We put the mules in a secure corral in the hamlet but again guiltily tied them up without feed. Already in the corral was a small donkey, and its elderly lady owner was worried it might be bullied by our larger animals. We assured her that our animals were impeccably well mannered. I hoped this would remain true even though they were hungry.

After supper, Arturo and I returned to the hamlet to search for food for the mules. A group of local children followed us, some banging on drums and others playing flutes – a sort of reverse Pied Piper situation where the young followers rather than the leaders played the music. Through the gloom, we eventually found an elderly man who said he had maize leaves to sell. We transacted business (1 Boliviano) and returned to the corral with a bundle of leaves only a fraction of the size of the one Arturo had carried so effortlessly two evenings ago. The expectant mules greeted us delightedly. The small donkey didn't look as if it had suffered any bullying by our animals.

The next day, we continued to climb a rough, bumpy track at the northern extreme of the Cordillera Real. For the first time, we could see the extensive bulk of the northern face of Illampu. We reached bleaker, wilder landscapes blanketed with thin, light brown scrub. All around us were dark, brooding mountains, heavily scarred and scattered with rough boulders and steep scree slopes. Occasionally, we saw small lakes and marshes dotted with tufts of reeds, frozen waterfalls and iced streams.

We were shadowing the beginning of the Camino del Oro ("Gold Trail"), the ancient route by which gold miners travelled from Sorata to the mines they worked, and ultimately the town of Guanay where they sold or traded the precious metal. The route still leads to several co-operative gold mining towns lower down the valley.

We climbed over three windswept and bitingly cold passes, each around 4,800 metres high, and gained a view of the eastern flank of the Cordillera Real. For the first time, we caught a glimpse of the glaciated summits of the Cordillera Apolobamba in the distance. Small herds of llamas and some horses grazed on the thin, high altitude scrub.

We descended from the third pass over an extremely rocky path towards the shanty gold mining town of San Vincente, whose houses of incongruously bright red bricks made a vain effort to lift the overwhelming sense of bleakness and gloom. The terrain around the town was pitted with rocky depressions where land had been water-blasted in the mining process. A woman and two young children crouched pathetically by the corner of a house sifting a pile of earth for any scraps of precious metal.

We rode into the small village of Tacoma where we lunched on chilli pasta and potatoes. Very thirsty from the riding and noon heat, watermelon and ice cream for dessert were exactly what we wanted. A young local girl seemed transfixed as I bought some tubs of ice cream in the village square. She gradually edged her way towards us. She didn't utter a single word, not even when I asked her whether she wanted an ice cream. I bought her one anyway. She took it and wandered off, still without speaking.

That afternoon, we traversed a narrow track around a mountain and passed the ruined wall of an Inca viaduct. High above us on the mountain, we could see traces of buildings once serviced by the viaduct. We were still pondering the Inca engineering when a buzzard flew past a little above our heads. It circled several times and then disappeared. Continuing a short distance further along the trail, I thought the buzzard had reappeared above us when it suddenly dawned on me that it was now much larger, was almost black and had large white markings on its shoulders. This was a condor, and it was flying not very high above our heads. The huge bird was suddenly joined by a second and the two condors soared ever higher, hovering in the air on their gigantic wingspans.

Andean people regarded condors as messengers of the mountain spirits, who could communicate through shamans and who watched over the sacred peaks. We marvelled for some time at these regal icons of the high Andes before we finally lost them behind a mountain. I had hoped to see condors in the Apolobamba mountains, but this sighting – my first ever of an Andean condor – so early in the expedition was a wonderful bonus and surely a good sign for the rest of the journey.

Shortly after the condor encounter, we rode past a ruined wall believed to date from the Mollo culture, which flourished in this region until just before the expansion of the Incas. Far below us, the Rio Llica (a continuation of the San Cristobal that flows down from Sorata) had carved a deep valley that my guides told me forms the watershed between the mountain ranges of the Cordilleras Real and Muñecas.

Continuing our traverse, we reached a hazy view of Cerro Paititi on the far side of the valley. This mountain has long been associated with the legend of the lost Inca city of Paititi. Many expeditions have vainly scoured the mountain for the ruins of the city, some using flamethrowers to try to force a passage through impenetrable cloud forest that swarms with bears, pumas and, some say, snakes with two heads! Although the mountain appeared harmless enough from this distance, my guides assured me that any sort of progress through its high altitude cloud forest would probably demand chainsaws rather than machetes. An old man in Sorata claims to have seen the Paititi ruins and alleges that they lie on a different side of the mountain to where most have so far searched.

Still pondering the mysteries of Paititi, we rode up to several areas of burning forest where campesinos were preparing land for growing rice and other crops. One particularly large area of burning land occasionally blew flames over our path. We waited for a lull in the flames, took a deep breath and rushed through the heat and choking smoke of the cauldron. Fortunately, the mules were not in the least bit perturbed by the threat of roasting.

By mid-afternoon, thick clouds had risen up through the valley, adding to the haze of several fires that continued to smoulder on the bone-dry ground of the Cordillera Real's rain shadow. We navigated our way round several flocks of sheep and passed fields of bright red peppers as we descended to the Rio Llica at the small mining settlement of Pallayunga.

Several miners sat around outside open doorways. Judging by their glum expressions, today had not been a good one for extracting gold. We entered the cavernous general store where a gregarious, greying woman missing several front teeth offered us a wide range of drinks.

The woman introduced herself as Juana and asked where I was from. "London in England," I replied. She asked me for a photo of London to put on her bare wall and I had to apologise that I didn't have one with me. She then asked if I would invite her to visit London. I explained that England was full of noisy, overcrowded cities and wasn't anywhere near as interesting as Bolivia. "Do you still want to come?" I asked, confident I had put her straight. Juana wasn't even mildly deterred.

After gulping down several large bottles of cola, we cautiously crossed the river and started the long climb into the Muñecas mountains. The stone enclosures of several farmhouses radiated the bright yellow glow of drying corn. We climbed through a section of dense cloud forest just as the afternoon sun gave up its battle against the unrelenting haze.

As dusk began to fall, we reached the attractive colonial village of Aucapata, whose ancient stone houses are set around a well-planted and maintained sloping square. A large church dominates the village from the high side of the square. Most of the houses around the square boast richly textured – much of it crumbling – stonework. Many have outside staircases, a feature I hadn't before seen in Bolivia.

That afternoon, we had passed from the Cordillera Real to the Cordillera Muñecas. We had also passed from the Aymara-speaking region of Bolivia to a region that speaks Quechua, the ancient language of the Incas.

A diversity of cultures and languages is characteristic of lands once ruled by the Incas, and reflects their policy of transmigration. To consolidate their control over lands far removed from the imperial capital, the Incas resettled millions of people to defuse dissidence and create enclaves of loyalty amidst potentially rebellious populations. These resettled people represented maybe up to a third of the population of newly annexed lands. This transmigration policy had the result of significantly altering the ethnic composition of many areas of South America, maybe including this area of the Cordillera Muñecas.

After having suffered several poor campsites, it was a relief and pleasure to be able to spend the night in the comfortable Residencial Iskanwaya, one street below the square. We also found excellent grazing nearby for our mules. Having not washed properly for several days, we probably drained most of the village's water supply in showering before dinner.

Feeling wonderfully clean again, we walked across the deserted and darkened square towards the welcoming glow of the only eating house open that evening. Apart from the owner of the eating house and the proprietor of a nearby shop who was closing up for the day, we met no other people that night. Our simple pasta dinner was probably more basic than the meals we had cooked while camping. However, being able to sit on a bench rather than a patch of grass, rock or disused farming terrace, and not having to worry about plummeting night-time temperatures made a refreshing change to our normal evening routine.

Next morning, after a luxuriously leisurely and warm start, late breakfast and visit to the fascinating Aucapata Museum next to the church, we descended a steep path to the ruined Mollo city of Iskanwaya. These ruins lie on a prominent balcony overlooking the Rio Llica. Rising steeply on the far bank was the heavily carved valley side we had descended the previous afternoon.

Marcello, a 26-year-old guide from Aucapata, accompanied us. Marcello was a very enthusiastic guide but was, for me, overly aggressive in both manner and voice tone, traits accentuated by his habit of regularly slapping the side of his leg with his machete. Marcello explained that, on average, Iskanwaya receives only around three tourists a year. I pondered how it was possible to work as a tour guide with so few potential clients. Marcello once again whacked his machete loudly against his leg and I decided not to ask him.

The arid path wound through parched plateaus dotted with cactuses and sprawling aloe vera plants. Marcello finally put his machete to better use as he picked several fruits from a sinkayu cactus. Once peeled, the fruit resembles a white strawberry and is quite delicious and refreshing. I was starting to warm to our guide.

The ruins of Iskanwaya command sweeping views over both upstream and downstream sections of the Rio Llica. In contrast to the many ceremonial shrines and temples found in most Inca sites, Iskanwaya displays evidence mostly of domestic life through its small plazas and narrow streets. Most of the excavated city comprises rows of tiny ruined houses with delicate walls.

A great many of the dwellings retain wall niches and slate-covered cubbyholes built into the floor that Iskanwayans used to store food and ceramics. Most of the many beautiful ceramic pieces displayed in the Aucapata Museum were found in such underground cupboards. Even after many excavations, numerous pieces of broken pottery still lay scattered around the site. The only wall still standing of the church looked out through ceremonial windows over a steep drop to the valley beyond.

Marcello explained that the Mollos built their houses with thigh-level doors to keep out the many snakes that infest the area. The doors are trapezoidal in shape, the classic Inca form that narrows from bottom to top. Experts have speculated whether the Incas reworked the site during their expansion into the area, or whether the Mollos adopted the trapezoidal form before the Incas. Like many Inca mysteries, we will probably never know.

We could see the remains of shelving in many of the houses. Clay still covered part of their interior stonework. Some of the clay walls even bore the vivid remains of decorative painting. Most fascinating for me, outside many of the houses still stood large, smoothed white rocks lying on top of hefty slabs of dark flat rock that Mollo women once used to grind maize. Despite lying here abandoned for so many centuries, the stones were still in such pristine condition it seemed as though the women had just taken a break from their chores and would soon be returning to resume grinding maize. A row of tiny kitchens emphasised the feeling of domestic life and the site was scattered with patches of tobacco plants originally cultivated by the Mollos.

The house of the village chief was larger than the terraced dwellings and set lower down the hillside, away from the main settlement. It contained more intricately carved wall niches and in front of it still stands a tall stone sundial. Adjacent lay the remains of a solid stone gallows clearly bearing the groove around which the rope was tied to hang people who broke the ancient, "Don't steal, Don't lie, Don't be lazy" commandments. Other ruined buildings were scattered on the hillside above the main complex, including the communal oven used for firing ceramics.

Walking back from the ruins, Marcello confided to me that his ambition was to move to Spain, hopefully in three months' time. He asked if I had any Spanish contacts that might be able to help him get a visa. Like Juana the previous afternoon, Marcello wasn't the least bit deterred by an initial negative response. When I explained that I didn't have any contacts in Spain, he immediately started quizzing me about work prospects in England.

As we left Aucapata and regained the path north, dense clouds once again filled the valley, although bright sunlight continued to shine overhead. As we gained altitude, the lush cloud forest of the previous afternoon yielded to a desolate Andean wilderness of dark rocks and scrubby olive green grass. By the afternoon, we reached the austere mountain pueblos of Huanku and Cotacucho, whose sleazy adobe hovels had outside staircases or sometimes only ladders to reach their upper floors.

Much of the surrounding landscape was a stark barrenness covered in bofedales: a boggy marshland interspersed with tiny lakes, trickling streams and criss-crossing icy rivulets, and thin tufts of vegetation. Grazing all around were many alpacas with thick, fluffy coats, thriving in the cool, moist environment.

We settled into a basic bunkroom in Cotacucho that was owned by Ignacio, a local alpaca herder. In one corner of the room stood a couple of open sacks of silky smooth alpaca garments. I wasn't sure how many degrees below freezing the temperature would drop that night, and it was comforting to know we could borrow these extra layers if needed.

Darkness replaced sunlight at a rapid, almost visible, rate. Ignacio kindly invited us to cook supper in the family kitchen, where his wife Francesca was also preparing supper. We started cooking to the late afternoon sun but soon needed a torch to check the progress of our pasta.

The family kitchen was cosy and romantic when its central wood stove was lit; forbiddingly cold almost as soon as it was extinguished. We huddled closely around its glowing embers as they struggled to keep at bay the piercing chill of the Andean night. Wilma, the elder daughter was learning to read by the light of a single candle. Her younger sister, Stephanie, was totally enthralled by my torch and doing her best to run down its batteries. After supper, these playful children wished us a happy good night with a giggly chorus of "Chau!" as we reluctantly left the warmth of the kitchen to return to our unheated room.

Back in our cold and dimly lit room, Arturo explained that the dwellings in this tiny village, and many other settlements scattered throughout the Andes, were almost identical to those in which people lived during Inca times. Outside the beautifully planned capital of Cuzco and the royal estates of the Sacred Valley, settlements were generally small and jumbled together without particular order. Villages were sited on land not suitable for cultivation, such as on slopes and on uneven, rocky ground, such as here. Where settlements were built on fertile land, the houses were widely separated to allow space between them for planting.

Dwellings were typically single storey and very humble – more like huts than houses. Most had neither windows nor chimneys; smoke simply rose through the dried grass roofs. The interiors of dwellings have always been sparsely decorated, with few adornments except for jars of maize, chuños and quinoa.

Houses traditionally had a stove located behind the door, shaped like a small clay furnace. Ordinary people lacked chairs, benches or seats of any kind. Except for the local lords, everyone sat on the floor, which they also used as the dining table.

That night, we huddled in our high, remote shelter, surrounded by a beautiful but harsh mountain world and the hostile grip of the elements. We were cold inside our adobe room and I shuddered to think what the temperature must have been outside. An icy wind whipped up ferociously and shook the room violently during the night. I was relieved we weren't camping.

The village had a single courtyard water tap. After supper the previous night, I had to kick it to encourage a final night-time trickle before the pipe froze solid. The next morning there was no chance. The ice wrapped all around the tap showed that no amount of kicking would have bullied any water to flow for several hours at least. We resorted to doing what the villagers and alpacas did, and drew water from a tiny stream to make our breakfast.

The alpacas that on the previous afternoon were grazing on the bofedales were now grazing in the village just outside our room. They showed only mild interest in my presence – but no fear. Perhaps they should have been afraid. Local residents rely heavily on these animals for many aspects of their lives. They weave traditional garments and craft items from their wool and leather, and fuel fires using their dung. More worryingly for the alpacas, villagers eat large quantities of their meat, which is supposedly cholesterol-free.

Llamas and alpacas – members of the Andean camelid family – have long been a source of food, transport, clothing, warmth and prestige to campesinos, and remain central to the Andean economy. The larger your head count of camelids, the greater the prestige you command. The largest camelid flocks in South America continue to graze these bleak, high altitude pastures of the Altiplano.

The Incas employed vast numbers of camelids, particularly for hauling supplies during military campaigns. Trains of thousands of supply-laden llamas supported travelling armies and became food or ritual sacrifices once their duties of burden had been completed.

Shortly after resuming our trail, we encountered a group of heavily sweating workers extracting rocks along the climb to the next pass. We chatted briefly, gave them a bottle of water and continued climbing. Reaching the far side of the pass, the landscape softened into a less menacing broad valley of pale green grass grazed by herd after herd of alpacas wrapped in fluffy white, brown and occasionally black coats. Some trotted off. Many simply stood and stared blankly at the motley mule train as we rode past, much as did many of the campesinos we encountered. In the distance, at the end of the valley, another barrier of dark, intimidating summits and serrated ridges once more blocked our path.

Our route climbed over two more high passes, beyond which we saw our first few sleek vicuñas, whose fine brown and white coats are prized even more highly than those of their alpaca cousins. The glistening, white-topped Apolobamba range once again came into view, with the sacred, glacier-streaked peak of Akhamani at its distinctive vanguard.

We descended gently through Inca and pre-Inca agricultural terraces to a viewpoint overlooking the town of Amarete. All around were pale yellow fields of recently harvested wheat; the calls of mules and donkeys filled the air.

With little time to stop and rest, we rode into and immediately climbed gently out of Amarete. A few terraces had lined the valley on our approach. Leaving the town in the direction of Charazani, distinctive Inca terraces suddenly filled both sides of the valley, covering all visible mountainside from high peak to river in seemingly endless layers of green and golden brown fields that stretched into the distance as far as we could see. Peru has so far managed to grab all the publicity for Inca terracing, but this Bolivian valley surely boasts the most impressive Inca terracing anywhere.

Farming the steeply inclined slopes of the Andes proved no great challenge for the Incas. They levelled the land by constructing vast systems of terraces, such as in this valley. They held the soil at intervals with dry stone walls, which they sometimes fitted together with as much care as important buildings. In this way, the Incas farmed high, rugged terrain that would otherwise have been impossible to cultivate.

Inca terraces always contour beautifully with the landscape and their width varies according to the terrain. On rugged mountainsides like some of the slopes here, the terraces are so narrow they resemble stairs. Where the slope is more gradual, terraces can be hundreds of feet wide. To irrigate their crops, the Incas constructed systems of ditches that extended over vast distances and over impossibly rugged terrain to channel river water to their fields.

As we rode fast to try to reach Charazani before nightfall, not even the dense cloud that once again drifted up the valley could shroud the mile upon unbroken mile of valley-filling terracing that contoured perfectly with the landscape.

Incredibly, after more than 500 years, most of the terraces still yield abundant maize, peas, potatoes, wheat and other crops for the local communities. More practically for us, unplanted terraces provided excellent campsites: perfectly flat, self-contained and with plenty of different levels available if required to accommodate separate human, mule and cooking quarters.

CHAPTER EIGHT

CHARAZANI

As the twilight hue started to drape the valley, we descended a series of sharp hairpins that provided increasingly lovely views over Charazani. Like Amarete, the town was surrounded on all sides by layer upon layer of attractively curved Inca terracing. With plentiful grazing for mules on fallow terraces all around the town, I decided to rest in Charazani for a few days before tackling the Apolobamba mountains. Neither Arturo nor Eduardo had travelled before to Apolobamba, so I would also need to find new guides for the next stage of the journey. Arturo, Eduardo and Arturo's two mules would begin the journey back to Sorata tomorrow whilst I continued into Apolobamba with Coco after spending a few days here.

We tethered the three mules to a stout bush on an unplanted terrace, lay huge piles of dried maize leaves in front of them and marched down the final few switchbacks into Charazani. Reaching the outskirts of the town, we discovered that tonight was the first night of the town's annual festival, which provided even more reason for me to pause here.

Charazani was vibrant. Crowds teemed around the square. I learned that many regard the Charazani festival as one of the finest fiestas in all Bolivia. A great number of people had travelled here from La Paz, and their many buses now lined the road into the town.

Many revellers wore their best traditional finery, including men draped in brightly striped red ponchos. The women in this region wear distinctive costumes: dark green, patterned shawls (much heavier than those of their Altiplano counterparts), black skirts trimmed with pink, brightly coloured headbands over which they wear white hats, and a red sack on their backs.

As we neared the town centre, we could start to hear the distinctive, though repetitive, panpipes and heavy drum beat of the local Kantus music, played by a band of processing musicians clad in matching light brown ponchos and black hats. A busy market continued late into the evening on the nearby local football pitch.

All around the town square, a string of stalls was selling freshly brewed alcoholic drinks. Several loudspeakers blared out loud cumbia dance music in competition to the more traditional sounds of Kantus. All the shops and small eating houses around the square were enjoying a vigorous trade in food and drink.

We crowded into one such eating house, which offered just two bench tables, for a simple supper of fried chicken and rice. The owner was the amiable Doña Rebecca, who was being helped by her daughter Muñeca and several other young family members who had all made the trip from La Paz for the festival. Charazani's power supply was evidently struggling to cope with the surge in demand created by the huge influx of new arrivals. Lights repeatedly flickered on and off in the square and across whole sections of the town. Shortly after receiving our plates, the power failed yet again, this time for an extended period, and we ate supper to the soft light of a single candle.

As darkness fell outside, dancers filled the square in front of the floodlit white church, elegantly circling and twisting, and holding brightly coloured candlelit lanterns above their heads. As the night continued, a modern band played on the steps outside the church, noisy fireworks streaked into the black sky and revellers increasingly succumbed to the vast quantity of alcohol being consumed. The music and drinking would continue throughout the night.

I was still hungry after the meal, but knew we had to make sleeping arrangements quite urgently. All the hotel rooms in Charazani had been booked up long ago. We thought we had managed to sneak in a last-minute reservation some days earlier by relaying a message via the local phone operator to a contact of Arturo's at one of the hotels.

However, the message clearly failed to arrive or be acted upon as we found the hotel we thought we had booked, like Charazani's other two hotels, completely full.

The best we could manage were some mattresses on a second floor hallway, squeezed between four rooms in the unremarkable Hotel Akhamani. The alternative was to rejoin the mules and camp on one of the many terraces around the town, although it was now very late for that option. We decided to settle for the mattresses on the floor. A sofa and three chairs provided some privacy although the outer door of the hallway banged noisily throughout the night from the gusting wind.

I was so hungry after dinner I ate some bread, two granadillas, a second dinner in another eating house, two packets of toasted haba beans and finally my six remaining granadillas. Only the inconvenience of running out of food prevented me from continuing to eat as I pondered how it was possible that the expedition leader had been reduced to sleeping on the floor of a hotel hallway.

Dawn arrived on Saturday, the second and main day of the festival. I had hoped that having to sleep on the hotel floor had been only a very bad dream but, alas, I woke and was indeed still lying in a corner of the hallway. Not surprisingly, I hadn't slept well. I had been woken several times, not only by the banging door but also by revellers from the surrounding rooms arriving back noisily at various times during the early hours.

Drunks were still reeling around the square in the early morning. Despite their inebriation, some remained beautifully turned out for the festival. Others, in wretched contrast, looked pitiful, with wildly pained expressions and glazed unknowing stares. Others were filthy dirty and reeked of coca.

After a final breakfast together, squeezed beside a family of boisterous revellers at Doña Rebecca's, I walked with Arturo and Eduardo back up to the terrace where our mules were tethered. They had somehow managed to munch their way through most of the food mountains we had placed before them the previous evening. Arturo loaded his two mules and suddenly we were shaking hands and waving each other goodbye. I sat on the terrace for some time, beside my still munching mule, as I gazed over the beautiful lines of terracing and watched my travelling companions make their way back up the long switchbacks. At Arturo's chasqui pace, it didn't take long before they rounded a final corner and disappeared from view.

At lunchtime, back in the town centre, a group of formally dressed local people carried the effigy of the Virgen del Carmen out of the church on their shoulders and paraded her around the square, preceded and followed by Kantus bands and groups of candle-carrying devout. After one circuit of the square, the bearers restored the Virgin to the church while the bands continued playing outside.

The bands gradually separated into two circles, into the centres of which squeezed groups of elegantly dressed dancers. The bands and dancers processed around the square again at intervals. While these festivities were dominating the square, the bustling market was once again moved to the nearby football pitch. The only stalls were those of various food sellers; other sellers simply spread out their wares on the sun-baked ground before them.

During a lull in festivities, I could hear several diesel engines splutter into life. Although today was the official day of the festival, by mid-afternoon, some of the convoy of buses were already setting off on the long journey back to La Paz.

I decided to stop for an afternoon coffee (accompanied by tasty Charazani wheat bread) in a cramped eating house in one corner of the square. A short, elderly man, smartly dressed in a grey suit, tie and hat, started a conversation with me, then came and sat down beside me with his coffee and bread. He introduced himself cheerfully as Crisoforo Oblitas Tudela, the owner of the eating house. We chatted for a while before Crisoforo strangely decided that he wanted to show me his abacus. He climbed a steep flight of wooden steps to his upstairs lodgings to search for it. Then, with obvious pleasure, Crisoforo used the instrument to show how he could calculate his age using the current year and the year of his birth. He might have been 82 (as confirmed by his abacus calculations) and slightly deaf, but Crisoforo's mind was still very sharp. Much less lucid were a couple of drunks who suddenly appeared in the doorway and started to cause trouble for the young waitress as I was getting up to leave.

Charazani descended into squalor that evening. Drunks openly urinated in the square, people sat around on the ground amidst broken glass and rubbish, and cholita vendors bedded down for the night on the street, barely discernible from the sacks of stock that surrounded them.

Sunday started badly. I was up early again after spending another night on the hallway floor. The only eating house open was a small one I hadn't noticed before. This establishment offered the unusually large number of four tables. I asked the woman owner whether she served breakfast. "Only coffee and egg sandwiches," she replied. I eagerly accepted. However, I was devastated when minutes later, while I was still eating my sandwich, a table of other breakfasters started tucking in to steaming bowls of chicken soup!

The square was by now foul. I sought refuge inside the church, the safest and by far the cleanest part of town. Even here, however, there was no respite from drunks. A man wearing a striped red poncho entered the church with a young boy in tow. He weaved his way up the aisle and started making exaggerated displays of devotion towards the effigy of the Virgin that stood at the front of the church. He then sat down on the pew beside me, bringing with him a nauseous stench of beer, and continued to make effusive gestures in the direction of the Virgin. After much bowing and gesturing, he asked me to give him some money, presumably so he could buy more beer. I was very happy to give him a donation just to see the red poncho disappear out of the church again.

Outside, the band and a dwindling troop of dancers made occasional circuits of the square in a valiant attempt to sustain the festival spirit. However, the many buses returning revellers to La Paz were far more prevalent.

Passing Crisoforo's eating house later that afternoon, his wife Irene Justa, a friendly but unsmiling lady with long grey hair flowing from beneath a baseball cap, was furiously swinging an axe at a leg of beef on a stump by the doorway. This "asado" (fried steak) was tonight's supper offering. Despite having seen the food in preparation, I decided to dine at Crisoforo's that evening. Sliding along one of the two bench tables past partly eaten meals, dirty mugs, glasses and scraps of vegetables (trying to find a relatively dry section of plastic tablecloth that wasn't totally swimming in beer and/or soup), I found myself suddenly next to part of the raw cow haunch that hadn't made it onto tonight's menu.

With people rapidly returning to La Paz, I was finally able to move from the hallway floor to a room in the hotel. The room was clean but had one of the most uncomfortable beds I have ever slept on, with a mattress so thin I could easily feel the slats beneath. I was tempted to ask to move back to the hall floor.

I woke next day to find that Charazani had neither electricity nor water. To make matters worse, a strong wind was blowing dust and refuse all around the town. Fortunately, the much-needed street cleaners had finally arrived and were starting to clean up the mess from the festival.

The power and water didn't return until early afternoon. By then, a thick blanket of cloud had enveloped the town, wrapping around the twin church towers and the trees in the square. With the festival having finally petered out, Charazani was restored to its usual calm, broken only by the sound of donkeys and occasional vehicle. A few donkeys wandered around the square. Others, and some horses and cows, grazed in the outskirts, on terraces close to where Coco was still tethered. All was very peaceful.

Back at Crisoforo's eating house, the raw leg of beef from the previous evening had been moved from the bench onto one of the tables, and was now joined by a raw leg of pork. Irene Justa kindly moved these to the other table to make room for my supper (soup and more asado left over from the previous evening). The neblina made it feel damp and cold. I decided I had rested here long enough and that it was time to move on tomorrow to Curva and the Cordillera Apolobamba.

A freezing wind blew through Charazani the following morning, its cold chill waking me up very early. I shivered into the square hoping to find a warming coffee, but none of my usual haunts was yet open. I was about to search elsewhere when I heard the welcome voice of Doña Rebecca calling me. She invited me to her eating house and explained that she was just on her way to buy the breakfast bread and some chicken for lunch.

Back at Crisoforo's for a final morning coffee, the leg of pork from the previous day was still there, but had had a large chunk hacked out of it. Today, I shared a bench (previously occupied by the leg of beef) with a bag of rotting lettuce. Half-eaten meals and a tray of chickpeas were spread over the table. Chickpeas were also scattered around the floor. As I was saying farewell, Irene Justa was on all fours, scraping up chickpeas from around a table leg.

I had bumped into Crisoforo on several occasions since our first meeting when he had demonstrated his abacus skills. With each meeting, he had looked progressively less and less smart. By the time of our last, brief, meeting today, he appeared positively scruffy and looked as if he had been in a fight.

I ate a farewell lunch in Doña Rebecca's eating house, which had become by far my favourite spot in Charazani. During lunch, she and her daughter Muñeca told me a story about a foreign visitor who had met a local girl and settled down nearby in the valley. The foreigner's sister later met a local man and settled there too. "Be careful of the local girls!" they warned as we hugged and said our goodbyes.

CHAPTER NINE

CURVA

With both mule and rider rested and refreshed, I rode out of Charazani on a gravel track that descends past the town's thermal baths to the floor of the valley. We crossed the boisterous river over a small stone bridge and climbed a series of arid switchbacks bordered all around by an endless tapestry of terraces.

Once we had climbed away from the river, the rhythmic clip-clop of Coco's hooves was the only sound I could hear. The profound hush even seemed to envelop my mule. His long fluffy ears usually twitched towards every faint noise, but this afternoon the antennae remained almost still.

We passed Niño Corin, with its small church high up on the hillside and donkeys grazing quietly in fields. Rounding a corner, we caught another view of the soaring, jagged Apolobamba range led by the sacred peak of Akhamani, today dulled beneath a cloudy sky. As we approached the sacred mountain, I could make out massive ice fields shaped like downward pointing daggers glinting on its steep flanks. The side of the valley on which we travelled was still heavily terraced. In contrast, the mountains on the opposite side were now covered in dark green grass with some clusters of trees.

I could now glimpse the village of Curva in the distance, lying still some height above us in a shallow saddle between two green peaks. The gradient of our path climbed only slowly, but we paid for this luxury through the length of the switchbacks on the tortuous track, which meant we spent an inordinate amount of the afternoon travelling away from Curva rather than towards it. Child shepherds tended a few donkeys in a terraced wheat field outside the adobe village of Santa Rosa de Kaata – a silent cluster of thatched dwellings.

The path climbed through increasingly steep and rocky mountain terrain, dotted with occasional tufts of vegetation. There were now fewer terraces; not even the Incas could overcome these topographical challenges to farm here. Looking back, low clouds had once again swamped the Charazani valley.

As the afternoon shadows started to lengthen, we once again reached areas of extensively terraced valley. We passed the adobe farming villages of Upinhuaya and Caalaya, where nothing stirred. Cobs of maize were hanging up to dry on several washing lines and we started to see qeñhua trees, with their distinctive, intensely red brown bark. Small streams crossed our path. Most were only tiny trickles; many were completely dry.

In the late afternoon, we finally reached Curva, the mountain village that lies at the foot of the Apolobamba mountains. Curva is a peaceful settlement of antiquated (in many cases rundown) stone houses perched on a sloping, wooded spur at some 3,800 metres. Pigs wander around the village and occasional herders drive sheep through its narrow, car-less streets. Horses graze on fertile pastures all around. The few people I met offered warm greetings and energetic handshakes.

I skirted the banks of a reed-lined lagoon in which grazed several horses up to their bellies in water, and arrived at an unexpectedly large building that offered accommodation in two spacious dormitory rooms. Coco was spoilt for choice by the lush grazing all around us. The young man who ran the establishment introduced himself as Paulino Puyasaca. The only other person staying there that night was a gold miner on his way to a remote mine high in the cordillera. The gold miner and I had one dormitory each.

Curva is the spiritual home of the Kallawayas – the mystical healers and fortune-tellers who once treated Inca nobility. Paulino was himself a practising Kallawaya who had recently been elected Mallku (local community representative) of Lagunillas, a satellite village. Helping

Paulino in the kitchen that evening was his wife. She was dressed in a traditional cholita costume and was also busy keeping an eye on the energetic antics of their two youngest children.

As the miner and I drank coffee and hot chocolate and ate many slices of bread, we pored over my map of the region. The miner pointed out the gold mine he would set off for very early next morning.

After cooking us a hearty supper, Paulino joined us at the table, where the three of us drank tea made from muña plants, which Paulino explained was very good for the digestion. This made a refreshing change from the universally served mate de coca, a panacea tea made from the coca leaves habitually chewed by many people in the Andes.

I asked Paulino if he could help me find a guide for the journey through the Apolobamba mountains into Peru. Paulino said he knew of someone who might be able to take me there. However, the more we talked, the more I realised that Paulino himself would be the ideal guide. He had travelled through Apolobamba many times before and, as a Kallawaya and Mallku-elect of Lagunillas, he had many contacts that might prove useful. Paulino was happy to guide and would bring along one of his young mules to accompany Coco. Luis, a local arriero (horse/mule handler) on his way to trade goods in a remote mountain village, would also travel with us for the first couple of days of the journey.

After supper, Paulino said he wanted to introduce me to a friend of his, another of the local Kallawayas. Paulino threw on his thick red poncho decorated with many brightly coloured stripes and I followed him into the night, beyond the back of the church and into one of the narrow, cobbled closes. We walked through a number of dimly lit passages and emerged into a darkened stone room illuminated by only a fire in one corner. Beside the fire knelt a solemn figure also dressed in a brightly striped scarlet poncho and matching woollen hat. The Kallawaya invited us to sit before him.

A shiver ran down my spine as the stern-faced Kallawaya hurled alcohol over the fire to invoke the spirits of the high mountains, which he petitioned one by one in his native Quechua tongue…

"Pachamama (Mother Earth), Tata Santiago (protector of the Spanish and Aymara god of thunder), Achachilas (protector gods of the high mountains and ambassadors between the spiritual and material worlds) and Tio (lord of the underworld)."

Leaping flames lit up the darkened stone room and showed off the kneeling figure's striped scarlet robes in their full splendour. The Kallawayas are renowned for their ability to foretell the future. This one was about to foretell mine.

The Kallawaya invited me to ask him a question. I thought for a moment then enquired slightly nervously, "How will my journey through the Apolobamba mountains go?" I was asked to place a small tip under a cloth on which the Kallawaya had already placed a cross. The Kallawaya took out a bag of coca leaves, placed one on the cloth to represent my question, chewed some others then threw individual leaves over the cloth.

I later learned that leaves landing dark side up are generally considered good omens whereas those landing light side up are generally considered bad, although much depends on the interpretation of where and how they land on the cloth and how close individual leaves land to the one representing the question. Not knowing whether things were looking good or bad added greatly to the tension.

After several uneasy minutes, the stern expression on the Kallawaya's face relaxed slightly, and he pronounced that the journey would go well overall. However, some light-side-up leaves scattered around the cloth suggested we would encounter some problems or delays (maybe more blockades?) along the way. "Good luck. Go forward," the Kallawaya encouraged, "go forward." I sighed with relief.

Next morning, Paulino and I set out to buy provisions for our journey into the mountains. Curva's few tiny shops lie scattered around its square and open their doors when the shopkeepers are at home and feel like opening. We needed to buy food and fuel and entered the first shop. With a small table pushed into a corner, the shop doubled as an occasional eating house. However, the unlit shelves offered few of the items on our list, and no items at all of fresh food. The second shop was even darker and couldn't add any of the missing items. The third shop had been open when we first arrived in the square but in the meantime had closed whilst the proprietor went to visit a friend.

"No hay," meaning, "I don't have any," was a phrase I had grown accustomed to hearing regularly (particularly in the context of food items) since arriving in Bolivia – even more so after the blockades exacerbated existing shortages. Bolivians use a physical expression for "no hay" – a slow, side-to-side swivelling of an open hand, palm face down – that many of the shopkeepers in Curva now used whenever I requested anything.

Eventually, through the combined inventories of all three shops, we scraped together just about enough food to enable us to set off, although we still lacked many staples like cheese, tomatoes and fruit (there seemed to be no fruit in the entire village). We also struggled to find bread, without which we would really have had problems. We scoured all the village shops with no success and eventually had to track down the house of the local baker, where we finally managed to buy a large bag of rolls.

It was still early in the morning when we gave up all hope of finding any further provisions in Curva. We were about to leave the last tiny shop cum drinking house when I found my exit barred by a drunk propped up against the doorway. The drunk stared at me through an idiotic grin plastered firmly on his face. He insisted I take a drink from his beer glass, and then began conversing with me. The man introduced himself as Curva's chief of police. Beer glass back in hand, he started quizzing me about what I was doing in Curva, what permissions I had obtained from the local authorities to be in Curva and, bizarrely, how many photos I had taken. After several minutes of this charade, it became evident that the inebriated officer of the law was only angling to "invite" me to "invite" him and his equally drunken friend (introduced to me as an ex-policeman, and it wasn't difficult to see why he was an "ex") for two more bottles of beer – the policeman's idea of local "permissions".

With as much politeness as I could feign, I declined to help finance the early morning revelry. The chief of police made a comical attempt to appear authoritative and even threatened to take police action against me, although of what sort I, and I suspect he, had no idea. I reiterated that I wasn't going to buy him any beer and eventually he was forced to scuttle off – painted grin barely disturbed – with his equally drunken friend into a shop across the square for some sobering breakfast.

Much more edifyingly, we ran into Miguel Tejerina as he was walking across Curva's small square. Miguel was the resident Kallawaya physician at the recently built medical centre, and was also the minister at the local evangelical church. Miguel was returning to the medical centre and we walked with him along a peaceful path overlooking the valley. The centre had one room for Kallawaya medicine and an adjacent room for modern medicine. Miguel explained a little about Kallawaya diagnosis and treatment techniques, and showed me the wide range of medicinal plants he uses for treatment. He also talked a little about the long history of Andean medicine men.

In Inca times, many native witch doctors were believed to possess the power to cure sickness, although all treatments first required casting lots and making sacrifices. Treatments often used medicinal plants and were invariably accompanied by various superstitions and magic. Many witch doctors were also highly skilled at concocting deadly potions of poisonous herbs, with which they could kill anybody they chose.

Obscure ancient medical practices included smearing a patient with the grease of a guinea pig or toad, after which the healer sucked the pain or illness out of the patient's body.

Although many ancient "healing" practices were no more than shams, several current Kallawaya treatments continue to cause guinea pigs much reason for concern. In one diagnosis technique, a Kallawaya kills a guinea pig by hurling it against a wall. The healer then cuts open the splattered rodent and dabs its blood over the patient's body. After an hour, a black spot appears on the part of the body where the health problem exists.

In another practice, the sick person sleeps with a bag containing a live guinea pig. The Kallawaya sacrifices the guinea pig the next day, after which the patient recovers and the former illness appears in the body of the deceased guinea pig. I looked forward to learning more about the fascinating Kallawaya culture from Paulino during our journey north.

After leaving the medical centre, Paulino invited me back to his house in Lagunillas, a short walk away down a gently sloping, leafy path. As we passed the local school, members of the school band were in the playground practising brass instruments and large drums. Several villagers were busy with domestic chores outside their small thatched huts.

Reaching Lagunillas, a vigorous game of football was taking place on the village pitch. The players were undeterred by a sharp rain shower and low cloud that suddenly threatened to envelop all of Lagunillas, including the pitch. Neither weather feature boded well for the start of our journey tomorrow. When not used for football, the Lagunillas pitch was otherwise grazed by horses, donkeys and pigs.

Paulino's home was a tiny adobe hovel set on a small patch of sloping land on which some dogs and baby goats were scampering around excitedly. Paulino, his wife and three children lived in two cramped rooms, the smaller being a kitchen and eating area and the larger, a sleeping and living area. Paulino invited me to sit down in the larger room.

Inside its unlit interior, the earthen floor was scattered with straw. The single window was covered, presumably against the cold. I couldn't see a bed, although it could have lain buried under any of several piles of clothing, food and other possessions strewn around the darkened room. A neat stack of cassettes next to an oversize radio-cassette player and some cobs of maize hanging up to dry on a line strung across the low ceiling were the only visible signs of order in the room. I sat on a low wooden stool and Paulino offered me a bowl of steaming vegetable broth and a plate of maize. The rest of the family sat down to eat on the floor in the adjacent kitchen.

Paulino and I spent the afternoon and evening making final preparations for the journey. Although Paulino had travelled widely throughout the Apolobamba region, he wasn't sure which was the best border point at which to enter Peru. As night fell, Johnny Quisbert Caceres, the local ranger, rode back into Lagunillas on his motorbike after spending the day working in Curva. If anybody knew, Paulino assured me, Johnny would.

As well as being the local ranger, Johnny was also serving his first term as Curva's Mallku, the elected local community leader. Clad in black leathers, he leapt off his bike energetically and bounded into his house. He was clearly in a hurry but squeezed in time to scribble down some suggestions of route and border crossings beyond the village of Pelechuco in the north of the Apolobamba mountains. By the time we thanked and said goodbye to Johnny, it was raining strongly, which boded even less well for our departure the following morning.

CHAPTER TEN

CORDILLERA APOLOBAMBA

The morning of our departure dawned unexpectedly bright and clear. As we were enjoying our last indoor meal for several days, I noticed that I was spreading inexplicably large dollops of butter onto the bread I was eating for breakfast. I realised this was something I had been doing ever since arriving in Curva. I recalled theories about how your body can send you subconscious urges that direct you to the foods you need most urgently. I didn't know if this was happening to me, but if it were, my only conclusion could be that I would need a lot of energy and maybe an extra layer of body fat in the coming days.

Paulino, Luis and I loaded our equipment and provisions onto the two mules under a blindingly bright sun. Paulino kissed his family goodbye and suddenly we were off. We climbed a crest out of Curva and the Apolobamba mountains immediately rose into glinting view. Not far outside the village, we passed several sacred sites where local Kallawayas sacrifice llamas twice a year in ceremonies to ask for Pachamama's blessing for harvests, work and health.

Extensive agricultural terraces continued to carpet the valley. We climbed towards Akhamani, the sacred mountain of the Kallawayas, its lower slopes verdant, layered with terracing and grazed by llamas, alpacas and sheep. The mountain is shaped like a gigantic dome, down one side of which streaked a huge finger of glacial ice. We descended to the Rio Cañisaya, which we crossed by stepping-stones. We then climbed again before dropping to the nearby Rio Lloholla, which we crossed over a tiny bridge.

Climbing again after the second river crossing, three small Suerte Maria birds fluttered past – a lucky omen according to Paulino. After yesterday's persistent rain, it had been bright, dry and sunny all day. Maybe these birds were just confirming our good fortune.

Ancient stone enclosures, small streams and rivulets criss-crossed the landscape. Isolated, thatched stone cottages housed local herders. Some of the stonework we passed was stained red from rain and covered with lichen. Dotted about the valley were tiny shelters used by herders in emergencies: crude stone walls and thatching built around the cover of leaning rock overhangs.

We ascended into the Jatumpampa valley to the south of Akhamani and the Apolobamba range. Huge outcrops of dark rock loomed over the light brown landscape and its cloak of clumpy, pale green paja brava grass. Paulino explained that the locals named one of these outcrops "Choco de Condor", meaning, "Perch of the Condor". Condors are known to live on the crag although we saw none today. A lone viscacha (a large Andean rabbit) hopped over the rocks beside us. More alpacas and llamas grazed in the valley in the distance and high up on the mountainside above us.

Climbing the Jatumpampa valley to an area of level pasture beside the small river, we set up camp and made tea. An arriero travelling towards Curva with four horses stopped for a chat and we offered him some tea and bread. The day had been warm and sunny, but it felt cold as soon as we stopped moving, particularly after a thick mist drifted up the valley.

By 3:30pm, I was wrapped up in every layer of clothing I possessed (six in total) and couldn't care how ridiculous I must have looked wearing a poncho over a rain jacket. If someone had offered me a tablecloth, I would happily have worn that too without hesitation. Our camp that night was at just over 4,000 metres – a very modest altitude in these mountains. I shuddered to think how cold the nights would get as we climbed higher into the cordillera.

The neblina set in with a vengeance for the rest of the day. The setting sun cast a beautiful, slightly otherworldly light through the thick mist.

After moving the animals to better grazing higher up on the valley side, Paulino, Luis and I walked back down the path to the house of Luis's aunt, who coincidentally lived in the last stone house we had passed on our climb to camp.

The aunt was sitting on the ground outside her house, crouched over a pile of coca leaves spread out before her on a cloth. Next to her on the ground was a small loom on which she had been weaving traditional Andean patterns using some brightly coloured alpaca wool.

For centuries, weaving has been an essential skill for all Andean women. Weaving was one of the most important arts in the Inca empire. Textiles played a central role in rituals, ceremonies and other important events such as marriages and coming of age, when participants sacrificed, gave or exchanged fine textiles. Fine textiles were also burned as part of nearly every major sacrifice. The Incas valued their finely woven textiles so highly they burned most of them after the Conquest, rather than let them fall into the hands of the Spanish.

Behind the aunt, standing next to the family sheep pen, were a cheerful young boy and girl. As we said hello, a pair of temptingly plump hens waddled past, causing thoughts to turn immediately to supper.

The few inhabitants of Jatumpampa are known for their ability to catch trout from the stream using only their bare hands. Paulino had earlier said that we too could catch some fish this evening. I wanted to see this to believe it, besides which fresh fish for supper would be a great and unexpected bonus in this wilderness. The aunt confirmed that there were some trout in the stream right now. Without hesitation, Paulino, Luis and I followed the smiling young boy and girl (who wielded a crude cage net and long stick) down to an impossibly tiny water pool beneath an overhanging bank.

The children prodded the water and bank with their stick. Almost immediately, their chattering Quechua reached fever pitch as a dark torpedo shape dashed from side to side in the pool. Luis calmly placed his hands into the cold water and seconds later stood up clutching a wriggling trout about 20 centimetres long with shiny, dappled pink flanks. I was amazed.

After this initial triumph, we followed the children downstream to a slightly larger flow of water in search of bigger prey. The children darted excitedly about the bank and leapt expertly over stepping stones, prodding beneath rock slabs and into pools beneath the bank. The chatter of Quechua reached fever pitch several times more as startled fish dashed for their lives. Rocks were manoeuvred to block escape routes and the net was placed in strategic positions. In the gloom of the dusk and mist, we caught two more fish, a small one in the net and another larger one by hand. The largest fish we saw annoyingly evaded all attempts at capture, although we nevertheless returned to the house full of excitement and the anticipation of an excellent supper.

The aunt's house comprised a small terrace of three stone rooms, the outer two used as sleeping quarters and a central hut, thatched with paja brava grass, used for cooking and eating. Telltale chirps of "cuwee, cuwee" confirmed the Quechua custom of letting guinea pigs roam freely around the cooking area, to control pests and hoover up fallen scraps of food.

Whilst we had been fishing, the aunt's elder daughter had returned home through the mist with the family's large herd of alpacas and llamas, and had restored the flock of sheep to its pen. She had also collected a pile of dried camelid dung for use as fuel that she now carried in a sack over her shoulder.

The aunt immediately got to work gutting and cooking our catch for supper. While she was busy boiling rice and potatoes and frying the trout, the two young girls giggled loudly as they chased and eventually caught several young lambs in the pen, which they wrapped in plastic sheeting to keep their torsos warm overnight. Meanwhile, the girls' brother tried to read a book in the feeble light of the nocturnal gloom.

As darkness smothered even the mist, we were invited inside the small dark cooking area. Quechua homes traditionally have no chimney and the room was very smoky. Through the wisps of pungent dung smoke, I could make out hanging from the ceiling above me a withered and rather scary-looking four-legged form with a disproportionately large head. This, Paulino explained, was a llama foetus, a traditional lucky charm that campesinos often hang inside their homes for good fortune.

After the cold and damp of the dusk, the inside of the house was wonderfully warm and dry. Flames burst forth from the small dung stove in the corner behind the door, encouraged by the aunt blowing through a piece of metal piping. In the warmth of the cosy, darkened kitchen, and to the dim glow of the crackling embers and a single flickering-in-the-breeze candle, we sat on the straw-covered dirt floor and devoured a delicious fish supper.

It was late by the time Paulino and I reluctantly bade farewell to the aunt and her family (Luis would sleep here tonight). We bought some small items of knitwear to thank the aunt for her hospitality, and then left the warmth of the kitchen to return to our frosty camp. It was totally dark outside. We hadn't expected to be so long with Luis's family and neither of us had brought a torch. Clouds shrouded what would otherwise have been a nearly full moon. Paulino and I carefully edged our way back uphill, even at one point somehow managing to feel our way across the stream over stepping-stones. Arriving safely back at camp, we celebrated a captivating evening with a cigarette.

I woke up next morning to ice on the tent and a valley once again spilling over with low clouds. Paulino and I walked back down to the aunt's house to share some of our bread for the family breakfast and to collect Luis. We didn't set off on the trail again until mid-morning, by which time the clouds had thankfully started to lift.

We climbed steeply over dark rocks towards the first of the high passes of the cordillera. The heavy, grey morning added to the menacing appearance of our surroundings. Reaching close to where I was sure the pass had to be, I met three campesinos descending the path towards Curva. Certain that it wasn't, I confidently asked if the pass was far. To my dismay, the campesinos gave me the answer I didn't want to hear! Fortunately, on this unique occasion, I was right and the locals were wrong (or, more likely, they didn't understand my poor attempt at Spanish). A few more switchbacks, bounded to left and right by steep scree slopes, and I reached the cairn of rocks that marks the summit of the pass.

Paulino told me to place a white stone on the cairn to ask for good fortune and strength. On passing a hilltop or high pass in the Andes, it has for centuries been customary to leave coca, maize, feathers or, most frequently, stones as an offering to ask to be allowed to go by in peace, be relieved of any tiredness and be given strength to complete one's journey. This custom of laying stones on mountain passes dates back to at least the time of the Incas, who revered snow-capped summits and mountain passes (which they called apachetas). The accumulated offerings made by travellers form piles of stones still found to this day on most Andean summits and passes.

The Incas also built shrines on high summits to pay homage to the gods of the mountains and lay claim to the sacred landscape. They carried food and drink up to hilltops where they offered them to their gods. The food, including highly esteemed coca leaves, was burned and chicha was poured over the ground. From these elevated shrines, the Incas could pronounce themselves the mediators between the earthly and supernatural worlds, again reasserting their ascendancy and right to rule.

From the relatively tame first pass, the formidable barrier of the second, higher, pass loomed threateningly above us. We didn't pause long at the cairn before hurrying down the saddle between the two passes. Just a few strides before the summit of the second pass, near disaster struck. The cargo on Paulino's mule suddenly slipped completely and dangled under the animal's belly. The panic-stricken young mule immediately tried to buck and bolt his way back to Curva. Paulino had to use all of his strength and mulemanship to cling on to the lead rope as the mule kicked in circles around him, before he was finally able to soothe the youngster to calmness and safely unfasten the load.

Just as we were re-securing the cargo, a large condor glided magnificently not far above our heads in the direction of Curva, perhaps sensing that the terrified young mule was about to provide a free lunch. The condor was followed shortly afterwards by another lucky Suerte Maria bird. Had our good fortune been the lucky escape from disaster or the condor sighting over the pass? I wasn't sure.

Low clouds streamed in waves over the second pass. We didn't linger long there either. After placing a stone on its cairn to ask for more luck and continued strength, we descended into a misty bleak wilderness. Dark, lichen-covered rocks towered above us in near-vertical cliff faces, some overlain by frozen waterfalls. Small ponds and tufts of paja brava grass broke the monotony of the thin, pale green grazing. Not a sound could be heard and the enveloping mist added to the eerie silence.

As we descended further into the hushed mist, the landscape finally started to mellow. We crossed an area of open country and reached Inka Kancha. This site was once used by the Incas to graze livestock, and still bears the ruins of corrals. With excellent grazing and being near the river, this would have been an ideal place to set up camp for the night, although at barely lunchtime, it would also have been ridiculously early to stop. We had little choice but to continue across the river and tackle our third high pass of the day.

We paused on a chilly mountainside for a crude lunch of bread and biscuits before we climbed steeply once again up a path known locally as "Mil Curvas" (Thousand Curves). The path clawed its way up the mountain by way of short zigzags much steeper than those we had climbed to the earlier two passes. Being much too steep to ride, we had to walk and scramble our way up. "Mil" is fortunately a bit of an exaggeration, although not by much. Loose rocks and gravel made the going slippery and the climb even harder.

I normally like to be able to see my target, but in the case of Mil Curvas, it was perhaps for the best that a cold, muffling mist had once more set in for the day and blocked entirely the view of the pass high above us. We could see nothing except for the next few curves as the path climbed relentlessly into the clouds. The temperature plummeted; where there had been occasional pockets of snow lower down, there were now large slabs of permanent ice.

We panted our way up to a patch of level ground at a chilly 4,500 metres. We decided to set up camp here, as there was a tiny rivulet of water and reasonable grazing for the animals. We rushed up the tents just in time before a steady drizzle set in. By 3:30pm, I was again dressed in all the clothes I had, despite which I was again very cold. We hurried an unpleasant supper in the spitting rain and dashed for the relative sanctuary of our tents.

Next dawn, thick ice on the tent made it difficult to unzip and emerge into a bitterly cold, although dry and clear morning. The air sparkled with clarity and the crisp chill of sunrise. After the interminable drizzle of the previous evening, we could scarcely believe the sight of

Mount Akhamani, this morning bathed in dazzling sunshine against the backdrop of a cloudless deep blue sky and nearly full moon. The previous afternoon had been so misty and murky we hadn't even seen the colossal domed mountain that now looked so near.

The elation of the view briefly obscured the fact that our camp was still deep in freezing cold shadow. Everything that had got even the slightest bit wet the previous evening, including my rain jacket and gloves, was now frozen solid. We set light to clumps of paja brava grass (which burns surprisingly easily) to create instant though short-lived fires to warm ourselves while we prepared breakfast. Looking back down the valley, dense clouds once again smothered everything except the distant glassy peaks of the Cordillera Real spearing through the mist.

After letting the tents defrost in the late-arriving sun, we turned to what remained of Mil Curvas. The climb to the pass loomed like a daunting cliff before us, although perhaps still elated from the close encounter with Akhamani, the reality was not nearly so intimidating. We bounded to the summit in just 20 minutes and gazed over a wide bowl of much gentler vistas: golden brown turf interspersed by tufts of ichu (clumpy grass like paja brava but shorter). Looking back, the peaks of the Cordillera Real continued to sparkle in the distance above the low cloud that once more threatened to sweep towards us. For the moment, though, there was not a cloud in the sky.

Just beyond the pass, Luis pointed to the tiny village of Qellwaqota several kilometres to our right, towards which he would now head whilst Paulino and I continued along the main trail. I felt sorry to say goodbye to Luis after just a couple of days, particularly after the wonderful evening of fishing he had introduced us to at the house of his aunt.

After losing sight of Qellwaqota behind some rolling undulations, we traversed a bare slope and skirted several trout-filled lakes. The glaciated peak of Sunchulli came into view for the first time. Morning sunlight continued to light up Akhamani in rich tones although we were now starting to lose the sacred mountain behind other summits in the cordillera.

We traversed an open landscape fringed by a ring of dark mountains, and passed beneath two small gold mines. At the second, two men were working high up on the mountainside above a cluster of ruined stone houses. The sun continued to shine and an energetic but not too cold wind kept the temperature comfortable.

We climbed to the Viscachani Pass just as some wispy clouds were drifting into the valley we had vacated. Summiting the pass gave us a superb broadside view of Sunchulli and its glaciers, and the beautiful, snow-crowned form of Mount Cuchillo revealed itself to us for the first time.

After pausing at the pass to admire the view, Paulino led the animals along a high path to pasture whilst I descended the steep valley side to the gold mining town of Sunchulli to replenish provisions. As I slid my way down the faint path, I could see that two small mines had been blasted into the flank of Sunchulli. A much larger, mechanised mine dominated the entrance to the village.

Sunchulli comprised an austere collection of tiny stone dwellings – functional at best. Lower down in the valley stand the remains of the Inca mining village with its large church. I was greeted in the modern Sunchulli by an energetic barking dog and four far-from-energetic people sitting outside one of the houses taking in the afternoon sun. One of the four was a woman who held a large folded blanket over her head as a sun shield. The woman shooed away the dog that had been harassing me. I had wanted to throw a rock at the nuisance but thought better of it as the dog might have belonged to one of the quartet.

We chatted briefly and I learned that just several days earlier, Peruvian bandits had raided the mine and had tragically killed one of the miners. As if life in these mountains wasn't harsh enough already! I was glad we were just overnighting here.

Two children and two adults followed me into Sunchulli's single store, which offered a surprisingly large range of items. "What else, what else?" asked the young boy enthusiastically every time I requested something. I bought kerosene, bread, cheese, tinned fish, fresh oranges, drinking chocolate and, at long last since leaving Sorata, toasted haba beans. The other child and two adults seemed transfixed by my every enquiry and purchase. Non-resident customers were clearly still a bit of a novelty here.

Following the fast flowing Sunchulli River upstream to rejoin Paulino and the mules, I criss-crossed small streamlets and springy bofedales, and climbed gently through pretty pastures grazed by many alpacas and llamas. Judging by the size of many of the animals, the grazing here was of excellent quality.

I caught up with the others at our camp at the foot of Mount Sunchulli, at an altitude of 4,700 metres. It was only 3pm and still blindingly sunny. We took advantage of this rare luxury of late afternoon warmth by drinking several cups of coffee and gorging ourselves on toasted haba beans. We finally set up the tents and put on all available layers at 5:30pm.

The sun disappeared from camp all too rapidly, although we could follow the weak line of sunlight as it retreated up the Sunchulli glacier. Almost immediately, the temperature plummeted well below freezing. Our kerosene stove could do little to warm us as we ate supper huddled against the low wall of a ruined hut.

The clear sky we had enjoyed all day led, as expected, to a particularly bitter evening, exacerbated by the high altitude of camp. My feet were numbingly cold in boots and thick socks. I couldn't believe that Paulino, who chose to wear open sandals without socks while in camp, didn't catch frostbite. The upside of the biting cold was the dazzle of frosty stars that lit up the cloudless sky, with the Southern Cross brilliant at the fringe of the Milky Way, giving me my bearings.

For a welcome change, we woke next day to early morning sunlight streaming over the tents, although it was still shiveringly cold (ice still rattled around inside my water bottle several hours later, even after continuous warming in the sun). As I emerged into the morning, alpacas and llamas were grazing amongst our tents.

Not having to defrost our tents this morning, we set off relatively early by our standards at just after 9am. We climbed for an hour up a dirt track towards the 5,100-metre Sunchulli Pass, inching ever nearer towards the mountain's glistening blanket of thick ice and snow. The view behind us of the valley snaking back towards Sunchulli village, with the Andean ranges beyond, was as striking as that of the mountain we were climbing.

We reached the pass and were immediately rewarded by a staggering panorama of the next broad valley. To our left, Cuchillo continued to show off her perfectly formed, angular profile while the rest of the cordillera's serrated, snow-covered peaks stretched away into the distance. To our right, the Sunchulli glacier towered above the calm turquoise water of Laguna Verde, beyond which scowled a dark, brooding ridge protected at its base by impossibly steep "if you dare" scree.

We skidded and slid our way down a steep gravel slope to a beautiful landscape of bouncy bofedales and myriad rushing streamlets and tiny waterfalls. Much of this watery wonderworld still lay frozen or overlain with sheet ice even in the late morning.

Continuing our descent, we reached pretty, pastoral scenes of shepherds watching over flocks of sheep grazing by the babbling river. Not quite so idyllic were some worryingly large puma tracks heading along our path, although I convinced myself that the well-fed alpacas, llamas and sheep would provide much tastier puma food than any member of the expedition.

As we continued descending towards the river, Paulino demonstrated some of his Kallawaya knowledge by picking Qheya Qheya (a herb for treating coughs) and Maycha (an easily combustible plant used for making fires, known as "Andean firewood"). We reached the river and continued along the valley to the community of Piedra Grande, an attractive collection of stone-built houses and animal enclosures set on the steep pitch of the valley side. Villagers had made no attempt to terrace this valley and the enclosures tilted with the lie of the land. We paused for lunch beside a large herd of laden llamas heading up the valley towards Sunchulli. We had descended unremittingly from the Sunchulli Pass to reach this point and I didn't fancy the afternoon's work facing the llamas.

Llamas were the only pre-Columbian beasts of burden known in the Americas. Their small two-toed feet with their rough pads let them walk easily on slopes far too rough or steep for other animals. However, they have a reputation as unpleasant beasts, partly due to their ability to spit and sneeze acrid saliva over considerable distances and with alarming accuracy.

The Incas commonly used llama caravans for transport. Because llamas cannot carry heavy loads, these caravans could sometimes extend to thousands of animals. Llamas can cover around 20 kilometres a day, which explains why so many settlements in the Andes, and tambos along Inca roads, are separated by such distances.

That afternoon, we followed a long, undulating path through a valley dotted with thatched stone houses and enclosures. We climbed to the drab mining town of Hilo Hilo, where once again I entered the village in search of a shop whilst Paulino and the animals bypassed the settlement by a more direct route.

A group of miners sat in the grim square facing another miner carrying a clipboard. They looked as if they were just about to start a meeting. The miners were as uninviting as the dismal village. They stared at me with suspicion. Did they suspect I was here to try to steal their gold? I didn't wait to find out. I dashed into the shop, bought a bottle of drink and hurried away quickly to rejoin the others.

Safely past the horror of Hilo Hilo, the Pallqa valley regained its idyllic appearance, with many alpacas and llamas still grazing by the riverbank. Several sharp peaks rose before us, dominated by the spear tip form of Keansani at the head of the valley.

We set up camp in an enchanting meadow at Tacaquani. It was still sunny when we arrived at 4pm and we estimated we still had half an hour of direct sunlight. We rushed to the river to wash ourselves and some clothes, and managed to get all our layers back on again just in time as shadow rapidly replaced sunlight in the camp. We cooked a pasta supper after which Paulino made a refreshing tea from muña plants (good for altitude and digestion) he had collected earlier in the day.

The valley sides rose high above us to the east and west and closed to narrow points to the north and south, creating a lemon-shaped sky above the meadow. As darkness fell, bright stars filled the lemon and the Milky Way formed a dazzling diagonal sash across its middle. This spot was so tranquil and still (with just the sound of the river, grazing mules and the occasional hooting owl), and the sky and shooting stars so beautiful, I sat in the vestibule of my tent for several hours, not wanting to zip away the scene.

As has long been the Andean custom, the Incas revered the stars and planets. They identified constellations of both stars and dark spaces, and created an elaborate mythology around the celestial bodies. No visitor who has ever gazed up at the awe-inspiring clarity and brightness of the Andean night sky, with the brilliantly luminous Milky Way prominent, would find this in any way surprising.

To the Incas, the most important constellations were the Pleiades, the three stars in Orion's belt and a cross constellation believed to be the Southern Cross. The Incas worshipped and made sacrifices to many stars, in particular the Pleiades, which they revered as a major huaca (shrine), and whose celestial course they tracked more closely than any other constellation. The Incas worshipped the stars as heavenly patrons, derived from the Pleiades, which protected every living thing on earth.

Early next morning, we left our delightful camp and continued climbing up the valley beside the rushing river towards the impressive, albeit snowless, peak of Keansani. The river suddenly became silent as we reached a flat section of valley, where the hushed watercourse meandered noiselessly beside our path.

The mountains ahead were still protected by lower slopes of viciously steep scree. We climbed up a rugged path hewn into a small opening in the cordillera's defences. The considerable effort of climbing the long, arduous switchbacks to the Keansani Pass was eased by the beautiful view back down the valley every time we paused for breath, which was every few steps in my case. We could follow the entire sweep of the river, from the lower meanders upwards to the source of the tiny stream high above us in the glaciated peaks of the cordillera.

We slogged our way up one of the most lung-busting climbs so far to a thinly oxygenated pass that offered disappointingly unimpressive views beyond. Pausing only briefly to place a stone on the cairn, we hurried down a steep, scrambly path into another broad, watery world of bofedales and small lakes. Mist drifted up the valley to greet us.

Shortly afterwards, the broad Hitapilluni valley fell away abruptly before us in what looked alarmingly like the edge of a cliff. We navigated to the side of the cliff and continued descending on a steep, stony path strewn with boulders. The path was sufficiently steep that we couldn't walk at a comfortably controlled pace, and coated with enough gravel that it was difficult to keep our footing. The next few hours were challenging and frustrating for two-legged and four-legged members of the expedition alike. A thick, damp, enveloping mist obscured most of the view and made the skidding and stumbling yet more disagreeable.

I was struggling to find anything positive to extract from this sapping experience when one appeared out of the mist as if by magic to revive our spirits.

"Condor!" shouted Paulino out of the thick fog behind me. Instinctively, I looked skywards, but out of the corner of my eye, I saw through a break in the haze a huge dark shape gliding down the valley beneath us, like us also heading towards Pelechuco.

I gasped at the massive wingspan (which looked more like a small plane than a bird and which never once deigned to flap), the characteristic fingered wingtips, black colour and large white epaulets on the shoulders that indicated it was an adult male.

Seconds later, the condor vanished into the mist. Thick cloud returned once more to shroud any view of the valley. However, after the fleeting clearing during which we had glimpsed the magnificent vulture, it didn't seem to matter any more. The condor had seemingly appeared as an omen to encourage us to keep on going during this unpleasant stage of the journey. I recalled the words of the Kallawaya: "Good luck. Go forward. Go forward."

CHAPTER ELEVEN

PELECHUCO AND THE KATANTIKA PASS

Tired and damp though still invigorated by the condor encounter, we arrived in Pelechuco almost before we could see it. As far as I could make out through the thick mist, Pelechuco comprised a cluster of ancient stone houses, many with thatched roofs, which sloped down several cobbled lanes to a main square.

By chance, the village happened that day to be celebrating the festival marking its foundation and we could hear a band playing in the square. Animals weren't allowed in the village centre, so we corralled the mules in a small field and walked down to inspect the festivities.

A bedraggled-looking band was playing pipes and drums in one corner of the square. The usual drunks were staggering around and dancing, one curiously carrying (or was he dancing with?) a stove. Two rather more formal-looking bands then entered the square, one wearing blue and yellow jackets, the other bright green ponchos. These two bands played the traditional Kantus music of the region, marked by panpipes and a heavy beat of drums.

As the bands played, teams of men were busy blocking the four corner entrances to the square with strong temporary barricades made of heavy wooden poles. Householders and shopkeepers were barring their doors.

Then, with little warning, most of the musicians and revellers vacated the scene and a bull was dragged by a rope into the fenced-off square. A gang of makeshift matadors and many riotous members of the crowd (some still in the square, others from behind the safety of the barricades, but all fortified with Dutch courage) taunted the animal and hurled random missiles at it.

The enraged bull made several charges at the tormentors and matadors, some of whom used ponchos and striped tablecloths as capes. The matadors either performed basic bullfighting passes, with varying degrees of skill and grace (one matador was bundled over by the bull, although he escaped serious injury), or rushed helter-skelter for cover behind benches or the railings of the square's central enclosure. Each charge of the bull was accompanied by a mighty scattering of bragging muchachos and drunken campesinos, and shrieks of delight from everybody else in the crowd.

After being tormented in this manner for several minutes, the bull was forced into a corner where a local cowboy jumped onto its back in rodeo style. We were expecting to see bucking fireworks but when the bull was released, instead of violently trying to dislodge its rider, it merely exited the square at a tame, bouncy canter.

As one bull tired, another was brought in to replace it and the same tormenting procedure repeated. Thus, afternoon turned to early evening before Paulino sensibly suggested we should continue on our way.

Leaving the still-celebrating festival village behind us, we followed attractive, though not extensive, agricultural terraces upstream along the Pelechuco River. The valley was still shrouded in the neblina that a local shopkeeper had earlier told me arrives regularly every afternoon. "We have sunshine every morning and cloud every afternoon," he had explained as I was topping up on provisions whilst waiting for the bullfighting to begin.

Through the mist, we caught hazy glimpses of the Ruinas de Guanan on the opposite side of the valley – stone ruins of strange, mushroom-shaped structures of uncertain purpose, believed to date from Inca times.

Munching a couple of melting chocolate bars to help keep us going, we continued along a deserted road. By dusk, we had reached the small village of Agua Blanca, where we decided to spend the night in the relative luxury of a dormitory room.

We had neglected to obtain a formal Kallawaya blessing in Curva before setting off into Apolobamba. During our evening at Agua Blanca, Paulino performed some of his Kallawaya practices to help us on the rest of our journey towards Peru, and to predict how the journey would go.

Using coca leaves, he divined whether we would enjoy a good journey from Pelechuco to the Peruvian border. In a similar manner to my previous Kallawaya reading, Paulino threw individual coca leaves over the table to determine the answer. The first leaf landed light side up – bad news. "Best of three," Paulino hurriedly interjected before I had time to consider the implications. The second leaf squared the score although to our shock, the decider again landed light side up. How was this possible? Had we already used up all our good fortune from the many sightings of Suerte Maria birds?

Paulino then divined what the weather would be like on the journey. He had already warned me to brace myself for bitter, buffeting winds and freezing temperatures – colder than in the mountains – on the high, exposed plains of the border pampas. Was there any chance we might enjoy slightly milder conditions? To our dismay, the coca leaves gave the identical prediction as before. We turned our thoughts immediately to finding additional thick layers of clothing, and spent much of the following morning buying thick hats, gloves and socks from a nearby alpaca workshop.

Our panic buying of extra layers meant we set off even later than usual that morning. The bright sun was already high in the sky by the time we continued following the Rio Pelechuco upstream on a poor, rocky path. The path climbed through many long switchbacks, but fortunately also included many shortcuts. In the distance, the impressive glaciated peak of Nevado Presidente stood sentinel at the head of the valley, before which rose Flor Nevado, with two gold mines blasted high up on its flank. The two mountains glinted ever more impressively the further we progressed along the valley.

Shadowing us across the river, a ridge of dark, gnarled peaks soared high above a base of steep scree slopes. Herds of alpacas and llamas grazed on pastures beside the river. Two aggressive sheep dogs barked at us angrily as we approached, while their owner sat languidly under the shade of a large rock outcrop. I hurled stones towards the dogs as they threatened to charge, but my throwing was so far off-target they must have thought I was playing a game of fetch with them.

Snarling wild and sometimes rabid dogs can be a problem in Bolivia. A La Paz climbing guide had advised throwing whatever we had – including every item of our belongings – at such dogs to try to keep them away. "Throw whatever you can lay your hands on, and keep on throwing," he had advised. "If necessary, run and keep on running," the advice continued. I hoped that we would never be reduced to that.

The path remained arid and monotonous but our target – the beautiful glaciated summits of Presidente and Flor – called us forward without complaint. Their white snow was tinged with glacial blue, with several sections torn apart by fields of crevasses.

We climbed slowly towards the Katantika Pass, crossing over which we would leave the jagged summits of the Cordillera Apolobamba and head west towards Peru over high, rolling pampas. We stopped for a much-needed lunch on a sunny pasture overlooked by plunging glaciers. Not a single cloud disturbed the intensely blue sky. Across the valley, a lone herder's hut and stone corral on Presidente's lower slopes were the only signs of human activity. In such surroundings, even our simple lunch of cheese and local bread made from wheat and maize tasted delicious.

We inched breathlessly upwards towards increasingly awe-inspiring views of glaciers, crevasses and snowy peaks. The view back down the valley was also becoming grander and grander as we rose high above the dark scree slopes and meandering river into the icy world of the high Andes.

As we finally neared the rounded pass, I literally stumbled across a section of unmistakable paved Inca road, some three metres wide, running west through the bofedales towards the ancient imperial capital of Cuzco.

We were still marvelling at the unexpected remnant of Inca road when a condor flew across our view to a rocky perch high above the pass. This was not nearly as close as yesterday's encounter on the descent towards Pelechuco, but was another wondrous condor sighting over a high pass, and we had neither seen any Suerte Maria birds today, nor lain any stones on cairns.

The Katantika Pass itself is marked by several turquoise lakes and some of the most striking scenery in the Andes. The glaciers and crevasses of Presidente and Flor glinted in the afternoon sun, plunging steeply towards the valley far below, and seemingly rimming a tranquil, trout-filled lake bordered by Inca paving. And a condor perched somewhere not far above my head. A stone cross marks the most sacred point of the pass, the landscape beyond mellowing markedly from jagged, icy summits to rolling undulations. This was Andean grandeur at its most sublime.

Out of habit, I laid a stone at the cross, more in gratitude for this staggering vista than to ask for any more good fortune. After all, what more could go right?

Morenada dancers, Island of the Sun, Lake Titicaca

Totora reed boat on Lake Titicaca

Deep in the Apolobamba mountains

Kallawaya healer and fourtune-teller from Curva

The Karantika Pass

CHAPTER TWELVE

BORDER PAMPAS

Paulino and the mules started the long gentle descent from the Katantika Pass. I remained at the summit for what seemed like an age, transfixed and speechless at the view and trying to take a picture that would do it justice, which of course was impossible. When I finally pulled myself away from the spellbinding scene to rejoin the others, I walked down even more slowly than I had struggled up to reach the pass. At every step, I scoured the rocks high up the mountainside to my left where I was certain the condor had perched, and looked back over my right shoulder to the unforgettable vista of towering snow-crowned mountains and sparkling glacial lakes.

The path descended gradually through an elevated, rolling landscape, high above a floor of golden brown bofedales punctuated by yet more turquoise lakes. Small herds of vicuñas grazed high up on the mountainside above us. Invigorated by the magnificence of the summit of the pass, we continued walking until late afternoon, when I suddenly realised that beneath the adrenaline rush, I was exhausted. The mules seemed equally tired and could hardly keep their eyes open whenever we paused.

We set up camp on a plateau near the village of Apachetapampa; behind a large rock that we hoped would provide some shelter against the wind that Paulino warned me blows up the valley every night. Not so! As I later recorded the day's events huddled in the vestibule of my tent, a gale struck up so violently that I was praying its gusts wouldn't tear the tent pegs out of the rocky ground.

The evening temperature plunged rapidly with the wind chill. As darkness fell, the direction of the Southern Cross confirmed that we had turned southwest towards the Peruvian border.

We gulped down a quick noodle supper and were so cold we couldn't even bring ourselves to complete our normal routine of carrying the rest of the food back to our tents. Instead, we hurriedly covered the food and cooking equipment with a plastic sheet and dived into our bellowing accommodation. This indiscipline nearly cost us dearly.

As we had passed Apachetapampa on our way to camp, we had encountered another pair of aggressive dogs. My stone throwing remained woefully inaccurate and still must have seemed more like play than an attempt to frighten the dogs away, but we thought our camp was sufficiently distant from the village not to have to worry about marauding canines that night. However, as the wind buffeted the pampas in the middle of the night, a couple of large hungry dogs crept around our tents. Fortunately, they rattled a cooking pot and awoke Paulino, who managed to shoo them away before they could make off with any of our food.

We woke to yet another freezing dawn. The morning sun was inconveniently blocked by the only mountain for miles around and we shivered in our camp until 8:30am. We continued along a dusty path through bofedales and a landscape of lakes and rolling pampas. We skirted the bare banks of Lago Katantika, which is noted for its trout fishing and whose far bank is fringed by an elongated, flat-topped mountain.

We were shedding worryingly little altitude along the undulating path. I wasn't so much concerned about breathlessness as the likely night-time temperature. After yesterday's elation at the Katantika Pass, everything today – not just our surroundings – seemed flat and far less interesting. Despite trying to perk myself up with several chocolate bars, I felt listless and lacked energy all day.

Plodding our way to the end of the lake, we arrived at the tattered little stone pueblo of Antaquilla where we enjoyed the rare luxury of lunch ("thimpu", a lamb stew) in a small eating house. Nearby, we encountered a couple of drunks chewing coca while reclining beside their bicycles in a pasture of long grass. They told us that they were returning from a local market. One was dressed in a bright red poncho with colourful stripes – a little like Paulino's poncho. The other claimed to be the Mallku of a local community.

They asked us for cigarettes. We would happily have obliged except they were buried deep in a pack on one of our mules. The Mallku then declared sternly that we needed local authorisation to be in the area and demanded that we report to the mayor in the morning. This was so similar to the encounter with the drunken policeman in Curva that I wondered whether all local leaders demanded consumable permissions from travellers in the form of beer or cigarettes. We smiled politely and walked away from these sad, but fortunately rare, examples of the local population.

We continued a short distance beyond the drunks and set up camp beside Laguna Janqo Qala (which means in Aymara "Lake of the White Rock"). We hadn't been there long before a chill wind blew up again, soon followed by sleet and rain, which dimpled the previously glassy lake surface. I scoured our surroundings for any sign of a Suerte Maria bird that might herald a change in our weather fortunes, but could find none. Paulino's coca leaf prediction was proving to be shiveringly accurate.

There wasn't even a sign of the eponymous white rock behind which we might shelter. Paulino folded up his stiff poncho and stood it in front of our stove as a wind break, but the howling gusts still blew out the flame several times. We were forced to cook inside one of the tents, which warmed us up so cosily we wondered why we hadn't done this before.

That night, we endured one of the coldest and most unpleasant nights of the entire journey – much colder than those we had spent at higher altitude! I barely slept all night and several times thought I was suffocating. I wore virtually every layer I possessed – including my rain jacket – inside my sleeping bag, and sacrificed just my poncho, which I used as a pillow. I found it difficult to breathe and at first thought this was because I was too tightly wrapped up in clothes. However, the breathlessness continued even after I loosened some of the layers. I was reduced to spending most of a horrible night sitting huddled in my sleeping bag, wrapped up in all my layers and watching the hands on my watch turn painfully slowly towards the next, reluctant dawn.

As daylight finally arrived, I struggled to unzip my iced-up tent and emerged to glistening frost all around. Having to allow time for the tents to defrost and dry, we set off very late. That day deteriorated into another prolonged grind beside a lake, then once again over pampas.

Paulino tried to shorten the distance by taking us along shortcuts, although at one point this strategy required taking off our boots and socks to wade across a river. In my very annoyed state, which I blamed on tiredness, I crossed the river, dried my feet and then realised I had forgotten my camera, which was still sitting on a rock on the far bank. Having to wade back to collect it did nothing to help lighten my mood.

We endured a lengthy climb past endless false summits before we finally reached the last pass before Peru. At an altitude of around 4,800 metres, we enjoyed superb views over lakes to cloud-shrouded mountains and gentle alpaca pastures beyond.

At the pass, Paulino (who had reached the summit long before I did) whispered to me that some locals had invited us to attend a meeting at their village.

"Why do they want us to attend their village meeting?" I asked in some disbelief, still breathless from the climb to the pass. Paulino shrugged his shoulders.

I had severe doubts, but reluctantly agreed to go along to the meeting. A short detour across the pass took us to a shabby little pueblo with rundown – almost derelict – buildings set around a compact square containing only a communal tap.

Five idle muchachos and a coca-chewing cholita with wild eyes and bedraggled hair were sitting on the ground in the sunny corner of the square. I presumed the meeting had convened, although I couldn't see much business being discussed. One of the muchachos conversed with Paulino, and then started a conversation with me, asking where I had travelled from, what I was doing, and how long I had been in Bolivia, etc.

The interrogator then pronounced that we had "permission to pass through". I struggled but failed to recall ever having requested permission from the gentleman. The interrogator then claimed to be the local authority and asked whether I wanted to buy a drink. I misunderstood his meaning and assumed he was asking whether we wanted a drink. I explained we were nearing our camp and could wait until then.

It transpired that the "authority" was inviting me to buy them a drink. Still ill-tempered from the pervious night's lack of sleep, I fumed at this latest request for consumable "permissions". I demanded to know what authority he represented. He claimed he was the Mallku of the village, which sadly explained everything.

"How many people do you represent?" I demanded to know. The authority dissembled that his jurisdiction was split into two and that he represented the larger section. I repeated my question but received the same non-response. I sought to clarify: "So you are the local Mallku but don't know how many people you represent?"

"Yes," came the embarrassed response. I took this total disregard of duty as relieving me of any drink-inviting obligations. I turned away without even bothering to ask Paulino the name of this ghastly little settlement. Like most of the other local "officials" we had met in Apolobamba, the Mallku was clearly in his post primarily for whatever personal gain he could seize. I was saddened, not so much by the repeated requests to gift these "authorities" drink and cigarettes, but by the depressing prospects the local people had of ever rising above their poverty with such officials in control of their fate.

We continued walking late into a long hot afternoon, trudging across a flat, bare and featureless landscape grazed by large herds of alpacas and llamas. As the shadows were starting to lengthen across the plain, we arrived at the Hichocollo hot springs, where natural spring water bubbles to the surface of small pools at a comfortable bathing temperature.

We were planning to camp by the hot springs and loosened all loads from the two animals. I threw my own pack down and collapsed on the ground. Just as we were pondering whether we could dive into the natural pools without any swimming costumes, three men who had been bathing approached us and introduced themselves as local rangers. They were from ANMIN, the government agency that looks after Bolivia's protected areas, and they owned the three motorcycles that lined up incongruously beside the pools.

We chatted briefly and explained our plans for travelling into Peru. Having known us for just some minutes, Justino Callancho Kana, the Hichocollo ranger, invited us to spend the night in his lodge. After the discomfort and lack of sleep of the previous night, this was an unexpected offer we couldn't refuse. The ranger's lodge had to be warmer and much more comfortable than our tents, even given the adjacent hot springs. Without hesitation, we abandoned all thoughts of a long, warm soak in the thermal pools and immediately began to strap our bags onto our startled animals again.

The dipping afternoon sun was still beating strongly across the pampas and Hichocollo appeared no more than a faint, hazy blur in the distance as we set off on this unplanned extension of the day. No matter. The prospect of spending a night inside a cosy lodge was all we needed to keep us moving; although I'm not sure our mules quite saw it that way.

Hichocollo turned out to be an unremarkable border town surrounded by wide, open pampas and vast herds of alpacas and vicuñas, some of which wandered through its dusty streets. The ranger's lodge was a curious, squat building shaped in the form of a cross built of two upturned half-pipes, and had solar-powered electricity and thick adobe walls painted brilliant white.

Justino kindly invited us to cook supper in the lodge and even more kindly invited us to use any of the food he had lying around his kitchen. Paulino immediately got to work boiling up a large pot of soup with rice, meat and vegetables. Justino bought some bread and bananas from the local shop, then heated up a bowl of steaming maize. Outside, the by now very low evening sun was setting over the flat pampas and lit up a sky of atmospheric clouds in beautiful shades of deep blood orange.

After several shivering suppers in the numbing cold of the windy pampas, we couldn't have dreamt we would tonight be enjoying endless cups of hot coffee and hot chocolate, bread and large bowls of steaming hot broth in the cosy warmth of the ranger's lodge. For once not having to dash into our tents and sleeping bags to preserve body warmth, we chatted late into the night while the ranger put on his favourite cumbia music.

For the first time since we entered Apolobamba, I was totally warm and snug that night; so much so I even woke up a couple of times overnight and had to shed some layers of clothing.

The next morning, I awoke to sunlight streaming through a small window and the beat of more of the ranger's cumbia collection. We enjoyed an unhurried breakfast and said our thank yous and goodbyes to the friendly ranger.

Within a few steps of leaving the lodge, we saw another Suerte Maria bird fluttering past us. I wondered what more good fortune this lucky omen would bring, although I was starting to question whether these birds didn't just confirm good luck retrospectively (such as the sunny start to our journey through Apolobamba and the condor sighting over the second high pass) rather than presage forthcoming happy events. On such a beautiful morning after such a restful and comfortable evening, such details really didn't matter.

Before us lay miles and miles of featureless pampas – a desolate immensity of unimaginable proportions. Like sailing a yacht across the open ocean, we picked a mark on the horizon and aimed for it. Apart from the thinnest vegetation and occasional clumps of ichu grass, the pampas was bare and scattered with red-hued rocks. We might have been on Mars.

We splashed across bubbling streamlets, crackled over thin ice and strode across dried riverbeds of rubble and sandy dried lakebeds. Many small herds of vicuñas skipped gracefully across the landscape, for once outnumbering the omnipresent alpacas. Pale green plains swept to distant encircling ranges of rounded pink-brown mountains – Bolivian to our left, Peruvian to our right – like two massive armies about to wage a huge battle. Behind the Bolivian ranks towered the glittering crowns of the Cordillera Apolobamba, as if saluting us in a final glorious farewell. Maybe the Suerte Maria bird was a foreteller of good fortune after all.

For several hours, we weaved and bounced over the endless span of green pampas. We crossed numerous rivers and streams, and scattered herds of alpacas and vicuñas, before we finally reached the modest river that separates Bolivia from Peru.

Pairs of simple white concrete posts spaced a few kilometres apart marked the porous border: uncomplicatedly, one on the Bolivian side marked "Bolivia" and another on the Peruvian side marked "Peru". Each pair of posts is numbered. We arrived at border crossing number 13. Looking around, I wondered how people reached these desolate crossings and what border formalities were necessary. There was no road by which to approach and, not surprisingly being in the middle of nowhere, there was not a person, let alone a border official, in sight.

This seemed a disappointingly low-key way in which to change countries. No matter, however. A couple of splashes later, we stood in Peru.

CHAPTER THIRTEEN

PERUVIAN ALTIPLANO

We celebrated crossing the border by pausing to devour several chocolate bars and assorted fruit, before we continued to the small Peruvian border town of Cojata where we guessed we were required to complete immigration formalities. It would have been a surprise if our appearance over the border hadn't caused some stir amongst the customs and immigration officials. And so it turned out. The welcoming immigration officer shook his head in smiling disbelief as Paulino and I explained from where and how far we had travelled. His stamp almost missed my passport as I continued to explain how far we – or at least I – still had to go (Paulino would turn back at Cuzco).

Cojata was once a thriving centre of llama ranching, but harder times have recently descended on the town. The once-massive llama herds have dwindled somewhat in recent years.

Surrounded by desolate plains, the view from Cojata had the unmistakeable stark beauty of the Altiplano – a starkness that questions how anybody or anything survives up here at such an altitude, on such barren land and in such bleak surroundings. Looking back towards Bolivia, flotillas of late morning cloudlets that had drifted up from the jungle were still floating gently along the Apolobamba range.

Having replenished our food supplies in Cojata, we followed a faint path northwards to Crucero and then Macusani, a small city located at over 4,000 metres set against the backdrop of snow-capped mountains and lakes that freeze overnight.

I discovered that Macusani is the highest provincial capital in Peru. Due to its isolation and abundant water supply, Macusani has enjoyed a long tradition as a refuge for Andean camelids. Although local people hope that a recent new venture of uranium mining will secure the town's future, Macusani remains a major centre for rearing alpacas and llamas.

Being so spoilt for choice as to where we could set up our camp that night, we dithered as we surveyed the expansive plain before us. Just at that moment, a vicious, icy gust of wind blew straight in our faces. Paulino and I looked at each other and, without uttering a word, we scurried straight for the local hostelry.

As Paulino unloaded the mules and corralled them in a nearby enclosure, I ascertained that there were a couple of free rooms in the basic hotel. The only other guests staying there that night were a couple of overseas alpaca buyers. That evening, we chatted to some friendly locals in the hotel before the alpaca buyers appeared and we all ate supper together.

It transpired that this hotel is well known in alpaca circles for its basic level of accommodation, which includes one toilet shared between all the guests and a single concrete corridor basin should anybody care to wash. Feeling cold to my core after just a couple of freezing beers, I certainly didn't.

I thought it strange how a concrete basin would have been a welcome luxury on any of the past few days, when we regularly endured the highly unpleasant – often painful – experience of washing in icy mountain streams. Not having spent even one night in a hotel again, we now suddenly found the basin inadequate if not unpleasant. How quickly our standards change as soon as we enter "civilisation"!

As is common throughout the rarefied Altiplano, temperatures range from a comfortable daytime 10 degrees centigrade to considerably below freezing as soon as the sun nears the horizon. Wind chill causes dramatic further discomfort. Basic our rooms might have been, but as the wind howled again, the adobe walls must have provided much greater protection against the elements than our tents ever could have.

The next morning, we said goodbye to the alpaca buyers and descended along a gentle valley cut into soft volcanic rock. By late morning, we were approaching the ancient stone village of Corani. We had reached the eastern edge of the Altiplano and were near the foothills of the isolated Carabaya range.

For the next two days, we climbed steadily on a pre-Columbian trail along an ancient Andean trade route that for centuries linked the northern Altiplano and gold-rich areas of Bolivia with the Inca capital of Cuzco. As we climbed the long, gradual valley, we passed rugged terrain and weird rock formations sculpted by ferocious wind and rain. As we reached higher and wilder landscapes, we passed several small mining operations where miners work mineral deposits by hand and carry out the mined ore on llama trains.

Half a day beyond the mines, we encountered an incongruous sheet of dazzling whiteness set in the midst of the Altiplano's forbidding earthiness. Paulino explained that we had reached the Quilquaya ice cap, one of the world's few ice caps found at tropical latitudes. Climbing onto the frosty surface, we were rewarded with sensational views of glinting mountain peaks in every direction.

After the unexpected interlude of the ice cap, we continued northward and climbed a lung-busting path up and over the Chimboya Pass at 5,100 metres. The scenery beyond was even wilder and more rugged as we entered the snowy Vilcanota range. The Vilcanota mountains form Peru's second largest glaciated system after the appropriately named Cordillera Blanca ("White range"). On this western side of the Vilcanota range lay mountains, grassy foothills and high plains grazed by large herds of alpacas that flourish on the sweet, tender pasture. The eastern side of the range falls away to the steamy forests of the Amazon.

The sacred 6,384-metre Ausangate is the highest peak in the Vilcanota range and is visible from Cuzco. Andean people have long revered Ausangate as an apu or holy mountain, traditionally the site of worship and sacrifices dating from pre-Inca times. Although shamanic pilgrimages are made to the mountain throughout the year, Ausangate is primarily renowned as the setting for Qoyllur Rit'i, an ancient ritual celebrated every June. Enacted in Cuzco and Ausangate, the festival's rituals merge Christianity with the ancient cult of the Sun.

Qoyllur Rit'i is one of the greatest native Indian festivals. The ritual is associated with the fertility of the land and the worship of apus, the spirits of the mountains. The main ceremony takes place at the foot of Mount Ausangate. On the day of the Holy Trinity, more than 10,000 pilgrims climb to the snowline, accompanied by all variety of dancers clad in full traditional costumes portraying various characters from mythology.

Climbing the mountain, pilgrims atone for their sins at various stone cairns along the way. A group of hefty, dressed up queros (members of what is probably Peru's purest Quechua community) then sets off for the summit at 6,384 metres in search of the Snow Star, which is reputedly buried within Ausangate. On their way back down the mountain, the queros haul massive blocks of ice on their backs for the symbolic irrigation of their lands with Ausangate's holy water.

Our timing didn't allow us to witness Qoyllur Rit'i, which was probably just as well. The strenuous climb and high altitude festivities would not have been a good idea for me, even after what was now a reasonable period of acclimatisation, but would have been very difficult to resist.

After descending all too briefly from the Chimboya Pass, we climbed again to an even higher pass, surrounded by mountain scenery that was becoming yet more astounding. The thin air was so clear that many of the mountains visible from the pass seemed to assume a surreal glow.

We descended a beautiful valley to Lake Ccascamacocha, which was surrounded by vast pastures of alpacas and inhabited by many ducks, flamingos, geese and giant coots. We set up camp beside the lakeshore, near which several viscachas bounded over rounded rocks. As we cooked supper beside the peaceful lake, we watched giant coots nesting on piles of mud in the inshore shallows and several pairs of Andean geese. Several families lived here permanently to tend their enormous alpaca herds. As night fell, their isolated fires lit up along the darkened lakeshore.

Gaining in cardiovascular confidence as we neared our immediate objective of reaching Cuzco in one piece, the next day we undertook a gratuitous and very strenuous scramble to the 5,450-metre snow-crowned summit of Cerro Yayamari, an inviting peak in the centre of a plain of lakes and mountains.

I was initially disappointed by Yayamari's appearance. It didn't look to me, admittedly a climbing layman, like a 5,000-metre plus summit, although given we were starting from almost 4,500 metres, that shouldn't really have been a surprise.

An angry, howling wind did its best to hinder our progress and seemed at times to be trying to suffocate us. With the final push in sight, we cowered behind the relative sanctuary of a large boulder to gather our strength and contemplate what remained of the climb. As we neared the summit, the many apachetas (ritual cairns) confirmed that Yayamari has long been worshipped by natives as a holy shrine. Fortified by some lunch, we clambered up a final range of large boulders and emerged onto the windswept summit and an almost endless view over bleak plains, jagged ridges and occasional lakes.

After a day in which we gained a lot of altitude but little distance towards Cuzco, we made good progress during the next couple of days towards the glacial Lake Sibinacocha, with many flamingos seemingly growing from its icy waters. High grassy plateaus now dominated the landscape. The glacial melt at the head of the valley attracted many pairs of graceful Andean geese. We camped beside the tranquil lakeshore and, save for the occasional stone herder's hut, could have been the only people in this vast valley.

Crossing over three more high passes, we traversed the flank of the mighty Mount Ausangate, along the way passing many brightly coloured lakes. Once more, we shared these endless plains with huge herds of alpacas and llamas grazing on irrigated pastures, all very unmoved by our presence.

At our camp just before Tinqui village, we bathed blissfully in a natural hot spring, which was a joyous relief since most of the other lakes and streams of the past few days had been much too cold to even contemplate washing.

Beyond Tinqui, we rode past several Andean villages scattered over a high landscape dotted with archaeological remains from Inca and pre-Inca times. Gradually, the bleakness of the Altiplano started to yield to patches of vegetation and eventually a beautiful, fertile valley. We were approaching the imperial capital of Cuzco, the city the Incas called the "navel of the world".

CHAPTER FOURTEEN

CUZCO

Arriving in Cuzco, the ancient capital of the Inca empire, I was immediately struck by the awesome beauty of the city. Endless church steeples and bell towers soar above a sea of red roof tiles, surrounded all around by high mountains. Columned arcades line the many ceremonial squares. There seems to be an ornate palace or church at every turn.

One of the most conspicuous features of the city is the layering of architectural styles. The Spanish built their flamboyant churches, monasteries and other ceremonial buildings on top of Inca structures they had destroyed except for their solid foundations. In every direction stand fabulous colonial structures built upon base layers of unmistakably perfect Inca ashlars.

In ancient times, Cuzco was no more than a modest cluster of humble huts spread over a landscape of marsh and springs. After their spectacular rise to power, the Incas decided to remodel their capital into the most distinguished city in all the land, at every turn imbued with architectural magnificence and sacred import.

They laid out their new capital in the shape of a puma, with a body, legs and tail, at the head of which stands the massive fortress complex of Sacsahuaman. The tail stretches down what is nowadays Avenida Sol to where two rivers came together at Pumachupan ("Puma's Tail"), near where the great Pachacuti Inca's monument stands today.

The redesigned Inca capital was a vision of thatched houses interspersed by flamboyant palaces. In contrast to the red roof tiles of the modern city, the roofs of ancient Cuzco were tightly thatched and steeply pitched. The Incas filled their capital with vast plazas, temples and royal palaces, and intended the very sight of their capital to inspire awe in all who set eyes upon it.

Cuzco's architectural extravagance reflects not just the Incas' remodelling of their capital but also their tradition whereby successive monarchs didn't occupy the palaces of their predecessors (which remained shrines to the deceased rulers) but instead had to construct their own elaborate abodes. Thus, each successive generation heaped architectural splendour upon architectural splendour.

Pachacuti Inca is credited with the original remodelling and rebuilding of Cuzco in the imperial era, which created the largest and most majestic city of its time in South America. It was he who planned the puma outline (he called the city the "lion's body", and regarded its inhabitants as the limbs of that lion), although at that time the puma lacked a noteworthy structure at its "head".

On returning to Cuzco from putting down an uprising in Collasuyo (the southern expanse of the empire), Pachacuti's son Topa Inca recognised that unlike most settlements, Cuzco lacked a stronghold in which its people could take refuge if the city were attacked. He set about designing the mighty fortress complex of Sacsahuaman that now dominates the head of the puma-shaped capital.

On the day we arrived in the city, Cuzco was full of tourists and even fuller of businesses supporting the tourists. Restaurateurs and tour companies marketed their services enthusiastically, although also with good grace should you decide to eat elsewhere or try another tour company or artesania shop. Adding to the crowds that day were hundreds of local schoolchildren, who were joining hands around the massive puma-shaped outline of the city in an event designed to raise cultural awareness and celebrate an anti-smoking campaign.

To say that Cuzco's bustle was a culture shock didn't begin to describe the feeling of arriving here after so many days spent in the silent wilds of the Andes. If I was shocked, I could only wonder at how Paulino must have felt. Having lived most of his life in a tiny village in remote mountains, Paulino had never before visited a town larger than Charazani, let alone a city like Cuzco.

Our two mules would have been even more bewildered by the sights and sounds of Cuzco. We spared them the experience by leaving them with a farmer in a field in the outskirts of the city. Modern day Cuzco really isn't geared up for making grand entrances on muleback.

Our plan all along had been for Paulino to return to Bolivia after we reached Cuzco. I needed to spend some days exploring the city, and Paulino had no experience of the route beyond Cuzco, so I would have needed to find another guide even if Paulino was travelling further. Several sections of the journey from here (in particular the trail to Machu Picchu) didn't allow pack or riding animals, so we agreed that Paulino would also take my mule Coco back with him to Curva, where he would feel much more at home than here.

I urged Paulino to stay at least a night in Cuzco to rest, but he insisted adamantly on beginning the long return journey that afternoon. We enjoyed a long leisurely lunch together and walked back to the farmer's field where the mules were devouring the grazing as if they had never before seen grass. We then solemnly loaded the mules together for a final time.

I could have spent much of the afternoon watching my friends slowly disappearing along the road we had travelled together, but I dislike such drawn out farewells. Instead, we hugged our goodbyes not far from the field, after which I quickly jumped onto a local bus, which minutes later returned me to the hustle and bustle of Cuzco.

I was exhausted from the exertions of the past two weeks and felt sad at saying goodbye to Paulino and Coco. I checked in to a comfortable colonial-style hotel just off the main square and collapsed straight into bed.

I was still sleeping soundly when John Leivers, a locally based explorer, called at the hotel. I had arranged to meet John in Cuzco in order to pick his brain about routes and guides for the journey through Peru, in particular through the jungle-choked mountains of Vilcabamba. John had only that afternoon returned from an expedition to a remote corner of Vilcabamba and was still dressed for the jungle. This tall, well-built man wearing bush wear, wide-brimmed hat and a GPS receiver stuffed in his breast pocket wasn't difficult to spot amidst the locals in the hotel lobby.

John and I chatted all evening about the Incas and my journey, and pored over my several newly acquired maps of Vilcabamba. By the time we had drunk a couple of large mugs of coffee and a couple of beers and had eaten a large three-course meal, I was feeling much more confident about my journey through the wilds of Vilcabamba, despite John warning me that even the best maps of the area aren't always terribly accurate!

The next morning, refreshed and once again clean, although still sad at being muleless for the first time in several weeks, I set off across the main square to Cuzco's excellent Inca museum, to discover more about the people and their great empire.

Inca society was a strictly elitist theocracy defined by a rigid class structure and ruled by a tiny but all-pervasive hierarchy. The Inca ruler was known as the Sapa Inca. His subjects revered the Inca as a living god – the Son of the Sun. His royal insignia was a fringe of fine red wool that hung from a headband of cords and covered his entire forehead, and partially covered his eyes. Nobody was allowed to appear before the Inca without bearing something in their hands as an offering, such as fruit, vegetables, flowers or birds.

On the same day as he received the royal insignia, the Inca also received his coya or principal wife, often one of his sisters or first cousins. Such family marriages were usually ceremonial only, and the Inca ruler had countless other women to satisfy his carnal desires. One account records how by the time Pachacuti had reached the age of 70, he had sired some 200 sons and 100 daughters.

The Incas applied a collectivist system of government whereby all land, animals and crops were held in common by the community or state. People were regarded as the real source of wealth and subjects were accordingly taxed in labour.

The Incas forced native Indians to work for the common good, extracting labour and resource tributes from their subjects by way of the mita system. Under this system, households provided the empire with a rotating labour service as required by the Inca. Subjects typically provided two to three months of service a year in duties that included farming, military service, mining, construction of roads and buildings, and manufacturing artefacts.

In return for requiring their subjects to work for them, the Inca elite provided collective benefits to everyone in their realm, from conqueror to vanquished alike. These benefits were conditional, of course, on their subjects' absolute compliance with and loyalty to every commandment of the Inca state. Any failures to comply were dealt with by harsh punishments. The Incas meted out death penalties by hanging or stoning for a wide range of crimes against the state or community, even for laziness. Dissenters were executed or forced to migrate to distant corners of the empire where they would be of less danger to the state.

During the century of Inca domination, there was little opportunity for individual effort. The concept of private property didn't exist. Everything belonged to the government or community. Crops were taken by the priests, the Incas and other nobles. In contrast to the effects that such a system might have on workers today, Inca subjects weren't as unhappy as we might suspect. People seldom had to labour alone since everything was carried out in common. Workers went out in huge family parties when it was time to cultivate the fields or bring in the harvest. Village gossip and choral singing lessened the hardships of their labour. Large quantities of chicha quenched the thirst and further cheered the mind.

The Incas tried to match the service and tribute they demanded with the specialisms of their subjects. They had, for example, specialist litter bearers, stonemasons and warriors. The Uros of Lakes Titicaca and Poopo, some of whom I had met earlier at Lake Titicaca, liked to think of themselves as superior (and this aloofness contributed to their difficulties with their Aymara neighbours). However, far from recognising such superiority, the Incas considered the unfortunate Uros as too inept to engage in any public works projects, and instead relegated them to menial tasks such as fishing and reed gathering.

Of much greater importance to Inca society were the goldsmiths and silversmiths who crafted many of the fine artefacts on display in the museum. According to Inca mythology, gold symbolised the sweat of the Sun and silver the tears of the Moon. The Incas revered these metals (all the more so because they reinforced their link to the cosmic deities), and crafted beautiful gold and silver idols, vessels, jewellery and architectural ornaments.

The Incas maintained large numbers of skilled goldsmiths and silversmiths throughout the empire, who worked exclusively for the Inca and other imperial nobles. These goldsmiths and silversmiths, along with the stonemasons and weavers of fine fabrics, were the only artisans who dedicated their entire lives to their art. Without knowledge of iron, the silversmiths unbelievably did all their work using just tools made from wood, copper and hard stones.

The Incas produced many more fine examples of gold and silver artefacts than survived the 16th century. To the Spanish Conquistadores, however, gold, silver and other metals merely represented the earthly riches they so craved. Following the Conquest, a century of fine Inca metalworking was melted down as fast as the Spanish could dump the plundered treasures into their raging forges. The Incas buried many pieces and even hurled others into the depths of Lake Titicaca to avoid them falling into Spanish hands.

Andean people have long been deeply religious and superstitious. They believe they co-exist in the world and the cosmos with the gods, the spirits of the landscape and their dead ancestors. The earth and the skies above them teem with powerful gods who control their lives and send omens through the weather and other natural phenomena such as comets and earthquakes. The people dutifully revere these gods through prayer and sacrifice in an effort to appease them.

Inca religion and ideology were based on thousands of years of Andean beliefs, interwoven with history (often manipulated to suit their purposes) and politics. The Incas worshipped the Sun, the Moon and the stars; natural landmarks (huacas); the Inca ruler, who they believed was a living deity and the Son of the Sun (as had been the Egyptian pharaohs); the mummies of their deceased kings; and, above all, the universal creator god Viracocha (although Viracocha's pre-eminence may have been overstated by the Spanish in their search for an Inca equivalent to the Christian God).

In addition to their major gods, the Incas also worshipped a bewildering range of natural phenomena, including exceptionally large trees and uniquely formed potatoes and ears of maize, which they honoured by drinking, dancing and performing other special ceremonies. They also revered springs, rivers, lakes and hills that were different in shape or substance from their surroundings, snow-capped mountains and high plains, boulders and large rocks, cliffs and deep gorges. They worshipped hilltops and mountain passes (which they called apachetas) by laying stones on their summits. The accumulated offerings made by travellers form cairns of stones still found on most high points and mountain passes in the Andes.

On the ground, they believed that stones could come alive (as they had done to help Pachacuti defeat the Chancas) and that the opposite could also happen – people could become petrified.

The Incas cast lots and made sacrifices as precautionary measures before undertaking any important activity such as planting, harvesting, construction, marriage or setting off on a journey or military campaign. They cast lots to determine whether the outcome would be good or bad, and to find out which sacrifices would be most agreeable to their deities to ensure a favourable outcome.

The hooting of an owl or howling of a dog were both believed to portend the death of a relative or neighbour. Lunar and solar eclipses were regarded as evil omens, foretelling grave misfortune and calamities. Rainbows were generally regarded as evil omens foretelling death or serious injury. They considered the end of a rainbow to be a particularly frightening place to be feared and venerated.

The Incas planned their crops and celebrated religious festivals by measuring time through careful observation and an advanced understanding of the heavens. The Incas were accomplished astronomers who understood and could predict solar cycles, solstices and equinoxes. They based their calendar on the passage of the sun, and celebrated important annual ceremonies such as Capac Raymi (the Great Festival) in December and Inti Raymi (the Festival of the Sun) in June. The Incas also had a good grasp of lunar cycles and fixed many of their festivals to the appearance of the new moon.

The Incas couldn't predict solar eclipses, however, and found these events frightening and grave. They associated eclipses with the Sun having gone into mourning, probably predicting a royal death. The Inca reaction typically involved lengthy fasting and copious sacrifices of a great number of children and livestock in an attempt to divert catastrophe. People responded to earthquakes by pouring water over the ground, believing the earth to be thirsty.

The sight of comets or shooting stars also caused great shouting and the making of sacrifices in an effort to divert calamity. Comets, in particular, were believed to portend grave, historic events. The Inca Atahualpa himself reported that a comet had foretold the death of his father Huayna Capac. Another comet appeared during Atahualpa's captivity in Cajamarca (the Spanish captured him at the beginning of the Conquest). The Inca predicted the impending death of a great prince, not knowing that he himself would be dead within a few days.

The Incas were so prescribed by superstitions, idols, ceremonies and sacrifices, they observed their religious obligations as inviolable beliefs and laws. Without the benefit of a written language to record their religion, the Incas employed more than a thousand men in Cuzco just to remember all their myriad spiritual obligations.

Such was the profound devotion of subjects and strict enforcement of worship that people willingly offered and sacrificed their own children and burned their own property, as required.

Inca priests were selected from twins, triplets and other unusual births, and were consecrated when they became old and unable to perform other duties. The empire had an excessive number of priests since every shrine, no matter how small, had its own priests and attendants to care for it and offer it sacrifices. Priests often also carried out the duties of confessor, doctor and sorcerer. The Lord High Priest, called Villac Umu, was selected from boys born during a thunderstorm.

The Incas justified their conquests in the name of religion, based on honouring and obeying Viracocha (as the universal creator), the Sun, the Moon, the Thunder and their numerous other gods. The Incas claimed that these gods gave them the power to conquer, safeguard and bring civilisation to the world.

Reflecting the huge scale and ethnic diversity of the Inca heartland, the empire incorporated many different religions. The Incas forced all conquered people to acknowledge the supremacy of the Sun and its Inca descendants. They required all the nations they vanquished to worship the Inca religion, but only forced them to give up their own religions where they contradicted the official religion.

The Incas brought back to Cuzco all the various native gods and idols they captured from conquered tribes. They even worshipped them to a limited extent alongside the empire's official gods. Having conceded control of their gods to the Incas, the conquered vassals were obliged to obey the Incas, on pain of severe punishment by their gods.

Seizing control over the gods of their subjects helped the Incas subjugate their vassals and force them to abandon all hope of ever successfully rebelling against their rulers. This became a great contributor to imperial rule over the empire's diverse and widespread subjects. Should any of their provinces rebel, the Incas brought out the native gods of the rebelling province, and whipped and humiliated them in public until the rebellion had been quashed. To further subdue their subjects and demand obedience, the Incas reserved the worship of their most revered god Viracocha for themselves and only those others who they permitted.

The Incas considered their glorious capital the "navel of the world", from which radiated a network of zeqe lines burgeoning with huacas, which together defined a sacred world alive with numerous spirits.

Zeqe lines were similar to the stations along a Christian pilgrimage route and emanated from Cuzco and other settlements throughout the Andes. Huacas were sacred shrines comprising both natural landscape features, such as carved rocks, mountain peaks, springs, wells and caves, and manmade features, such as palaces, temples, idols and fountains. Set within an empire-wide sacred geography, there were some 400 named huacas in the Cuzco area alone.

Not distinguishing separate spiritual and material worlds, the Incas endowed huacas with magical significance and supernatural powers and a unique place in Inca mythology. This allowed the Incas to imprint both their history and legend over a landscape of sacred space.

The Incas worshipped these huacas with prayer and sacrificed copious offerings to them of llamas, guinea pigs and coca. Hundreds if not thousands of people came to pay homage to important huacas, which sometimes evolved into self-sufficient areas controlling their own land and herds.

Andean people often paid more attention to their dwellings after death than they did to their dwellings during life. While their houses were small and humble, they took great care to adorn the tombs in which they were to be buried, and arrange the most lavish and impressive burials as possible. Some tombs were dug underground whilst others were built above ground, sometimes in the form of small towers.

The death of an Inca king or great noble precipitated many days of lamentations, during which time people honoured the deceased with dancing, mournful songs and much chicha drinking. No fires were lit in the house of the deceased during these lamentations.

At the death of a king, his entrails were removed and his body embalmed. The dead bodies were preserved with such care and skill that when they were found several hundred years later, they looked like they had died only a month before. The dead king's family group would carry his clothes and weapons to the places where the deceased lived his life or performed heroic acts, where they would sing more mournful dirges and recount his triumphs. They killed the king's wives and most important servants and officials, all of whom were needed to accompany their master into the afterworld.

The deceased took all their personal property with them on death; none was bequeathed to their heirs. Part of this property was either buried or maintained in his house. Other parts were buried in locations where he spent time during his life.

One of the Incas' practices that most appalled the Conquistadores was their veneration of the bodies of their dead. This worship of the mummies of their deceased rulers was striking, even by the standards of ancient societies. The Incas revered their dead like gods; they respected them and offered sacrifices to them.

Whilst the Incas' practice of ancestor worship horrified the Spanish, it was perfectly natural to the native Indians, for whom the living shared the world with the dead, the gods and spirits.

The bodies of noble lords were embalmed with such great skill the mummies were preserved intact for centuries. These Inca mummies continued to live in considerable style in gracious palaces and estates, and were served by large numbers of attendants. The mummies even visited one another. During such visits, they partook of extensive dancing and drinking, and counselled the current rulers on important matters of state.

A line of royal mummies was regularly brought out into Cuzco's main square where they ate and drank with living royalty and aristocracy. Attendants lit fires in front of the deceased, in which they burned food for consumption by the dead lords. The deceased were also offered chicha to drink from large gold and silver tumblers.

According to one native story, Huascar, later the loser in the final dynastic war, had his mother marry the mummy of his father, Huayna Capac, in order to fully legitimise his claim to the Cuzco throne.

The Incas didn't share the Christian concept of a single body and soul. In addition to worshipping the mummies of their dead kings, the Incas created royal statues from the fingernail clippings and hair cuttings of their deceased rulers, and created various other representations of royal mummies (including vessels containing preserved afterbirth), all of which they revered as divine objects.

Leaving the engrossing museum in the early afternoon, and still wondering exactly where in the square mummified Inca rulers used to eat, drink, be merry and counsel the current ruler, I strolled around Cuzco's ancient and atmospheric cobbled streets. Now with more time to appreciate them, I was even more struck by the beauty of the city and its historic buildings, in particular the Incas' instantly recognisable stonework. This dazzling architecture never fails to astound to this day with its beauty, scale and intricacy, and is arguably the Incas' most conspicuous legacy.

Most Inca structures reflect an obsession with religious ritual and sacred space. Using masonry techniques they probably learned from Tiahuanaco, the Incas cut and polished huge stones with brilliant precision, tightly fitting together adjoining blocks with bevelled edges – even in complicated polygonal shapes – without using mortar. So accurately did the Incas fit blocks together it is impossible to place a knife blade between adjoining stones. Even more remarkably, the Incas achieved this stoneworking precision without the benefit of machines, wheels or iron tools.

Possibly even more impressive than their beauty is the remarkable resilience Inca constructions have demonstrated over the centuries. The central Andes occupy an active earthquake zone, yet Inca constructions have contemptuously shrugged off numerous violent tremors that have brought many much more modern buildings crashing down.

The Incas employed vast numbers of architects and stonemasons to erect an unending stream of magnificent fortresses, palaces and temples throughout the empire. Constructing relatively simple roofs of substantial wooden beams covered by well laid bunches of grass, the Incas focused their architectural genius on the walls of their structures.

The Incas used different types of stone and stonework, depending on the importance of the building and the local availability of materials. The Incas reserved their most elaborate masonry for their palaces and temples, and built these of rectangular ashlars of black andesite. This weathers to a deep rust colour, which is clearly demonstrated by many of the stones at sites such as Pisac and Machu Picchu (which I would soon see for myself).

Many of the foundations and terraces in Cuzco were constructed of hard grey limestone (which the Incas also used for the massive stones in the fortress of Sacsahuaman). In many constructions, the outer face of each stone was bevelled inwards, thus providing a beautiful texture and shading to even the longest section of flat wall.

The two principal stonework styles were "coursed" and "polygonal". Coursed stonework laid rows of precisely cut rectangular blocks on top of each other, and was used for the walls of the most important structures. The stones of each level are uniform in size, but the ashlars become progressively smaller the higher up they are.

Polygonal stonework created interlocking structures out of haphazardly shaped rocks. Although often regarded as inferior to the neatness of coursed masonry, the elaborate beauty of polygonal stonework can be mesmerising, and these stones were fitted together just as perfectly as ashlar stonework.

Exploring the narrow lanes of the ancient capital, I came across one of the most famous examples of Inca polygonal stonework – the huge stone in Cuzco's Hatunrumiyoc ("Street of the Great Stone"). This massive stone has been carved with no fewer than 12 corner angles.

The mind boggles at the intricate skill required to fit such a large and annoyingly irregular stone so perfectly into the wall.

The trapezoidal shape of doors and windows, in which the vertical sides taper inwards towards the top, is another unmistakable characteristic of Inca architecture. Trapezoidal niches decorate the interior walls of many buildings. Niches could be large enough to accommodate a person, although they were more often of smaller size and were used as alcoves for storage or to display religious icons.

The finest examples of Inca stonework surviving today are probably the walls of Cuzco's fabled Coricancha ("Golden Enclosure" or "House of Gold"), most notably the perfectly curved and tapering outer wall of its Temple of the Sun. Cuzco lay at the heart of the Inca religion and the Coricancha was its most venerated shrine.

Sun worship was central to Inca religion, as it had long been to many Andean cults before it. Each year in June, the Incas celebrated Inti Raymi, the most important festival dedicated to the Sun. Annual re-enactments of this ancient festival still take place in Cuzco and Vitcos in Vilcabamba.

The Incas always claimed divine kinship with the Sun, which in their world was the foremost religious cult. The Incas imagined the Sun as a man, with the Moon as his wife and the stars as the offspring of them both.

Through their knowledge of astronomy and their ability to predict the solar passage across the sky, the Incas were able to support their links to this most worshipped deity, and thus reinforce their claims to supremacy as the Sun's chosen people on earth.

The Incas so venerated the Sun that they dedicated to it many more magnificent temples than they did to any other god (including the creator god Viracocha). Every major Inca town and site had a Sun temple, amply served by numerous priests and attendants.

Next to each Sun temple, the Incas constructed a convent for mamaconas, the cloistered virgins whose lives were dedicated to the service of the most important Inca gods. These women cared for the temple and assisted in services, made fine clothing, cooked food and brewed copious amounts of chicha for the priests to drink and for use in rituals and sacrifices. Mamaconas had to remain virgins for their entire lives, or else face being buried alive or some other equally horrible death.

The Temple of the Sun in Cuzco's Coricancha was by far the most sumptuous temple and most venerated sanctuary in all Inca religion. The Coricancha is believed to have originally extended for hundreds of metres in length, and housed some 4,000 priests and attendants. Religious ceremonies, offerings and sacrifices were performed there daily. Although now known as the Temple of the Sun, the Incas worshipped all their deities at the Coricancha. People visited to pay homage from throughout the empire.

The Coricancha contained lavish temples to the Sun and Moon, as well as shrines to the gods of thunder and lightning, and the Pleiades, and chambers to house the gods of conquered tribes.

Although its full magnificence is difficult to imagine, three Conquistadores saw the Coricancha in its resplendent, golden-lined glory. Unfortunately, these three ruffians had been sent by Pizarro to plunder the temple rather than pay homage.

It was from the Coricancha that the captive Inca Atahualpa had most of his ransom collected in his doomed bid for freedom after being captured by Pizarro at Cajamarca during the first days of the Conquest. Pizarro sent his three men to Cuzco to speed up collection of the ransom. With their bare hands (the terrified Indian attendants refused to help, fearing death if they violated the shrine), the three Spanish looters prised off some 700 great plates of gold that sheathed the temple (each measuring about half a metre across and weighing around 2kg), and dismantled a golden fountain weighing some 55kg. They also reported but were unable to carry off with them a golden altar weighing almost 90kg and large enough to hold two men.

Pizarro's main party later carted off all manner of exquisite golden treasures and precious objects, all of which the Spanish melted down as quickly as they could transport them to their furnaces.

Whilst the first three Conquistadores plundered the largest and most easily removed gold pieces from the Coricancha, they failed to remove the most sacred religious symbol of the Inca empire: the Punchao. This was a golden disc that represented the Sun and was the principal Sun god worshipped by the Incas.

Punchao means "moment of daybreak", the instant when the first rays of the morning sun broke over the horizon and filled the gold-lined Coricancha with radiant light – a moment that must have been of unimaginable beauty in the crystal clear air of the high Andes.

The Punchao was made entirely of the finest gold encrusted with exquisite jewels. Light reflecting off it shone with such brilliance it looked like the sun itself. From its temple in the Coricancha, it was brought out every day to greet the sun, before being carried back inside again at the end of the day. Manco Inca spirited the Punchao away with him after the failed Great Rebellion of 1536, when he fled to Vilcabamba to lead the guerrilla resistance against the Conquistadores.

The most solemn Inca rituals required them to make human sacrifices to their gods and ancestors. These rituals were generally Sun worship ceremonies marking the death or coronation of a ruler, a great conquest or a time of great need, for example, during floods, failed harvests or earthquakes.

The death of an Inca required the sacrifice of one thousand of the most attractive boys and girls aged around five to six, generally the children of caciques (native chiefs). These were chosen for their beauty so as to send humanity's finest to accompany the deceased ruler on his journey to join the gods. These children were dressed up finely, paired as a boy and girl, and buried in their pairs with gold and silver table service all over the land in places where the Inca had travelled in life. Some were even thrown into the sea in their pairs. In this way, the children were offered to the Sun and would be able to serve the Inca in the afterlife.

The coronation of a new ruler was celebrated with equally great pageantry. The lords and nobles gathered in the main square in Cuzco. The statues of the Sun and other major gods were brought out from the Coricancha, together with the mummies of the deceased kings. The sacrifices made at coronations included two hundred children, a thousand llamas, a large amount of gold and silver, many fine textiles, and large volumes of seashells and delicate, coloured feathers. The children were strangled and buried together with items of gold and silver on the hill of Chuquichanca, which lies above the San Sebastian district of Cuzco. The llamas, textiles and other sacrifices were burned.

Human sacrifices on less important occasions involved offerings of children collected by the Inca by way of tribute, generally more girls than boys. The child sacrifices were made drunk before they were strangled or had their throats slit. Some even had their hearts cut out while still beating as a further offering to the gods. The Incas would then smear the blood of their sacrifices over their idols and the mummified bodies of their kings and lords.

Although some have claimed that Inca rituals sometimes demanded the sacrifice of several thousands of victims, even this would come nowhere near the bloodthirstiness of Mexico's Aztecs, who might have sacrificed many tens of thousands of victims in a single event. In the Inca domain, llamas and guinea pigs had much more to fear than humans from upcoming rituals.

The sacrifice of large numbers of llamas and guinea pigs was valued second only to the sacrifice of humans. The Incas also used the sacrifice of such animals to predict the outcome of future events, for example, by slicing open the carcasses and looking inside for certain signs. All sacrifices were invariably accompanied by feasting and great drinking bouts involving dancing, singing and games.

After partaking of my own modern day feasting and drinking that night amidst Cuzco's tourist hordes, I set off next morning for the short walk to the imposing ruin of Sacsahuaman, which stands on a hill overlooking Cuzco.

Although usually regarded as a fortress, Sacsahuaman probably served religious and administrative as well as military functions. However, it's difficult to regard it as anything other than a fortress when you gaze up at its main defences: three mighty rows of zigzag ramparts that rise one above the next and form a colossal wall 15 metres high that extends for over 300 metres, protecting the site's northern aspect.

For structural strength, the Incas placed the most massive stones at the apexes of the zigzags. One expert estimates that the largest stone block, which stands some 8.5 metres tall, weighs over 360 tonnes, making Sacsahuaman one of the most remarkable structures of the ancient world. Despite the colossal size of the boulders, the Incas characteristically fitted them together with the utmost precision.

One theory for the zigzag construction is that it allowed any attackers to be fired on from at least two different positions. A more romantic explanation is that the zigzags formed the teeth of the puma, whose outline is drawn by the shape of Cuzco, and at whose head Sacsahuaman sits.

At the time of the Conquest, the summit of Sacsahuaman comprised a large complex of religious, administrative, defensive and storage buildings. Its labyrinth of buildings was crowned by three great towers, and was spacious enough to garrison five thousand troops during Manco Inca's 1536 rebellion. Most of the population of Cuzco could probably have retreated within Sacsahuaman during times of threat.

Unfortunately, in the centuries following the Conquest, Sacsahuaman was reduced to serving as a quarry of pre-cut stones for Cuzco builders, and the site has been stripped of all but its massive terrace walls.

Although now nowhere near its ancient glory, the mere sight of the colossal stone blocks of Sacsahuaman never fails to cause wonder at how the Incas managed to extract such large stone blocks from quarries, work them with such skill and precision, and set them in place without the aid of machines, wheels or iron tools. To heavily superstitious native Indians viewing Sacsahuaman for the first time, they must surely have believed that this was the work of the gods.

The construction of Sacsahuaman required an estimated workforce of at least ten thousand men, working non-stop for around six years. In the context of the end result, some claims that up to 30,000 people at a time worked on the fortress appear believable. Most of the labour was required to haul the huge stones from the quarries to the site. Some stones were so massive they needed five hundred or even a thousand men to move them.

Sacsahuaman was the site of one of the fiercest battles of the Great Rebellion of 1536 – a battle that was to prove pivotal to the outcome of the uprising. Native troops had easily retaken the site, which was at the time only lightly garrisoned by Spanish forces, and used it as a base from which to launch repeated attacks on the Spaniards in Cuzco.

The beleaguered Spanish realised that their only chance of survival was to recapture Sacsahuaman. Juan Pizarro, a younger brother of Governor Francisco Pizarro (the leader of the Conquest), led a slender cavalry unit out of Cuzco in a desperate do-or-die attempt to recapture the Inca fortress. If they failed to retake Sacsahuaman, the Spanish would be doomed.

Fighting their way around an array of obstacles erected by the natives between the capital and its fortress, the Spanish horsemen somehow rode through the volleys of Indian slingshots and javelins. They captured the knoll facing the mighty walls of Sacsahuaman, although Juan Pizarro himself was killed in an evening attack on the fortress. Bolstered by five thousand reinforcements, the natives launched repeated counter attacks to try to dislodge the Spanish from the knoll. The Spanish saved themselves only with great ingenuity and cunning siege tactics.

The Spanish had noticed how the Incas revered the night of the new moon and reserved it for ceremonies, even in the middle of military campaigns. The Spanish used the night of the May new moon in 1536 to launch a major offensive on Sacsahuaman, which they reinforced with European siege warfare tactics. Under the cover of darkness of the new moon night, Hernando Pizarro led an infantry force that used scaling ladders to take the mighty walls of the fortress, driving the startled natives inside the towers and other buildings.

An intense and bloody battle raged for two days, with appalling loss of native life. Finally, after exhausting their water supplies and arsenal of stones and arrows, the defenders weakened and capitulated. When Hernando Pizarro and his men finally entered the fortress, they put to the sword all those inside – around 1,500 men – while many others flung themselves to their deaths from the walls. The heaps of unburied corpses provided a grisly feast for flocks of giant condors – a macabre fact commemorated in the 1540 coat of arms granted to Cuzco, which until the 1990s bore a tower and eight condors.

I spent several more days soaking up Cuzco's unique atmosphere and consuming vast quantities of ice cream, coffee and cakes in its excellent cafés. On the day of Corpus Christi, I joined the throng to watch the sacred parade (or, more accurately, traffic jam) as the effigies of 14 saints were borne out of their respective churches and carried around Cuzco to the accompaniment of several brass bands.

On my last evening in Cuzco, I met up with John again for a drink and to go over some final details. As we were about to leave a bar in the main square, I heard the ringing of bells outside. "Rubbish van," explained John. As we left the bar, I was introduced to one of the sadder sides of Cuzco life. Parked on the Plaza de Armas directly outside a bar full of gringo tourists stood a large rubbish lorry, its bell still ringing and diesel fumes pouring out of its funnel. Hardly had restaurateurs and shopkeepers placed their rubbish sacks on the pavement of the historic square than they were whisked away, not by the rubbish collectors, but by several women who were searching for bottles and anything else with the slightest bit of value to sell.

CHAPTER FIFTEEN

SACRED VALLEY OF THE INCAS

At dawn next morning, I jumped onto a bus and headed into the valley of the Urubamba River, now better known as the Sacred Valley of the Incas. The Incas never used that name themselves. However, as a cloak of ethereal white clouds hovered over the picturesque, slumbering valley, above which shimmered a distant haze of snow-capped, pointed peaks and below which a patchwork of fields was ablaze in the early morning sun, beyond which I could just pick out the meandering line of the river itself, the sacred depiction seemed very fitting.

The base of the valley was broad and gently sloping at this point, its striated sides rising steeply like a wall on the far side of the river, above which peeked occasional glaciated summits. A reddish brown soil was visible beneath a thin covering of vegetation.

The Incas' meteoric rise to power over the Andes brought them fabulous wealth and resources, much of which they channelled into building graceful estates for their living and dead rulers. The Incas built arguably their finest estates in the Sacred Valley, particularly the section between Pisac and Machu Picchu. These include several of the most spectacular and extraordinarily engineered sites ever witnessed in South America.

The dazzling stonework, terracing and water channelling displayed by these sites bear awesome testament to the Incas' unmatched artistic and engineering prowess. They also demonstrate the Incas' genius at creating artistic masterpieces by adapting and modifying to natural features at the same time as solving more prosaic construction challenges.

In keeping with his supreme status at the pinnacle of the dynasty, many of the most majestic Inca sites were royal estates of Pachacuti, most notably Pisac, Ollantaytambo and Machu Picchu.

At every stop of the bus, I was disappointed to be accosted by enthusiastic artesania sellers, and even more disappointed that they all offered similar, if not identical, stock lines of textiles, jewellery and other trinkets. However, given the widespread appeal of Cuzco and the Sacred Valley, this shouldn't really have come as a surprise.

My target that first day was the market town of Pisac, which was visible from far away as, after a long gentle climb, the road descended rapidly into the valley. Pisac is a small town of narrow streets and walkways. It was founded after the final defeat of the Incas in 1572, when the Spanish forced many native Indians to live there together, where they would be easier to monitor and control.

Pisac is nowadays most famous for its market. There is a food market and small artesania market every day, with frenetic (tourist) artesania markets every Tuesday, Thursday and, like today, Sunday. Pisac market is a warren of stalls covered in brightly coloured fabrics sprawling from the town's central square.

The air was rich with the smells of cooking food: frying pork, guinea pig, fish and chicken. Cobs of corn boiled in large bubbling open pots. Musical favourites of well-known panpipe and charango tunes blasted out from the stalls of foot-tapping CD vendors. Stall-less salesmen wandered the market touting trinkets, cigarettes, fruit, textiles and small pieces of art. Traditionally dressed cholita women and young children, occasionally carrying baby lambs to add to the effect, offered themselves to visitors as photo opportunities. The whole market was a riot of colour, smells and sounds.

High on the steep hillside above the town, tumbling rows of elegant Inca terraces silently overlooked the bustle, discreetly hidden from view of the commercial clamour.

I became disoriented after just a few turns in the market. Even when there was a vendor I wanted to return to, I found it nearly impossible to find the right stall again. It soon became difficult to know with whom I had already haggled. Most vendors greet you with a smile and a happy, "Amigo, I have a special price for you." Any eye contact is dangerous. If you show any interest whatsoever, such as by touching an item or asking for a price, any subsequent attempt to leave without buying usually proves a protracted affair.

A wedding was taking place in the church in the main square, after which the bride and groom processed through the ancient narrow streets followed by guests and a small band.

Colourful canopies provided welcome shade from the fierce sun as I perused the artesania stalls. In contrast, many food sellers were fully exposed to the beating heat. One woman with an array of vegetables spread out on the ground before her had only a small lettuce leaf on her head as meagre protection.

Taking a pause from price negotiations, I retreated into the local pizzeria for a coffee. Inside, one of the chefs was carefully rolling out a base (without the aerial flair of Italian counterparts) before cooking the pizza in a wood-burning oven.

I decided it was time to search out somewhere to stay. The Hotel Pisac, part of the same establishment as the pizzeria, was full, and I was directed next door to the Hospedaje Kinsa Ccocha (Quechua for "Three Lagunas"). Like the Hotel Pisac, the Kinsa Ccocha stands on the main square. Unlike the Hotel Pisac, it has no entrance onto the square. I was led down a side street to a darkened rear entrance.

While being shown the way to my room, I had to navigate around an inanimate caretaker with a vacant stare in his glassy eyes. The caretaker was standing holding a mop but showed absolutely no signs of doing any mopping or cleaning. When I returned several hours later, the caretaker was standing in virtually the same position, still in the mop pose and still not doing any mopping or cleaning.

After the market closed that evening, the square was left to an array of food vendors whilst the main market stalls were quickly dismantled. Men carried away stalls and bundles of long wooden poles on their backs, and wheeled away larger paraphernalia. Above in the darkened sky, the bright moon was almost full.

I set off early the next morning to explore the Pisac ruins. Walking through the now peaceful town square, I climbed a gentle paved path that the day before had been thickly lined with vendors. The path became steeper, turned a corner and I was soon lost in an undisturbed solitude of woods and terraces.

The Pisac complex's elevated position overlooks steep slopes cascading with streams of sweeping, graceful terracing that elegantly hug the hillside contours. These terraces fed the city with maize and encircled the settlement with a ring of vertiginous defensive walls.

The ruins comprise three sectors: religious, agricultural and defensive. They sprawl over the high hillside, connected by narrow paths with unprotected edges to frightening vertical drops of hundreds of metres. The main track through the complex passes through tunnels bored through rock faces so steep that not even the master-engineering Incas could extract paths around them, and negotiates near vertical flights of narrow stone steps.

Believed to be a royal estate of Pachacuti Inca, the main complex exhibits high status Inca masonry including a fine Sun temple with a characteristically curved outer wall. Its beautiful rust-hued ashlars are comparable to those of Cuzco's Coricancha in the quality of their construction and working.

Beyond the temple complex, I climbed by way of a steep and rocky stairway to the summit of the ridge. From there, I could look across a gorge to the pockmarked cliffs opposite of the largest known Inca cemetery. Bodies were walled up in caves set high in the sheer cliff face, although grave robbers with admirable mountaineering skills long ago sacked all the tombs.

Returning from the ruins in the early afternoon, I caught a bus deeper into the valley towards Chinchero. I thought I was in luck when I strolled down to the Pisac bridge to find a bus just about to leave for Urubamba, where I would have to change. Plaintive cries to the driver of "Vamos!" (Let's go!) as I boarded suggested other passengers had been waiting for quite a while. The girl next to me was fast asleep.

On reaching Calca (the town where Manco Inca set up his headquarters in the Great Rebellion of 1536), I realised that I was not so lucky after all. What must have been most of the children from the local school first rushed on and then squeezed into every possible space, which resulted in a horrendously cramped journey from then on. I had placed my pack by the door of the bus during a more sedate stage of the journey. It was now hidden from view for most of the time and, more worryingly, at most stops. I was relieved to still see it there when we reached Urubamba.

All through the journey, I had noticed many red and sometimes blue plastic bags hoisted aloft on the end of long wooden sticks jutting out over the doorways and entrance arches of houses. A fellow passenger explained that these red and blue bags signify that the house owner brews and sells chicha.

Changing buses at Urubamba, I was truly fortunate this time. The minibus to Chinchero left almost immediately, again filling to well beyond reasonable capacity. This time, however, I sat by a window and was insulated from the rumpus by another passenger who suffered the worst of the jostling.

We turned onto a side road and into the sleepy backwaters of the Sacred Valley. After a surprisingly comfortable journey, we arrived at the serene village of Chinchero, set on the edge of a commanding plateau at the head of a valley with views to the permanent snows of the Vilcabamba range.

Chinchero was built as the country estate of Topa Inca Yupanqui, the son of Pachacuti. Believed at one time to be a sizeable planned settlement, the village contains significant ruins of a large plaza, royal palace, houses and terraces.

The massive wall lining the main square contains a series of enormous trapezoidal niches, and is likely to have formed part of the Inca's palace. The Spanish built a beautiful whitewashed church over the foundations of an Inca temple. The inside of the church is decorated with lovely paintings, murals and much gold plating. Around the church stand the ruins of many buildings and impressive Inca foundations.

Chinchero is renowned for producing the best potatoes in the entire Cuzco region, some 250 varieties in total. In the church porch, a group of villagers huddled around a large steaming pile of their famous roasted potatoes. They kindly invited me to join them. A plate of sliced raw onions was passed around for accompaniment, and was soon followed by a large vessel of refreshing chicha. I thanked the villagers for the tasty snack and continued exploring the site.

On a grassy plain behind the church, near where the Chinchero plateau starts to fall away into the valley below, an elderly couple was performing what looked like a strange dance. They stamped their feet on the ground while performing slow, synchronised spins. It transpired that this couple was performing the daily routine of trampling piles of potatoes during the process to make chuños – blackened, frostbitten potatoes that keep for several years (although most foreign visitors who have ever tasted them would probably wish they didn't).

Chuños have long been a staple dietary item throughout the Andes and Altiplano, where current year harvests alone have seldom provided a reliable source of food. To make chuños, campesinos first leave small piles of potatoes outside overnight to freeze. Then, every day, they let the potatoes thaw in the bright sun and then trample them, as this couple was doing, to squeeze out all the remaining liquid. After repeating this process daily for two weeks, the result is the blackened chuños that possess great longevity but taste as bad as they look.

Around the chuño makers were ancient terraces and a beautiful polygonal wall whose irregular stones the Incas had fitted together with incredible beauty and precision. The shadows of the afternoon sun falling on the weathered, rust-coloured surface gave the wall a mesmerising texture and appearance.

Another minibus ride took me back into the heart of the Sacred Valley and on to Ollantaytambo – the last surviving Inca settlement. Ollantaytambo's residents still live in original Inca houses and water continues to babble through the village along Inca water channels.

The residential heart of Ollantaytambo is a wonderfully atmospheric grid of tightly packed ancient stone houses set along very narrow cobbled lanes, above which soar mountains on both sides of the valley. These lanes haven't changed much since the Incas first planned the village in the form of a trapezoid over five hundred years ago. Inca foundations and walls are clearly visible throughout the settlement. The small-sized entrances give an idea of the stature of the houses' original occupants. With many locals still dressing in traditional ponchos and headwear, you struggle to convince yourself that you haven't been transported back in time to the 16th century.

Ollantaytambo preserves possibly the only Inca houses still lived in today. Many dwellings retain their solid walls with characteristic interior niches, foundations made of huge interlocking blocks and particularly massive cornerstones. Most incredibly for me, water continues to course along an original Inca channel that lines one of the streets. Residents still draw water from the channel for washing and cleaning, although no longer for drinking.

A statue of the Inca warrior Ollantay dominates the main square, which remains surprisingly tranquil despite the comings and goings of tourists and even more so their buses. The settlement is believed to have been named after this warrior, who fell in love with a daughter of Pachacuti Inca, fell out of favour with the Inca, rebelled, was crushed and passed into Inca folklore.

Ancient yellow and cream-painted buildings cluster around the square. One of these is a tiny church beside which huddles a small, ever so civilised market with several thatched stalls offering a variety of food and snacks. Covered, motorised tricycles – like tuk-tuks – provide local taxi transport around Urubamba and Ollantaytambo, although even these struggle to navigate around the narrowness of some of Ollantaytambo's lanes.

I checked in to the Inkas Park hotel on the main square where I was given a comfortable room with a view overlooking Ollantay's statue. I drank a coffee at a street café then crossed the small river to visit the ruins complex.

Ollantaytambo commands a strategic position at the edge of the Inca heartland, where the Andean highlands start to yield to the steamy forests of the Amazon. Upstream lie the mountainous terrain and steeply terraced valleys in which the Incas felt so at home. Downstream, the Andean ranges become entangled in dense, low cloud forest and the climate becomes more tropical.

Ollantaytambo was one of the first conquests of Pachacuti Inca. The fortified ruins perch on a steep mountainside, protected by a flight of huge defensive terraces that contour beautifully with the precipitous terrain. There are some 15 terraces, each rising about three metres high and still standing proudly intact, their solemn grey-brown masonry sweeping purposefully down the sheer hillside. Gazing up from the bottom, the terraces meld into a single impenetrable barrier of daunting stonework.

Ollantaytambo was the scene of one of the most notable Inca victories during the Great Rebellion of 1536, when Manco Inca repelled a Spanish cavalry attack. As the Spanish tried to catch the Inca defenders at Ollantaytambo by surprise, native soldiers hurled a barrage of missiles down at them and archers shot arrows at them from the terraces. Manco then flooded the plain at the foot of the fortress, leaving the Spanish cavalry floundering in water up to their horses' bellies and with no option but to retreat.

Climbing up the steep steps to the ruins wasn't easy, even without being fired at from above. I couldn't imagine the fright the Spanish must have felt as they tried to storm the heavily guarded fortress.

Ollantaytambo's palaces, houses, and religious and defensive constructions were all beautifully tailored to hug their steep and rugged location. Constructed of finely cut polygonal stones and rhyolite blocks, the fortress and nearby settlement represent high status stonework that identifies the complex as an important site, probably a royal estate of Pachacuti.

At the summit of the defensive terraces is a panoramic plaza on which stand the religious complex and six gigantic vertical monoliths of rose coloured stone. Lying scattered around this elevated plaza are several huge stone blocks that the Incas were still working at the time they abandoned Ollantaytambo to the Spanish. Some clearly retain the grooves the stonemasons were using for alignment and cutting.

Gazing over the head of the long inclined ramp used to haul stones up to the construction area, I could see the quarry source of these blocks in the distance across the valley, hundreds of metres above the valley floor. Blocks weighing as much as 100 tonnes were quarried from this site, probably using a technique of pecking with hammer stones. The blocks were then skidded down to the base of the valley and somehow transported across the Urubamba River. The journey these blocks took from their quarry to the temple site must have spanned some six kilometres, most of it highly inclined. A great number of huge stones still lie abandoned between the quarry and the ruins, including several "tired stones" that stonemasons had started to work, but which never reached their destination.

Beyond the main plaza, I continued climbing up a steep, rough path beyond a series of cruder constructions to a wall marking the very top of the ruins. Grazing on low bushes near the wall were half a dozen miniature mountain goats that seemed totally unperturbed by my inelegant slipping and sliding up to the summit and then down again.

High up on the opposite side of the valley, a string of ruined stone buildings clings to the impossibly steep mountainside. These long, narrow buildings with steeply pitched roofs are believed to be examples of the Incas' famous storehouses, which they used so effectively to feed their imperial subjects.

The Inca state undertook to supply its subjects from central resources, which meant the Incas needed to be able to distribute food and other items around the empire. Their problem was that they never developed the wheel and didn't have powerful draft animals to carry loads. They overcame these challenges by constructing a vast network of well-stocked storehouses brimming with staggering quantities of food (maize, chuños, potatoes, quinoa, peppers, salted dried meat and fish), blankets, clothing, tents and weapons.

The Incas built these storehouses every 200 kilometres or so apart. To preserve perishable food, the Incas placed food stores on open hill slopes, such as here, sometimes with drainage canals, so providing cool, well-ventilated conditions.

These storehouses supported vast numbers of soldiers marching to war and garrisoned in the provinces, provided insurance against crop failures and were used to feed and care for orphans, the sick and the elderly. Along with these storehouses, the Incas also maintained large corrals of livestock. The Inca food stores were so vast and so well stocked that some outlasted the fall of the empire by several decades.

Returning back down to the ruins' main plaza, I overheard a local guide pointing out to her group that to the left of the storehouses appeared an image of the creator god Viracocha, naturally carved high in the valley face, as also appears at the Sacred Rock on the Island of the Sun. I hadn't been able to make out the Sacred Rock image without the help of a man pointing out Viracocha's features by throwing stones at them. Without the benefit of similar guidance, I struggled to make out the revered image across the valley. More visible to me was the huge profile of an Inca's face that had been formed by rocks at the edge of the mountain on which the storehouses perched. The guide continued to explain that the sun rises from behind the Inca's profile on the morning of the winter solstice.

As well as their storehouses, the Incas also constructed tambos (rest houses) along their network of roads. There might have been some 2,000 tambos in all across the empire to sustain travelling armies, administrators, priests and specialist labourers working for the state.

I returned to the village and my own tambo, where I discovered there was temporarily no water in the bathroom. I thought it just as well that I could wash in the nearby Inca water channel if necessary. At least that was working, even if the modern plumbing wasn't.

The sun was still shining brightly and I decided to celebrate the fascinating afternoon by revisiting the café on the main square. As I drank my coffee, I watched as shadows rapidly engulfed the ruined storehouses high on the hill. From this angle, they perched on even steeper looking slopes than I had earlier imagined.

Ollantaytambo was quietening down for the evening. Buses had carried the day-trippers away, mostly back to the hustle and bustle of Cuzco. Walking around the peaceful grid of ancient streets continued to feel like a time travel experience, particularly whenever I met one of the residents wearing a traditional red poncho and cushion-shaped hat.

Since arriving in Ollantaytambo, I had seen many red bags on the end of sticks hoisted over doorways, reassuringly confirming the adequate presence of chicha in the village. As night fell, I wandered into one such establishment in the heart of the ancient residential quarter. I entered through heavy wooden doors set in a grand Inca entrance. The doorway led to an unlit, open courtyard, on one side of which I could see a shaft of light and hear chatter and music. I followed the sound of the music into a small, plain, low-ceilinged room with wooden beams and walls plastered with posters (including a particularly attractive lady adorning a Cusqueña beer poster).

Music resounded from an old television set on which Alicia Delgado was blaring out a raucous performance of new songs while dancing against well-known Inca backgrounds such as Machu Picchu, Ollantaytambo, Cuzco and Sacsahuaman. A table of campesinos looked rather worse for wear, with many telltale glasses of chicha scattered before them. One rosy-cheeked cholita at the table was being uncommonly friendly towards my direction. The man at the end of the gathering slumped forward, barely conscious, with his head almost touching the table.

Mario Gonzales, the affable owner of the chicheria, emerged from a darkened doorway and invited me to sit down at a small, rickety table. I yelled an order of chicha above the din of the music. Mario disappeared briefly and returned handing me a glass of white chicha the size of a medium goldfish bowl.

The volume of Ms. Delgado's singing made conversation difficult, and Mario invited me through a small, cluttered yard hung with drying washing into the family kitchen. Mario's demur wife Guillermina was busy brewing tomorrow's chicha consumption whilst two small children ate in an unlit corner. As suggested by the impressive stonework surrounding the courtyard entrance, Mario's house was formerly an important Inca residence. Numerous niches in the kitchen wall, and even more in the courtyard walls outside, further confirmed the house's provenance.

Mario's English was much better than my Spanish. He took great delight in practising it as he explained and demonstrated the procedures for making white and red chicha. He also explained with some pride how his was one of the few chicherias in Ollantaytambo to offer both white and red chicha.

White (maize) chicha is the traditional variety brewed and consumed in vast quantities by the Incas. In Inca times, highborn women began the chicha making process by chewing maize and spitting the mash into a jar to ferment for several days, although such processes no longer fit in a modern world full of health and safety regulations. Red chicha, also called frutillada, is flavoured with strawberries and is sweeter.

"Frutillada is for women while real men drink white chicha," declared Mario categorically with a chuckle. Guillermina continued stirring the bubbling pot without commenting on this sweeping generalisation.

After a few more goldfish bowls of chicha, the conversation inevitably turned to football. Mario despaired at the state of the Peruvian national team. "Maletas!" he cursed ("maleta", Spanish for "suitcase", is the curious term of abuse Peruvians hurl at poor football teams). In contrast, the Cuzco team had recently been very successful – certainly not "maletas" – and was about to win the Peruvian championship with four games still to play. We then talked about English football, which Mario occasionally watched on local television. Before we left the subject, I converted Mario's English footballing allegiance, surprisingly easily, from Manchester United to Liverpool.

Shortly before I left Mario and Guillermina, a thin straggly man with wild hair, gaunt face and clashingly bright clothes appeared in the doorway of the courtyard. Mario introduced him to me as the "Mayor of Ollantaytambo", but admitted later he was actually the village madman, who regularly does chicha crawls through the village, drinking a glass in each of Ollantaytambo's many chicherias.

I said goodbye to Mario and Guillermina and headed home just as the "Mayor" was settling down to his first glass of chicha. As I left the Gonzales kitchen, I looked up through the open courtyard. The moon was almost full in a star-studded sky, its light illuminating the many niches in the ancient walls of the courtyard.

Returning to the main square, a large number of children were noisily playing volleyball, football and other games by Ollantay's statue. Happily, the hotel's water supply had been restored so I didn't need to wash in the Inca canal after all.

Next day, I had time to kill before my train to Km88, where I would meet my guide for the next stage of my journey. After several passes through the unremarkable artesania market at the foot of the ruins, I lost the will to haggle and ate a simple breakfast in a plain, unlit room.

With still over an hour to wait before my train, I happened past Mario's chicheria again. The red sign was reassuringly once again on display. Needing no second invitation, I hurried inside to enjoy a last glass of chicha with my Liverpool-supporting friend Mario before departing Ollantaytambo.

As my train pulled out of Ollantaytambo station, I caught a last glimpse of the elevated ruins and the long ramp the Incas used to haul massive stones up to the mountaintop site.

As we travelled deeper into the valley, the Urubamba meandered beside us, often running against the steep rocky hillside. The Urubamba River in dry season wasn't exactly a raging torrent, although its valley sides soared high and near vertically above us, testifying to its might when fortified by summer rains. Banks of rocks lined the shore and massive boulders lay in its stream.

The sheer sides of the V-shaped valley were themselves carved by deep side valleys. These side valleys were also carved by subsidiary valleys, creating a strikingly marked mountain landscape. Huge slabs of often-vertical rock and massive outcrops broke the vegetation on the valley sides.

I had to strain my neck to follow the jagged mountaintop, which was often lost in thick cloud. At intervals, I caught flashes of snow-covered peaks through breaks in the ridge. Further on, the valley became so steep and deep that it was often impossible to see the serrated ridge at all, even when not obscured by cloud.

We passed series of well-preserved agricultural terraces. As we wound through the tightening valley, the mountains at its head became increasingly carpeted in dense vegetation. Before long, thick cloud forest started to replace grass as the dominant feature.

High above several large banks of agricultural terraces, the ruins of Patallaqta appeared on the opposite side of the river. I was nearing my destination: a modern footbridge built on Inca foundations across the Urubamba River that marks "Km88". I got off the train and met the lone smiling figure of Antonio, who would guide me the four days along the famous Inca Trail to Machu Picchu.

CHAPTER SIXTEEN

MACHU PICCHU

The Inca Trail to Machu Picchu is just one path in a vast network of trails and highways that once criss-crossed the whole of Inca Peru and much of the empire. This system of roads they built to link their burgeoning empire was one of the Incas' finest achievements. Most roads varied in width between one and four metres, with the most monumental sections extending 10 or even 15 metres across. The grandest sections, such as those across the Altiplano between Cuzco and Ecuador and sections linking the principal highway to the coast, were paved with cobbles or flagstones. Steep staircases carried Inca roads over vertiginous mountain passes.

The Inca Trail to Machu Picchu was never discovered by the Spanish, who perhaps followed the main highway in the area as it turned north out of the Sacred Valley over the Panticalla Pass, just downstream of Ollantaytambo.

The Inca Trail can get busy, but amazingly, it wasn't today. When the train pulled away after the briefest of stops at Km88, it left Antonio and me virtually alone in the famous wooded valley. The only other person there was another smiling man, this one waiting to collect an official trail fee from us.

Formalities completed and monies paid, we put on our heavy packs and followed the trail as it wound away above a eucalyptus grove. We crossed an irrigation channel and followed the contours as they traversed the hillside. Above us lay the well-preserved ruins of Patallaqta that I had seen from the train. Antonio explained that in contrast to most of the ruins along the trail, Patallaqta was not a major ceremonial site but was instead a service centre where workers prepared food for the more illustrious sites.

We descended to the river and crossed just below a small ravine. Beyond a moderate pass, we followed an undulating track beside the Cusichaca River. The broad valley gradually narrowed. We crossed the river over a log bridge and climbed again to the settlement of Wayllabamba. We paused briefly at the schoolyard and chatted to a couple of the local men. They worked as porters for a Cuzco trekking company and would themselves be walking the trail tomorrow. They told us that there might be others who could help us carry our packs if we wished. I didn't think I looked that tired already, but maybe I did. We thanked them but thought we could manage ourselves. We wished each other happy trails, turned off the Cusichaca River and followed a side valley northwest.

As so often happens after declining a well-meaning offer of help, I soon regretted the decision not to hire a porter. The path soon gained an unrelenting steepness as we hauled ourselves towards the mountain passes on the trail. Shortly thereafter, we reached a point where two steep and densely forested valleys converge. We descended to another log bridge crossing and continued through thick woods beside the bank of the Llullucha River. We emerged from the woods into a small, sloping area of crops and meadow, known as Llulluchapampa, where we set up camp at around 3,600 metres.

As we prepared supper over a small camp stove, Antonio explained that he had lived in these valleys all his life, and that he had guided the Inca Trail more times than he could remember. Most beauty fades in its impact when repeated too often, but Antonio showed no signs at all of Inca Trail overkill. His eyes lit up every time he described one of the numerous magical features we encountered along the trail. As I gazed up at the setting sun illuminating the top of the serene valley, I couldn't disagree with Antonio that this was a blissful way indeed to earn a living.

After spending a peaceful night at Llulluchapampa, we climbed steeply up a winding pathway towards the first pass, known as Dead Woman's Pass. As we approached the summit, we could make out traces of ancient steps that identified this unmistakeably as a pre-Columbian highway. At the summit of the pass, we gazed into the distance and could just see two further high passes ahead of us, beyond which lay our target for the day. A stone trail wound down steeply towards a pre-Incan construction at Pacamayo. We descended to the valley floor, crossed another section of dense woodland and climbed sharply again.

As the path clambered upwards towards the circular ruin at Runkuracay, we started to find unmistakeable Inca steps set firmly into the mountainside. Antonio pointed out that a circular construction like Runkuracay was very unusual for a large Inca edifice; the Incas much preferred precise rectangular symmetry. Runkuracay, like most of the sites along the Inca Trail, served as a lookout point, and commanded a magnificent sweep across the valley. The site might also have served as a tambo or resting house, although we still had much further to travel that day before we would be setting up our own camp again.

Steep switchbacks brought us slowly to the summit of the second pass (named after the Runkuracay ruins) and a breathtaking view beyond of a snow-capped range crowned by the magnificent 6,000-metre Pumasillo (whose soaring rock towers resemble an upturned puma's claw).

As we descended from the second pass, the quality of the thick interlocking stone blocks made it increasingly obvious we were walking along an important Inca highway. We were making good progress in excellent conditions, the high altitude pleasantly cooling any overheating from the bright sun and our climbing exertions.

We climbed a flight of steps hanging above a cliff to reach the cramped ruins of Sayacmarca. These perch at the end of a rocky promontory and again provided Inca lookouts with spectacular views across the valley. Antonio explained that the Incas used a series of observation platforms to communicate messages from here to Machu Picchu, although the breathtaking natural beauty of the setting needed no practical justification as far as I was concerned.

Climbing down from Sayacmarca, the trail descended abruptly through mosses, ferns, lichen and other exotic plants, beside the edge of thick cloud forest, out of which occasionally fluttered brightly coloured birds. For the next hour, we ascended gently towards the third pass. As the afternoon shadows started to lengthen, we marched along beautifully preserved sections of Inca paving, some two metres across at their widest. We passed a stepped tunnel too steep and solid for even the Incas to build a path around, and arrived at the third pass.

We had climbed to around 4,000 metres and were surrounded by some of the most awe-inspiring scenery even by the standards of the Inca Trail. Ahead lay the magnificent sweep of the Urubamba valley. Below us lay another Inca ruin while all around stretched a glassy ring of snow peaks.

Energised by the view and some chocolate bars, I could probably have walked further (Antonio certainly could), but we decided to camp at this small site. Even if we had chosen to continue, it would have been dark anyway by the time I managed to pull myself away from the jaw-dropping panorama to rejoin Antonio, who had already started to prepare supper.

Reluctantly leaving our beautiful campsite just as the pale morning sun was rising, we descended from the pass to the ruin at Phuyupatamarca (Cloud Level Town), just as the last remaining clouds were lifting. The ruins were surrounded by many agricultural terraces and, like the previous ruins we had passed, looked out over the vastness of the Urubamba valley.

Beyond the ruins, we descended two flights of steps that plunged into the heart of dense cloud forest. The first was a sheer granite staircase, over two metres wide in places (again confirming this was an important Inca highway), that had one particularly steep section hewn out of solid bedrock.

We briefly inspected a cave decorated with internal wall niches that stood near the top of the stairs, and a similar cave lower down. I tried to imagine what it must have been like for Inca sentries as they rested in these shelters, contemplating the intense natural beauty all around them, with possibly not another soul for miles around.

From a lookout platform close to the second cave, we could glimpse the ruins of Wiñay Wayna in the distance. We negotiated another steep tunnel and descended to the incongruously horrible eyesore of the Wiñay Wayna hotel and litter-strewn campsite. Set amidst a scarred hillside, this was unfortunately (particularly after the extreme beauty of the previous night's campsite) the only place to stay tonight.

Recoiling in horror at the prospects for the night, I was relieved when Antonio suggested we immediately visit the nearby ruins. Antonio explained that the fascinating ruins at Wiñay Wayna are some people's favourite along the Inca Trail – preferred even to Machu Picchu itself – and it's not difficult to appreciate their point of view. After walking a short distance off the main trail, a gorgeous sweep of curved terraces contoured beautifully against the hillside, leading down to a cluster of buildings with sharp-pitched roofs at the end of a steep ridge. In the background, a waterfall tumbled down the mountain through dense cloud forest.

Another circular structure dominates the top of the site, below which a flight of steps leads down beside a unique set of ten ritual baths. Ritual bathing was an important element of the Inca religion and ritual baths have been found in all major sites. More such baths have been discovered in sites along the Inca Trail than anywhere else in the empire, which supports a theory that the Inca Trail and Machu Picchu together formed a sacred pinnacle of the empire.

Following the steps down further, we passed a warren of residential houses and emerged onto a tiny platform with nothing beneath us but a huge, terrifying drop. It was time to return to our horrible campsite.

Getting up early the next morning was no problem, not only to arrive at Machu Picchu, but more importantly to escape the horror of the Wiñay Wayna campsite. We quickly regained a pretty section of the trail that traversed an open, sloping landscape before undulating back into beautiful cloud forest. Reaching the top of a ridge, we passed through a ruined gateway beside which stood the remains of several buildings. This, Antonio explained, was the Sun Gate at the limit of the Machu Picchu complex. We had arrived.

The only problem was that unlike our other mornings on the trail, this morning dawned with thick clouds enveloping the whole valley.

As we arrived at the Sun Gate, we couldn't see a thing. We huddled beside an open stone structure with a thatched roof, known as the "Watchman's Hut". We waited, unsure whether we would actually get to see Machu Picchu through the mist. No wonder the Spanish never found the place.

As we waited, Antonio explained that Machu Picchu was discovered in 1911 when a farmer and local boy guided American explorer Hiram Bingham to the heavily overgrown site. The name Machu Picchu (meaning "Old Hill") is actually the name of the mountain behind you as you enter the site. No-one knows what the natives called the site itself. Huayna Picchu, the tall peak forming the famous backdrop means "New Hill".

Finally, after two hours, some gaps started appearing between clouds as they wafted up and over the spur on which stood (or so Antonio assured me!) the famous ruins. Then, with little warning, the rising sun suddenly burst through the remaining mist and the fabled "lost citadel" of the Incas appeared before us in its full majesty.

Perched incredibly on a narrow rock saddle atop a precipitous Andean peak at the edge of dense rainforest, Machu Picchu was never discovered by the Conquistadores. Lying hundreds of metres above a loop of the Urubamba River and shrouded by overgrown vegetation that protects it from view from all but the highest of nearby summits, the citadel would have been invisible from the valley floor. Local farmers themselves would probably only have been dimly aware of the glorious city in the clouds above them, particularly after the passing of a few post-Conquest years.

I'd seen Machu Picchu many times before in pictures, but nothing quite prepares you for seeing it in the flesh. The drama of the setting is way beyond the capture of any photograph. The ruins seem to hover above dreamy clouds and the rounded loop of the river far below. The granite sugarloaf of Huayna Picchu soars high above the city in a towering backdrop, with plunging forested hillsides all around.

Because it wasn't plundered and destroyed, Machu Picchu remains the finest and most complete example of a planned Inca settlement and shrine complex. The abandonment of this religious, astronomical and architectural glory remains an enduring mystery.

Dense clusters of fine Inca ashlars define temples, royal palaces and residential quarters. Skirting the ruins are steep flights of agricultural terracing that once fed the city's noble inhabitants.

Not surprisingly for a site that even today inspires unbridled spirituality in many visitors, religious worship and ceremony were central features of life at Machu Picchu. A series of ritual baths cascades beside the royal quarters. The tapering walls of the Sun temple, with its characteristically curved outer wall, contain the finest stonework in the entire site. The winter solstice sunrise aligns perfectly through one of its trapezoidal windows.

On a steeply stepped platform rising above the rest of the ruins stands the small stone column of the Intiwatana, the most sacred of all the shrines at Machu Picchu. The Intiwatana or "Hitching Post of the Sun" is believed to have been used for the alignment of important solar events, for making astronomical observations, and as a means of calculating the passing of seasons.

Tonight would be the night of the full moon. Oh, to be allowed to stay up here tonight to witness the scene! As if the sight of Machu Picchu wasn't awe-inspiring enough in the day, I could only marvel at the magical power these silent stones would surely assume lit up by the ghostly glare of the full moon.

Just beyond the last of the great stones, the mountainside plunges away alarmingly abruptly into the abyss below whilst all around, densely forested peaks keep watch over the site at a respectful distance. The nearest of these peaks is the sugarloaf shaped Huayna Picchu, which rises near vertically from behind the ruins and adds more than anything else to the breathtaking setting of the famous city.

Antonio and I decided to follow a number of tiny, slowly moving dots up the sheer flank of Huayna Picchu. Although this is a well-walked route – I could see even tinier dots moving around on the summit – there didn't seem to be a visible path from where I stood. The climb assumed even greater seriousness after I discovered we had to sign our names in a register at a control point. Antonio explained that whilst the climb itself isn't very dangerous, people have been known to fall to their deaths off the mountain. This was information I didn't need to know!

The narrow path claws its way up the sheer face of Huayna Picchu by way of murderously steep steps and short but seemingly endless switchbacks. Some struggling fellow climbers sat on steps at intervals, trying to recover their breath. The slowest moving of these hadn't progressed much further by the time Antonio and I were descending again over an hour later.

Dense vegetation thankfully blocks most views of the plunges downwards. Ropes and rails ease the trickiest parts of the climb. Two very steep and narrow rock stairways just below the summit looked worryingly exposed to falls, particularly on the descent when there seems to be nothing between the outer edge of the upper flight and the river hundreds of metres below. Fortunately, there are walls to help stabilise the descent.

After a short final scramble up a smooth rock face, I found myself gazing down over the entire loop of the Urubamba River. From this angle, Machu Picchu appeared little more than an insignificant grey hourglass form spread over the green landscape, which highlighted even more the importance to the magnificence of Machu Picchu's appearance of the mountain on whose summit I now stood.

Looking away from the ruins, there stretched wave upon wave of green Andean ridges and mountaintops, eventually fading to blue and then white nothingness. Although I couldn't see them, I was gazing in the direction of the Vilcabamba mountains, in whose dense forests the Incas sought refuge after the Conquest, and made their final stand against the Spanish invaders.

The Temple of the Sun at Pisac in the Sacred Valley

Elaborate Inca stonework at Machu Picchu

Mountain track through the Apurimac Canyon

Choquequirao, the "Cradle of Gold"

The author in the Vilcabamba jungle

CHAPTER SEVENTEEN

CONQUEST

The Incas had quashed virtually all resistance within their known world of Tawantinsuyo. Yet, this most powerful empire was destined to fall to a tiny band of Spanish adventurers and treasure hunters within the space of a few short months.

The Spanish undeniably had on their side technological and warfare advantages in terms of horses and weaponry. However, also instrumental in the cataclysmic collapse was the fragility inherent in the internal structure of the empire. The rigidly elitist Inca society had few leaders and suffered many rifts between its ruling royalty and diverse subjects. Once shorn of much of its ruling class, the mighty empire was doomed to disintegrate back into its many constituent fiefdoms.

The great conqueror Pachacuti Inca Yupanqui foretold the fall of his empire. Approaching the end of his life, he proclaimed that after the reign of his grandson Huayna Capac, there would take place another pachacuti, although not the usual cataclysm of floods, fire or disease. This time, instead, tall, white, bearded men would come from afar, from a direction he did not know. These men would defeat the Incas in war and subjugate them, so that not many Inca lords would survive after Huayna Capac.

Mighty though the Inca empire was, it was fated to crumble long before Francisco Pizarro led his small party ashore at Tumbes in early 1532, in the latest of his several exploratory voyages.

When Topa Inca died in 1493, he had no idea that three ships of Christopher Columbus had made landfall in the Americas the previous year, carrying with them a deadly cargo of lethal human diseases against which the native Indians, including the Incas, had no natural defences.

At that time, the all-vanquishing Inca empire had ruled the Andes for less than half a century. By the third decade of the reign of Topa Inca's successor, Huayna Capac, European diseases were already spreading inexorably south from the newly conquered Mexico, and may also have been carried to Peru by Pizarro and his men. These deadly diseases struck the Incas at the very pinnacle of their power, and helped pave the way for the Conquest.

The emperor Huayna Capac spent much of his reign journeying around his mountainous domain, borne on a richly decorated litter and attended by armies of courtiers, concubines and bureaucrats as well as a large fighting force. During his journeys, he performed many good deeds for his people, such as helping the poor, widows and orphans.

During one of his forays north to Quito, chasqui runners brought Huayna Capac news of the arrival on Peruvian shores of pale-skinned, bearded voyagers in white-sailed ships. It is unlikely that the emperor ever saw these strange men. He certainly could have had no idea that the Spanish Monarchy had already granted these men consent to conquer his empire.

By this time, the death toll from the European pestilence was terrible. Historians estimate that in some places half the native Peruvian population fell victim to disease – probably smallpox – almost overnight.

Smallpox killed and laid waste to men, women and children throughout the empire. The virulent assassin recognised neither physical boundaries nor social hierarchies, and proved a powerful ally of the Spanish invaders. The death toll destroyed not only the human population but, by indiscriminately killing so many of its nobility and the cream of its military leaders and gifted administrators, also the rigid structure that held Inca society together.

Sometime around 1525-27, the decimation of the native population struck the Inca himself together with his nominated heir Ninan

Cuyuchi, so setting in motion the final disintegration of the empire. Without the destruction wreaked by disease, and the claiming of the able Huayna Capac as one of its foremost victims, it is unlikely the Inca empire would have succumbed so easily and completely to such a small band of invaders.

Following the untimely death of the emperor and his heir, and with the empire toppling around them, the ruling Inca elite quarrelled and fought over who should succeed to Huayna Capac's throne. Two would-be successors – royal princes and half-brothers Atahualpa and Huascar – emerged, and their struggle for the throne soon plunged the Incas into civil war. This was a crisis for which the disease-ravaged and leaderless empire was totally unprepared.

Atahualpa led the Quito faction while Huascar led the faction from Cuzco. Huascar commanded the loyalty of most of the country, but he was young and hot headed, and had much more experience of drinking and womanising than he had of warfare. Atahualpa had accompanied Huayna Capac to Quito where his father died, and he commanded the Incas' professional army, which proved the stronger in battle. His generals drove Huascar's forces back to Cuzco and captured Huascar himself, so enabling Atahualpa to seize the throne. The civil war had lasted five turbulent years – until just before the arrival of the Spanish.

In early 1532, Francisco Pizarro and a small band of adventurers and treasure hunters made landfall in Tumbes, in the arid northwestern corner of Peru. Pizarro had long been seeking his fortune in the Americas, thus far with little reward, but caught a glimmer of the riches ahead when one of his ships captured an Inca sailboat off the coast of Ecuador. The boat was on a trading mission and was laden with silver and gold ornaments, crowns, armour, emeralds, shells and ornate embroidery. Along with the treasure, the Spanish also captured a number of young boys who they taught to act as interpreters in their first encounters with the Incas.

As the Spanish started to inspect their surroundings, they began to see evidence of a major civilisation in the form of roads, storehouses and other state buildings. Pizarro worked his way down the coast before turning inland and marching up into the Andean ranges towards

Cajamarca. By incredible destiny, Atahualpa, surrounded by his army of 80,000 battle-hardened warriors, was also near Cajamarca, celebrating his recent victory over Huascar in the dynastic war for control of the empire.

Atahualpa was familiar with Inca legends that foretold of the arrival of pale-skinned, bearded deities returning from the sea. The Inca initially believed the Spanish to be the returning creator god Viracocha. After recovering from his initial terror, he became glad of the returning gods and was happy to serve them.

However, Atahualpa was soon left in no doubt of the invaders' less than divine intentions as he received repeated reports of their raping, pillaging and murdering their way along the coast and into the highlands. Messengers advised how the Spanish coveted and appropriated everything they saw, be it young women, precious metals or fine clothes, taking everything and leaving nothing.

Despite repeated warnings that the Spanish were nothing but itinerant, disorderly thieves, the Inca refused to give orders to kill them. He continued to harbour thoughts that the Spanish were returning gods and that if he obeyed and served them, they might make him an even more powerful ruler.

Thus, instead of destroying the Spanish immediately, which he almost certainly had the power to do, Atahualpa invited them to enter further into his territory and meet him in Cajamarca. After all, what harm could 170 men inflict against his many thousands of battle-hardened warriors who outnumbered the Spanish by around five hundred to one? That misjudgement was to trigger the downfall of the Inca empire.

Thus, on Friday 15th November 1532, the force of 170 terrified Spaniards entered the plaza in Cajamarca, deep inside the realm of the most powerful empire ever to rule the Americas. So confident was he of his position that Atahualpa met the strangers with a large force of mostly unarmed men.

On that late afternoon, in a ruthless but breathtakingly daring manoeuvre, Pizarro's cavalry charged the unsuspecting Incas with their battle cry of "Santiago!" Unleashing cannon fire and galloping horses, and carrying vastly superior arms, the Spanish overwhelmed the massive Inca force. They slaughtered some seven thousand of the

Inca's men (according to Atahualpa's own estimate) in a one-sided two-hour bloodbath, and captured the Inca himself, without losing a single member of their own tiny force.

During the ensuing few months, the Spaniards learned much valuable intelligence that helped them to bring down the entire Inca empire. First, they learned of the dynastic war and the divided allegiances throughout the empire. They learned that many imperial subjects welcomed the overthrow of the Incas and saw the Spanish as liberators. They also discovered that they could exert control over the natives by harnessing the continuing authority of the imprisoned Atahualpa.

As it became obvious to him that the Spanish were purely interested in monetary gain, Atahualpa sought to secure his freedom by offering a huge ransom. The Inca promised to fill with gold a room measuring some 6 metres by 5 metres, up to a height of around 2.5 metres. The room's volume was also to be filled twice over with silver.

During the next few months, gold and silver were collected from around the empire, much of it from Cuzco's magnificent temples. By the middle of 1533, Atahualpa's promised ransom had arrived in Cajamarca where it was hurriedly melted down. Pizarro separated the royal fifth due to his king and divided the remainder amongst his men.

Following his victory in the civil war, Atahualpa's supporters slaughtered a great many Cuzco nobles and all of Huascar's children and wives, ordering that their bodies be thrown out and left to the birds and foxes. On the imprisoned Inca's orders, his men killed Huascar himself as he was being brought north from Cuzco. Curiously though, Atahualpa made no attempt to organise a personal rescue, possibly in the belief that he could still reach an agreement with his Spanish captors.

However, hearing rumours that one of Atahualpa's generals was preparing to march on Cajamarca, the Spanish hurriedly tried and convicted the Inca of treason and garrotted him at the end of July. Thus, within a year of the arrival of the Spaniards, both warring Incas were dead and their once-great empire well on the way to destruction.

The execution of Atahualpa left the Spanish without a native ruler through whom they could rule. To appease the natives and add legitimacy to their occupation, the Spaniards promoted Tupac Huallpa, the eldest remaining legitimate son of Huayna Capac, to the Inca throne. However, the puppet Inca died suddenly while accompanying the Spanish expedition as it fought its way inland towards Cuzco.

Undeterred and continuing to demoralise massive armies of Inca defenders with their speed and advanced weaponry, the Spanish marched relentlessly towards Cuzco. Manco, a young Inca prince and another of Huayna Capac's sons, joined the Spanish expedition and rode alongside Francisco Pizarro as the Conquistadores rode unopposed into the Inca capital on 15th November 1533, exactly a year after first marching into the square at Cajamarca.

One month later, the Spanish crowned the young prince Manco as Inca, with coronation festivities raging for several weeks. Relations were at first good between the new Inca and the Spanish. Manco seemed to the Spanish to be another compliant puppet ruler and did little to interfere as the Conquistadores plundered the Inca capital of its gold and finery.

Manco soon learned that although the Spanish granted him the title of Inca, not only had he none of the power of his position, but the Spanish treated him with contempt whilst enslaving his people and looting their land and riches.

Manco endured Spanish rule for nearly two years, feigning loyalty whilst secretly planning to drive out the detested Europeans and restore the power of the Inca throne. Eventually, in autumn 1535, with two young Pizarro brothers subjecting him to increasing persecution, insult and injury, Manco decided to rebel to try to liberate Peru.

Manco assembled a huge native army, estimated at between 200,000 and 400,000 strong, and in May 1536 laid siege to Cuzco. At the same time, other native forces attacked the newly established coastal city of Ciudad de Los Reyes – present day Lima. Manco trapped the terrified Spaniards in a corner of Cuzco whilst most of the city burned. However, crucially, despite besieging Cuzco for over a year, the rebellion failed to retake the capital.

The Incas tried repeatedly to set the entire city ablaze, but incredibly, they were unable to ignite a small area of roof thatch facing the plaza, beneath which the Spanish huddled. Native eyewitnesses subsequently reported how each time the straw was set alight, a Spanish lady seated on the church roof and dressed all in white put out the fire with long white pieces of cloth.

Others reported how a fully armed, bearded man on a white horse preceded the Spanish whenever they left the city to wage battle with the natives. On his chest, this man wore a red cross, and his horse threw up so much dust the natives were blinded and unable to fight.

After the Spanish recaptured the fortress of Sacsahuaman in the outskirts of Cuzco, the Incas were no longer able to attack the city with their previous intensity. The siege continued but the natives grew disheartened. Troops gradually drifted back to their farms and fields. Manco retreated from Calca to Ollantaytambo, a fortress further down the Urubamba River. For a second time, despite outnumbering the Conquistadores by five hundred to one, the Incas had failed to defeat their Spanish invaders.

Ollantaytambo stands at the edge of the Inca highlands, where the Andes meet the steamy forests of the Amazon. This was the scene of one of the most notable Inca victories during the Great Rebellion of 1536. After Manco and his followers had retreated there from Calca, Hernando Pizarro and a large force of mounted and foot soldiers struggled along the valley behind him, determined to kill or capture the Inca.

The Urubamba River meanders through the Sacred Valley, often running against the steep rocky hills that hem in the valley. To reach Ollantaytambo, the Spanish had to cross the river five or six times across heavily defended fords.

Arriving they thought unseen at the plain beneath the mountain citadel, Pizarro's men were fired upon by archers occupying the terraces. A vast number of well-armed Inca warriors hurled down a rain of boulders and slingshots. Riding on horseback with a lance in hand, Manco Inca himself directed the assault from atop his mountaintop stronghold.

Having engaged the Spanish in a ferocious battle, Manco unleashed his secret weapon. Inca engineers had diverted the river to flood the plain. The Spanish cavalry suddenly found themselves floundering in water that rose up to their horses' bellies. Realising the impossibility of continuing to attack, Pizarro had no option but to order his battered force to retreat, pursued by the rampant Indians.

After Manco's victory at Ollantaytambo, the Spanish made one last attempt to find a diplomatic solution to the Inca problem. Manco refused to surrender peacefully to the Europeans, but realised that he couldn't stay at Ollantaytambo. Lying just a day's ride from Cuzco, he was far too exposed to further Spanish raids. He decided reluctantly to seek a more remote refuge.

Manco's decision to retreat further into the forests and abandon Ollantaytambo to the Spanish was both momentous and poignant. Although it went unsaid, all his followers understood that Manco was giving up his last remaining grip on the highland part of the Inca empire, and thus abandoning all remaining hope of driving the detested invaders from Peruvian soil. His highland subjects would forever be subjugated to Spanish rule whilst he and his followers sought to establish an independent Inca state free from foreign interference. The Incas lamented the sad exodus from their highland home with solemn ceremonies and sacrifices.

The untamed, misty, jungle-matted mountains of Vilcabamba seemed to the Inca to be the perfect hideaway. Vilcabamba is the region northwest of Cuzco, bordered by the Urubamba and Apurimac rivers, into which the strategic Chuquichaca suspension bridge provided the only easy entry route. This region is so rugged and wild, the 16th century Spanish chronicler Juan de Betanzos described how "even dogs cannot enter some areas and difficult passes; even the Indians go up arm in arm on ropes and tree roots and vines."

Thus, Manco Inca and his followers abandoned Ollantaytambo and retreated to a site called Vitcos hidden deep in the Vilcabamba highlands.

As they retreated from Ollantaytambo to Vilcabamba, Manco's men demolished the trail behind them. However, the broken road did little to deter a party of dashing Conquistadores sent by Almagro under Rodrigo Orgoñez to capture the Inca. The Incas were taken totally by surprise. Manco just managed to escape, carried to safety by 20 fast runners, but his forest retreat of Vitcos was easily breached by the Spanish. Fortunately for Manco, the Spanish penchant for plundering treasure and women delayed the chasing party at Vitcos just long enough to let the Inca disappear into the night with a handful of followers.

However, the Spanish killed or captured great numbers of his people and looted the wealth and livestock of the jungle capital.

Following his near capture, Manco decided to regroup somewhere stronger and more remote than Vitcos, which had been so easily overrun by the Spanish. He and his followers withdrew further into the stifling forests of Vilcabamba.

Manco established his new forest hideaway in a place called, like the province itself, Vilcabamba. Making Vilcabamba (also known as Vilcabamba the Old) his principal city, Manco constructed palaces, halls and houses there. Being much lower and deeper into the Amazon than Vitcos, the city at Vilcabamba was surrounded by dense forest and had a warm climate. This was a world apart from the highland citadels the Incas were more accustomed to calling home.

Although dejected and demoralised, such was Manco's courage and determination that in 1538, just a year after the failure of his first rebellion, he began organising a new uprising against the Spanish. This second rebellion would be the last native attempt to restore independence to Peru.

Navigating along a vast network of jungle paths unknown to the Europeans, Manco and his commanders travelled along the Andes trying to rouse the many native tribes to his cause. Manco and his commanders succeeded in fomenting rebellions across several areas of the former empire. The natives fought bravely against the Spanish and a large force commanded by Paullu, Manco's treacherous brother who the Spanish had by now installed as puppet Inca in place of Manco.

The Incas had long ago realised that their Bronze Age weapons were useless against the speed and power of the Spanish cavalry. They determined to fight the Spanish in the depths of the forest, using jungle Indians to fire poisoned arrows from the cover of dense undergrowth. Another of the Incas' favourite military tactics was to lure Spanish forces into confined ravines and roll huge boulders onto them from the safety of high ground.

Crucially for Manco, however, several native tribes that had only recently been conquered by the Incas felt no loyalty to Manco's cause and instead sided with the Spaniards. With the Conquistadores bolstered further by the arrival of Spanish reinforcements, the native resistance crumbled.

With Manco's final rebellion failing, Gonzalo, the youngest of the Pizarro brothers, set off in April 1539 to kill or capture him once and for all. Accompanied by a massive expedition of soldiers, Gonzalo rode deep into the Vilcabamba forests. The Spanish followed the Vilcabamba ravine to the pass beyond Vitcos, until the forest became so dense they had to dismount and continue on foot towards Manco's new refuge.

The Spanish faced many skirmishes with the natives but eventually fought their way to the fort at Chuquillusca. This fort was described as lying about 14 miles from Vilcabamba, which places it in the vicinity of the existing settlement of Vista Alegre. When the natives realised they could no longer resist the Spanish attackers, three Indians carried Manco from the fort down to the river. The Inca swam to the far bank from where he shouted back defiantly: "I am Manco Inca! I am Manco Inca!" For the second time in two years, Manco had narrowly escaped capture. Vilcabamba was starting to acquire a mysterious and unpleasant reputation amongst the Conquistadores.

Although the Inca escaped, the Spanish captured his sister-queen Cura Ocllo. Governor Pizarro tried to use Cura Ocllo as a hostage to negotiate Manco's surrender. When Manco rebuffed him, the furious Pizarro had her savagely murdered and floated her body down the River Yucay so that Manco's men would find it. Manco was grief-stricken, but his Vilcabamba hideaway would not be seriously threatened again for another 33 years.

During these years of relative peace, many natives fled into the dense forests of Vilcabamba to join Manco, who was creating a new Inca state in the jungle. His men built palaces, houses and terraces and revived the Inca religion and well-ordered administration that had dominated South America only a decade earlier. The renegade Incas also continued to harass the Spanish wherever possible, although there was now no hope of ever fomenting another rebellion.

The Conquistadores now suffered their own civil war as the Pizarro and Almagro factions of the original conquering Spaniards struggled for supremacy. Pizarro's followers prevailed. However, just as Governor Francisco Pizarro was planning yet another final attack on Manco, he was assassinated on 26th June 1541 by a group of Almagro supporters. With the death of the leader of the Conquest, Manco became a forgotten fugitive.

Having sympathised with the Almagro faction of the Conquistadores, Manco welcomed into Vilcabamba any survivors of the now defeated Almagrists who fled there. Thus, seven Almagrist fugitives escaped Cuzco to join Manco in Vitcos, where the Inca welcomed them warmly.

Although Manco treated the seven with hospitality befitting an Inca, the Almagrists grew bored of their jungle retreat after two years and sought to negotiate a pardon from the rulers in Cuzco. They knew their chances of receiving such a pardon would improve immeasurably if they could eliminate the Inca, whose presence in Vilcabamba continued to threaten the Spanish in Cuzco and on the road to Lima.

In a wanton act of treachery, the Almagrists stabbed the Inca to death in late 1544 or early 1545, while they were all playing a game of horseshoe quoits. Treachery had finally achieved what several military expeditions and prolonged negotiations had failed to: an end to the heroic defiance of the warrior Manco Inca. The Spanish assassins galloped for their lives towards Cuzco, but were caught by a group of natives who burned or speared them all to death.

Before he died, Manco confirmed the accession of Sayri-Tupac, his eldest legitimate son. The new Inca was only five years old and ruled under the regency of his father's advisers. Unlike his father, Sayri-Tupac and his advisers opted for negotiation with the Spaniards and got on well with the rulers in Cuzco.

While Manco had been struggling to liberate Peru from the Spanish invaders, his brother Paullu ruled as puppet Inca in Cuzco and collaborated enthusiastically with the Spanish. Paullu persuaded Sayri-Tupac to return from exile in the forests of Vilcabamba in return for large estates in the Sacred Valley, riches and honours to be lavished by the Spanish.

On coming of age in 1557, Sayri-Tupac agreed to capitulate peacefully to Spanish rule and emerge from exile. When he began his sorry journey out of Vilcabamba in October 1557, he was abandoning his father's heroic struggle for independence. Manco would surely have been horrified, not only by this meek submission but also by his son's later conversion to Christianity once installed in his comfortable existence in Cuzco.

The return from exile of Sayri-Tupac seemed to have removed the last remnant of native Inca rule from Spanish Peru. However, Sayri-Tupac died suddenly in 1561, only four years after emerging from Vilcabamba. Poisoning was widely suspected although never proved.

Ultimately to be of greater concern to the Spanish, no sooner had Sayri-Tupac vacated Vilcabamba than his younger brother Titu Cusi – a more belligerent and capable leader – assumed power. Titu Cusi was another son of Manco, although by a wife other than Manco's coya.

Primogeniture and legitimacy were less important to the Incas in choosing their leaders than ability to rule. After Sayri-Tupac, the next in line to rule Vilcabamba should have been Tupac Amaru, another of Manco's sons, but by his coya (Tupac Amaru was a full brother of Sayri-Tupac). However, the Vilcabamba Incas recognised that Titu Cusi was more experienced politically and in warfare, and would make a stronger leader. Tupac Amaru was relegated to a monastic life as guardian of his father's body.

Like Sayri-Tupac, Titu Cusi continued negotiations with the Spaniards, astutely using dialogue to forestall the threat of further military invasion. However, unlike his brother, Titu Cusi had no intention of ever surrendering himself or his Vilcabamba state to Spanish authority. The new monarch of Vilcabamba revived his father's defiance against the hated Spaniards that had virtually ceased under the docile rule of his brother.

It was now over 20 years since Manco's narrow escape from capture by Gonzalo Pizarro. During that period, Vilcabamba had enjoyed freedom from further aggression. Its population of Incas and their forest allies had increased markedly. Vilcabamba was no longer just a forest refuge; it had grown into an independent native state.

Paying further lip service to the Spanish, Titu Cusi allowed himself to be baptised and even permitted two Franciscan friars, Marcos Garcia and Diego Ortiz, to come and preach in Vilcabamba. Titu Cusi invited the two friars to visit his capital city in early 1570, although the two friars had to struggle their way through the sodden land of the wet season whilst the Inca rode in a litter. Once at Vilcabamba, the two priests were horrified by the polygamy, debauched festivities, witch doctors and pagan worship they witnessed, and left soon afterwards.

In an act of defiance that soured relations between the Vilcabamba Incas and the Spanish friars, and sparked a chain of events that ultimately led to the demise of the native state, the friars set fire to the temple complex that included the White Rock of Yurac-rumi, and exorcised the site.

The Incas were furious and the two friars were lucky to escape with their lives. Garcia was expelled from Vilcabamba and Ortiz sent back to his church at Huarancalla. Native sentiment was hardening firmly towards its final collision course with the Spanish rulers.

One day a Spaniard named Romero, an adventurous prospector for gold, was found penetrating the mountain valleys in Vilcabamba, and succeeded in getting permission from the Inca to see what minerals lay there. He was too successful for everyone's good. Both gold and silver were found among the hills and Romero showed enthusiastic delight at his good fortune. Fearing that his reports might encourage others to enter Vilcabamba, the Inca put the unfortunate prospector to death, despite the protestations of Friar Ortiz. Foreigners were no longer welcome in Vilcabamba.

Historians estimate that the population of Peru at the time of the Conquest was around 7 million. The appalling rate of depopulation following the Conquest reduced that number to around 1.8 million by the end of the 16th century, 50 years after the Conquest. The population of native Indians declined further to less than a million by the end of the colonial period in the early 19th century.

The most obvious cause of this terrible loss was disease. After centuries of isolation, the native Indians had no immunity against European diseases. An outbreak of smallpox that spread south from the Caribbean might well have already decimated the Inca empire by the time Pizarro arrived in 1532. Records indicate another epidemic in 1546, this time of possibly typhus or plague, followed by outbreaks of other major diseases in 1549, and between 1585 and 1591.

Another major cause of population decline was the severe cultural shock and chaos that engulfed the turbulent aftermath of the collapse of the Incas' rigidly ordered and tightly administered society. Since the death of Huayna Capac, the empire had been shattered by a fierce, internecine civil war, a humiliating conquest by a tiny and seemingly alien group of foreigners, two huge failed rebellions and a perplexing series of civil wars between the invaders themselves.

The Conquistadores rarely killed natives except in war, although their preoccupation with plundering personal riches led to neglect. Agricultural terraces and irrigation networks were allowed to crumble. Herds of alpacas and llamas were wantonly slaughtered. The high Andean lands that once supported impossibly large populations – in spite of the harsh terrain – became barren, leading to famines.

Witnessing the collapse around them of their ordered way of life, seeing themselves robbed of everything they valued and being forced to live in miserable poverty and abject servitude, many natives grew deeply demoralised. Once Manco's two great rebellions failed, most of the population resigned themselves to their fate. Many lost the will to live. Indians hanged, poisoned or starved themselves to death. Mothers even killed babies at birth, not wanting them to suffer the hardships they themselves were suffering. The birth rate plummeted.

Surviving natives were invariably overworked and underpaid. Indians worked in wretched poverty (often being treated worse than slaves) to pay their tribute to their Conquistador masters, or satisfy the insatiable Spanish quest for gold and silver. The small number of survivors who maintained any ambitions sought personal power by establishing regional chiefdoms, which further fragmented and destroyed the former ordered hierarchy.

In May 1571, Titu Cusi became drunk on an excess of wine and chicha while visiting the shrine to his father in Vitcos. He developed pains in his side and chest and started bleeding from the mouth and nose. His secretary Martin Pando and another close friend mixed him a potion of egg and sulphur in an attempt to stem the flow of blood. The Inca reluctantly drank the potion, but became even sicker and eventually died.

As the only nearby Spaniard, Friar Ortiz was blamed for poisoning the sovereign. Some natives thought the friar, who had a reputation as a skilled doctor, might be able to revive the dead Inca and forced him to pray and say mass. When the Inca inevitably failed to recover, a group of militant captains killed Pando and subjected Ortiz to a cruel, tortured execution that stretched over three agonising days.

Titu Cusi was succeeded by his younger half-brother, Tupac Amaru, whom he had supplanted during his own ascent to the throne. When Titu Cusi became Inca, he had relegated Tupac Amaru to a monastic life, which left the new Inca unprepared to lead the Vilcabamba state. Blaming the Christians for the death of Titu Cusi, the new Inca's accession marked a severe hardening of attitudes towards the Spanish, and a total rejection of Christianity. Gone were Titu Cusi's attempts at coexistence. The reactionaries killed and persecuted Spaniards and Christians and closed the border to Vilcabamba.

This set the Vilcabamba Incas on a disastrous collision course with the hard lined new Viceroy of Peru, Francisco de Toledo. Toledo, like his predecessor initially tried diplomacy to resolve the Spaniards' Vilcabamba problem. The Spaniards had hoped to entice Titu Cusi from the forest with the promise of land and titles, as they had done his brother Sayri-Tupac. When correspondence went ignored, the Viceroy sent envoys into Vilcabamba. The first four failed to return. Of the next two, only one eventually returned, badly wounded.

Still unaware that the conciliatory Titu Cusi had died and been succeeded by the antagonistic Tupac Amaru, Toledo sent his ambassador Atilano de Anaya on a diplomatic mission to Vilcabamba. Anaya was a prominent Cuzco citizen and friend of the Inca, and carried with him letters and peace proposals from the King and Viceroy.

The natives initially received Anaya well and provided him with a hut at the Chuquichaca bridge. However, with weakened leadership from the sovereign, power was dissipating down the Inca ranks. Without the consent of the Inca, two captains made a fatal error that finally sealed the fate of the Vilcabamba province. Not wishing to allow Spanish influence back into Vilcabamba and panicking at Anaya's inevitable discovery of the death of Titu Cusi and, worse still, Friar Ortiz, the two captains stabbed the envoy to death with their lances and threw his body into a gulley.

A Negro servant found his master's body and carried news of the murder back to Cuzco. Events had already been convincing Toledo that he had to invade Vilcabamba. Now his mind was made up. He resolved to rid

Vilcabamba of the rebel Incas and proclaimed a "war of fire and blood" on Palm Sunday, 14ᵗʰ April 1572.

Toledo prepared a massive force containing distinguished Spaniards, some Inca descendants and a large number of native auxiliaries, which marched into Vilcabamba over the Chuquichaca bridge. To block off any escape to the north or south, two further forces were sent into Vilcabamba via the Apurimac valley. The Viceroy offered a rich reward to whoever captured the Inca.

Under the leadership of Martin Hurtado de Arbieto, the Spanish fought their way past several ambushes where the natives had hoped to trap the expedition in narrow ravines and destroy it with torrents of huge boulders from above. Arbieto continued relentlessly past an abandoned Vitcos and over the Colpacasa Pass. In doing so, he had dealt the final blow to the Incas' defence of their jungle state.

Marching on to Vilcabamba the Old, the Spanish found it was also abandoned, ransacked and still smouldering. Tupac Amaru Inca and his scattered followers were in full retreat. They had fled into the jungle with all they could carry and had set fire to what remained of their capital.

Determined to avoid the failure of previous expeditions to capture the Inca himself, Arbieto sent contingents deep into the forest to capture Tupac Amaru and his son Quispe Titu, the only legitimate heir to the Inca throne.

The Inca and his small party retained a small advantage in the chase and probably would have reached the safety of the densest part of the forest had they taken to a canoe to cross a large river. However, their escape was hindered by the Inca's pregnant wife, who was afraid to take to the water. Tupac Amaru pleaded with his wife to climb into the canoe but she refused. This proved decisive in slowing down the royal party and resulted ultimately in the death of her husband and the end of the last remaining Inca state. Tupac Amaru and his wife were captured huddled over a campfire in dense forest to the north of Vilcabamba – a pitiful end to the once great rulers of the Andes.

The captured Inca was brought back to Cuzco in chains. The triumphant Spanish also brought with them the mummified bodies of Manco and Titu Cusi, the two Incas who had died in Vilcabamba, and the Punchao

– the golden disc of the Sun that the Incas worshipped above all other idols.

Toledo was convinced that the last remnants of the Inca empire had to be eliminated. He felt neither sympathy for the mystique of the Incas nor any guilt towards them. Toledo regarded the Incas as recent conquerors themselves who had no greater right to rule Peru than the Spaniards. Toledo put the captured Inca on trial, accusing him of several murders of Spaniards and Indians. The Inca accepted conversion to Christianity in a desperate attempt to appease his accusers.

After the briefest of sham trials, the Inca was found guilty and condemned to death. A wave of appeals by shocked ecclesiastics protested the innocence of the Inca, but to no avail. On 24th September 1572, Tupac Amaru, the last Son of the Sun and last king of the four suyos was led through crowds of mourning and wailing natives to the main square in Cuzco, where he was beheaded. With this execution of the last Inca was dealt the final blow of the Spanish Conquest of Peru that had begun 40 years earlier.

CHAPTER EIGHTEEN

CRADLE OF GOLD

Beyond Machu Picchu lies a remote, wild region of cold high uplands and hot steamy valleys known as Vilcabamba. Its extreme relief rises from tropical valleys and canyons below 2,000 metres, through densely choked cloud forest up to 4,000 metres, to glaciated 6,000-metre plus summits.

At the height of the Inca empire, this steep and mountainous region served as a jungle border province. In 1536, four years after the fall of the Inca empire to the Spanish invaders, Manco Inca, a son of the last great ruler Huayna Capac, led a rebellion against the Conquistadores. After their failed siege of Cuzco, Manco and a few thousand followers retreated into the darkened forests of Vilcabamba, beyond the reach of the Spanish authorities. They established court in this remote corner of their once great empire, where they maintained Inca traditions, religion and statehood, and constructed jungle settlements, religious shrines and ceremonial centres linked by a network of paths and trails.

Over the following few decades, these primordial forests provided the final refuge for these last Inca survivors, who clung to the dying vestiges of their empire in Vilcabamba's inhospitable valleys and tried, ultimately in vain, to resist the Spanish colonisation of Peru.

The strategic Chuquichaca suspension bridge traditionally provided the only easy route into Vilcabamba. I was planning to trek from the village of Cachora, which required a return by train to Ollantaytambo and another bus journey.

Leaving Ollantaytambo in the frosty cool of the early morning, we headed up the empty road through the Sacred Valley. The morning sun lit up the agricultural fields in rich shades of yellow and brown. Rising early morning mist cloaked a delicate blanket over the landscape, through which pierced high peaks, many of whose snow-capped summits glinted brightly in the clear dawn.

We climbed endless hairpins and made swift progress until we were halted for an hour and a half after just missing the window of passage at a major road works where men were clearing the ground to build a new bridge.

A small convoy of stopped traffic slowly grew at the road works, providing great trading opportunities for an enthusiastic group of snack sellers. I gave the granadilla and ice cream vendors particularly good business. Sitting on the ground in the shade of the bus, I was hit on the shoulder by a half-eaten choclo (corn on the cob), and had several near misses with various other food missiles jettisoned out of the bus windows, as is the habit of Andean bus travellers.

Eventually able to continue on our way, we drove up into the clouds. We zigzagged up hairpins surrounded by steep summits to a pass at over 4,000 metres, marked by a dismal huddle of tumbledown huts and a bleak chapel where we stopped to light candles. I shivered with cold after just a brief stop and couldn't comprehend how these admittedly hardy people could survive here with scant clothing and virtually open dwellings. Fortunately, I didn't have time to linger very long to ponder this as we clambered hurriedly back onto the bus.

I soon found out why we stopped to pay our respects by lighting candles in the chapel. As the narrow road snaked down the other side of the pass, an unprotected and alarmingly crumbly roadside edge threatened the unwary and careless with certain death down a severe drop-off that fell away much further than we could see down the vertiginous rock face.

I fell into a nervous sleep. When I awoke, we had left the bleak high Andes and were descending through dense cloud forest. The drop-offs to the side of the road were starting to ease and become a little less life threatening. The vegetation was turning increasingly tropical and we started to see many fruit trees.

We eventually reached the turn-off for Cachora, from where we could see the massive broadside flank of Mount Salcantay, whose glaciated, snow-covered peaks rose nearly 6,000 metres and shimmered ghost-like high above the clouds. We descended a winding dusty track bordered all around by sloping terraced fields and arrived in Cachora in the middle of the afternoon.

Cachora is an attractive and atmospheric, albeit rundown, village in the shadow of Salcantay. Full of ancient, thick-walled adobe dwellings with pretty roof tiles, many houses have the tiniest of windows and some have no windows at all. Much of the adobe had clearly once been plastered and whitewashed long ago, although most of it was now in a sad state of disrepair. All around the village, peeled paintwork on crumbling adobe presented a rich, shadowed texture in the glow of the afternoon sun.

Several chicherias announced their presence with blue bags (rather than the predominantly red of the Sacred Valley) hanging from the end of wooden sticks. Also scattered around the village were several small eateries and a few even smaller shops offering limited stocks.

Cachora's charm is slightly marred by an incongruously large and modern main square set on several levels, although even this is fringed by rows of ancient stone dwellings, particularly on the side closest to Salcantay.

Equine activity was everywhere. Villagers were driving laden horses and mules through the streets. Other horses were being ridden or stood tethered outside houses. I had unknowingly arrived in Cachora on the eve of a village festival. Mules carried firewood for several large barbecues. A cow was being led off to be slaughtered. Nearby, a pig carcass was being prepared for roasting.

I entered through a pair of heavy wooden doors into a hostel where I had arranged to meet Omar, a local guide introduced to me by John Leivers in Cuzco. Passing through a tiny reception area, I emerged into an attractive sunny courtyard set with trees and overlooked by several rickety dwellings and wooden balconies. Omar had already arrived and was sitting at a table under the shade of a tree. This smiling young man hailed from the latest generation of the Cobos family, the famous explorers and guides of the Vilcabamba forests.

Omar and I drank coffee and ate oranges as we finalised plans for our journey to the Inca citadel of Choquequirao. Omar had already arranged the hire of a local arriero and four mules, so there weren't many practicalities still to complete apart from buying provisions.

With our route and planned camps agreed, Omar and I stepped across the dusty cobbles to a chicheria opposite the hostel, marked by a blue plastic bag on the end of a long but limp pole. An elderly woman greeted us in a simple darkened room, into which the door through which we had entered and another door in the opposite corner allowed the only light.

A long wooden table and bench stood in the room but we decided to take our chicha glasses outside, through the second door. This door led into a tiny courtyard. Seated on the ground in the courtyard was a haggard old woman with a dirty face and stricken expression, surrounded by piles of corn, assorted blankets and colourful buckets. The woman was busy stripping corn from cobs into a large green plastic bucket as the first stage of the chicha-making process. A blinding shaft of low afternoon sunlight streamed into the courtyard and lit up her mound of cobs in dazzling shades of yellow interspersed by occasional patches of dark red.

Beyond the old woman, two men sat eating in the shade of the wall. Beside them, corn had been spread out over large cloths to dry in the sun before being brewed into chicha.

After the refreshing drink, Omar and I set off to buy provisions from the village stores. Just like in Curva, this proved quite a challenge and required several visits to each of the stores, as local unavailability inexorably drove our culinary plans progressively lower.

Dusk was falling by the time we had accumulated enough items (mostly not our first choices) for the journey. As we were walking back to the hostel, we came across an anticucho (beef heart shish kebab) seller on the busiest of the very quiet village streets. After my previous experiences in Bolivia, where anticuchos are devoured as late night snacks, this seemed a bit of a surprise, albeit a pleasant one as we munched our way through a couple of tasty kebabs before supper.

The following dawn, whilst Omar and I hurried a quick breakfast, our arriero Glicerio tied our packs and kit bags onto two pack mules and saddled up two riding mules, Sojo and Pepe. We rode out of Cachora on a crisp, hazy morning in the direction of the mountain backdrop of Salcantay, which was this morning shrouded in cloud and shadow.

We followed a broad sandy track out of the village and into a parched brown landscape. The track narrowed as it climbed gently towards the flank of a mountain. We encountered much equine traffic along the path, including a train of 25 horses and mules carrying irritatingly loud bells.

As we rounded the flank of the mountain, more glaciated summits emerged into view. For the first time, we glimpsed the famous Apurimac River far below us. This powerful river and its deep canyon represent one of the great geographic wonders of the Americas. It was also one of the two most important rivers (the other being the Urubamba) of the Inca heartland. Apurimac means "Voice of God" or "Mighty Speaker" in Quechua. The river thunders for hundreds of kilometres through the remotest part of the Andes to eventually join a multitude of sister rivers and become the Amazon.

As we climbed towards the pass, a condor sailed across our view and disappeared behind a neighbouring peak. We hurried up to the pass where a woman and young girl sat in a small wooden shack. "Did you see the condor?" I asked breathlessly. "Yes," replied the woman pointing to the summit above her, "it passed around the mountain." We were optimistic of another sighting.

From the summit of the pass, all around us soared sharp, angular peaks. We could now hear the distant roar of the Mighty Speaker. In the far distance across the canyon, Omar pointed out the barely visible ruins of Choquequirao (which means "Cradle of Gold") perched high on a forested mountain spur at about the same altitude as where we now stood. "Great," I thought, "we should be able to reach the ruins by this evening." How mistaken that was to prove!

We began descending a series of long, rough, sandy switchbacks into the deeply carved canyon. We had only descended a couple of turns when the condor returned, an unmistakably massive black profile against the now unblemished blue sky. The bird was soon joined by its mate and the two huge vultures soared, hovered, circled and occasionally perched on their lofty crag, high above the pass. We craned our necks skyward to watch the majestic aerobatics as we continued our descent towards the Apurimac.

Glicerio, the young arriero, walked in open sandals and, I was later to discover, slept in the open without a tent. He constantly urged on the mules with cries of "Mula, mula!" and sharp, piercing hisses. When verbal encouragement alone failed to deliver the desired speed, he slapped the mules' backsides with the lead rope, an empty water bottle he was carrying or twigs – in fact, anything that came to hand.

Many sharp-pointed cactuses lined the path as we descended through a dry, scrubby landscape. We had reached about halfway from the pass to the Apurimac, and were already very hot and sweaty, when we decided to pause for lunch at an isolated wooden shack. The woman owner surprisingly allowed – even encouraged – us to climb her fruit trees to pick huge, sweet custard apples and limes whilst she prepared us a simple but very welcome pasta lunch.

Following ever-shortening zigzags, we continued steeply down the dry, dusty track that was frequently rough with loose, ankle-spraining rocks and stones. Still a distance below us, the Apurimac was following its own boulder-strewn course, albeit over much larger obstacles.

We were fortunate to have a secure bridge over which to cross the Apurimac. Crossing the river in Inca times would have been far more precarious. So powerful are the currents and turbulent floods of many of the rivers flowing through the Andes that they could not be crossed by conventional post-built bridges or boats.

The Incas devised several ingenious methods for crossing even the largest and swiftest of their rivers, without which travel would have been nigh on impossible across much of the empire. One particularly frightening method of crossing rivers involved pulling yourself across a stretched cable beneath which you dangled sitting in a basket. More secure and impressive were the famous Inca suspension bridges constructed from twisted cable. Despite sometimes swaying alarmingly, such bridges could carry horses and heavy loads. These Inca bridges could sometimes span some 60 metres, although they needed annual renewal to keep them safe and strong.

No sooner had we reached and crossed the great river than we began immediately to climb a brutal, murderously steep set of switchbacks on the other side. Even the mules were breathing hard and sweating profusely in the intense afternoon heat. We had to pause often to catch our breath and take long drinks of water. My mule Pepe laboured on every steep incline, hanging his head low and blowing up clouds of dust every time he exhaled through his nostrils. His long fluffy brown ears twitched feverishly to Glicerio's continued hisses and shouts. His whole body jolted every time Glicerio slapped one of the pack mules with his whip or empty plastic bottle.

The journey was exhausting for riders too, even on relatively forward-going mules. The terrain was so steep and narrow we had to dismount on many climbs and on most descents. "Muy peligroso," (which means, "very dangerous") cautioned Omar. The arid path offered only a difficult, uneven surface of rocks and slippery gravel, although Pepe seemed to know what he was doing. We all ran out of water that afternoon. My estimate of arriving at the ruins by that evening was already looking ridiculously over-optimistic.

We slogged our way up for several more arduous and very thirsty hours and reached a point about halfway up the climb to Choquequirao. Wet with perspiration, we arrived at a small shelf of flat land on the otherwise steeply inclining mountainside. We were all dehydrated and collapsed on the ground. Without anyone uttering a word, we all agreed we would travel no further that day.

When we could at last summon the strength to examine our peaceful surroundings, we discovered to our delighted surprise that the owners of the land grew maize from which they brewed chicha. Seldom can the royal drink of the Incas have been more appreciated, more needed or drunk more quickly than that afternoon. We guzzled several large glasses of the refreshing liquid before we could even contemplate setting up camp.

Revived by the chicha, we could begin to appreciate the still beauty of our campsite. Since arriving at this spot, we had seen no-one other than the owners. Above and below us stretched extensive carpets of sloping maize fields, irrigated by a tiny but energetic stream around which buzzed clouds of mosquitoes (I was covered in bites after spending only a few minutes washing in the stream).

From this elevated position, we could gaze across the steep, gaping canyon to what looked like a vertical wall of rock on the opposite side, on which was scratched the thin pale course of the zigzagging path we had descended to the river. Seeing the steepness of the path from here, I could appreciate why we had skidded and tripped so often on the descent to the Apurimac. In fact, I was amazed we hadn't all plunged straight into the river from the pass. The Mighty Speaker was once again far below us, invisible and inaudible.

The owner of the land on which we camped was a friendly man who lived there with his family in a couple of tiny thatched huts. He explained that the house had belonged to his grandfather and that both he and his father were born in this isolated spot. The man kept a dozen horses in this steeply sloping world, which he used to travel to Cachora once a week to sell maize. He described the difficulty of farming on the stony (not to mention steeply inclined) terrain.

As we chatted, the sky above this wonderfully tranquil site darkened and filled with stars: the Southern Cross, Scorpio, Sagittarius, the Milky Way and occasional shooting stars. We could make out the distant flickers of light from a handful of scattered houses on the other side of the valley.

The family gathered in the larger of the two huts, where they sat around the fire in the tiny living area to eat supper. The woman of the house kindly heated some water for us too so that we could prepare some pasta and tea. As we began eating our supper, the family had finished theirs and were already settling down for the night, spread out in both huts. We followed their lead soon afterwards and by 8pm, all was silent and still.

Refreshed from the comfortable overnight stop, we rose early to a pleasant, cool morning and continued the relentless climb towards Choquequirao. The climb was made more difficult by the fact we could often see our destination from far off (not to mention from the pass the previous day). Numerous times that morning, I reached a point in the path where I could look across to the massive, sweeping terrace walls of Choquequirao and be certain I had reached the same elevation as the ruins.

There could be no doubt that just around the next corner, I would be able to see the trail curving gently to the ruins. Not so. The path inevitably swept downwards again and lost much hard-earned altitude through yet more switchbacks. We would have to make many more steep and unwelcome descents during the climb, after every one of which the imposing terrace walls once again soared high above us, seemingly forever out of reach.

Our two riding mules Pepe and Sojo didn't seem to get on very well that day. Sojo trudged along slowly at the front but was reluctant to let me pass on Pepe. Every time I tried to overtake, Sojo weaved blocking manoeuvres that would have been more at home on a motor racing circuit than a narrow mountain path. Pepe did likewise on the few occasions when we led. More comically, we occasionally erupted from our steady plod into impromptu trotting races, as neither animal was willing to give way. Observing the mules' antics took our minds off the lengthy morning trek to reach the ruins.

After almost giving up hope, we finally arrived at the base of Choquequirao's four huge terrace walls. Each rises about three metres high and curves harmoniously for some 300 metres in a gentle sweep at the foot of the city. High Andean cedars line the terraces.

The Incas certainly mastered how to position and design their citadels for maximum impact and drama. Choquequirao juts out majestically from a prominent forested hill spur almost two kilometres above the Apurimac (significantly higher above its river than Machu Picchu sits above the Urubamba) on the western flank of the Cordillera Vilcabamba. All around the sweep of the chasm soars a backdrop of ice-sculpted, sharply angular mountains of grey rock coloured with a red tinge.

From this elevation, the Mighty Speaker appears – where it isn't blocked from view by the plunging sides of the canyon – no more than a silent foaming sliver from a totally different world from this high altitude sanctuary.

Like all good Inca sites, the finely constructed ruin of Choquequirao is cloaked in obscurity and enigma. Not mentioned in any chronicles of the Conquest, the story of this remotest of major Inca sites will probably remain a mystery forever. Some claim it was a royal estate of Topa Inca, the son of the great warrior emperor Pachacuti. Other scholars claim the site was a secret refuge, which would certainly fit its secluded location. Another theory suggests that this was where Inca priestesses raised Tupac Amaru, the last ruler of the Vilcabamba Incas.

Although evidence of its exact purpose remains sketchy, its finely constructed buildings and the number of trails leading to it suggest that Choquequirao was an important site in the empire. Some scholars have commented at the relatively poor quality of the stone working at Choquequirao compared with sites in the Sacred Valley. This is certainly accurate, although it is probably more a reflection of the availability and nature of local rocks. Stones available around Choquequirao couldn't be shaped as precisely as the andesite found around the Sacred Valley, which could be worked much more finely into more ornate structures and precisely fitting ashlars.

Above the imposing terraces, the Choquequirao site occupies two levels. The lower and larger level is set around a central grassy plaza and contains ceremonial buildings, including two halls with walls full of large niches – one of which contains person-sized triple niches: niches within niches within niches. Nearby stand the houses of high status individuals, where sections of stonework remain covered by a clay stucco that probably once covered the entire walls. Steps beside a water channel lead to a smaller upper plaza.

The most striking difference between this site and Machu Picchu is the intense solitude of Choquequirao. Apart from a couple of workers repairing a wall on the upper level, we were the only people at this remote and almost forgotten Inca ruin.

Returning to the lower plaza, we walked past a levelled-off hilltop overlooking the site and down a narrow grassy ridge. We reached a pretty courtyard and the ruins of what looked like another small cluster of exclusive residences. Whoever lived in these houses would have enjoyed not only total seclusion, but also some of the finest views over the Apurimac to the confusion of valleys and ravines beyond. After our previous night's camp on a similarly secluded, but lower, ridge, I could begin to guess at the intense, almost spiritual, peace the residents of Choquequirao must have enjoyed at their remote mountain redoubt.

CHAPTER NINETEEN

CLAWS OF THE PUMA

At mid-afternoon, with the scorching sun still high in the sky, we set off from the still deserted Choquequirao ruins. We followed a climbing trail in the direction of Maizal and the Rio Blanco. We crested the Choquequirao Pass and descended through tangled jungle to a huge area of terracing known as Pinchaunuyoc, where a sacred spring flows through several small fountains.

We descended the flank of the canyon towards the boulder-lined Rio Blanco. The river was higher and faster flowing than we had expected for the dry season, and we had to take great care crossing on the mules. Still tired from our climbing exertions to reach Choquequirao, we decided to camp early beside the river. We bathed hurriedly in the cold torrent and then set about stuffing ourselves with bread, biscuits, cheese and avocado, and several large mugs of tea. We were still so full by the evening that we only had room for soup at supper, which we cooked over a log fire.

Whilst we were happily gorging ourselves, there was little grazing for the animals, which was surprising given our verdant surroundings. We had to buy extra food for the mules from a couple of local campesinos. We watched while they cut grass by torchlight from a nearby field, close to where we had set up our tents. That night, more shooting stars enlivened a bright but otherwise unspectacular sky.

Still using the excuse of the previous day's early start and the long difficult climb up to Choquequirao, we awarded ourselves a lie-in the following morning. We genuinely needed to conserve energy, as the next few days would see us climbing and descending over the entire massive bulk of the Vilcabamba range.

Another bright sunrise had burnt off all the dawn chill by the time we emerged from our tents to a relaxing breakfast. We finally loaded the mules and set off late in the morning along a climbing, muddy trail towards a moderate pass.

After a brief stop for lunch, we caught up with another, larger mule train travelling in the same direction as us. As we approached, I could palpably feel that the competition level between the two groups of mules was even fiercer than the jockeying that had erupted between our own animals on the climb to Choquequirao. We had a great struggle overtaking the other mules. There were eight of them and their rear gunner was a particularly vicious character that kicked out several times at Sojo as we tried to pass. After several scuffles, the arriero of the other mule train finally herded his animals against the side of the path to let us through.

That afternoon, we climbed an undulating trail to the hamlet of Maizal, beyond which rose a great snow peak and from where we could see several valleys stretching into the distance. Maizal seemed to comprise just one house lived in by a gregarious farmer. With the obvious lack of regular conversation opportunities, it was no surprise that the farmer spent much time quizzing us about our journey, our mules, where I had come from – in fact everything under the sun, and more.

By the time the farmer had finished questioning us (or rather paused for breath before continuing his good-natured inquisition), it was just about a respectable time to stop. We set up camp and invited the farmer to join us for some tea and supper around our warm fire. Apart from our conversation and the crackling fire, all we could hear were quietly munching mules and the occasional squeal of guinea pigs from the farmer's house.

Fully refreshed after the short day, we rose early next morning. The farmer had risen even earlier and was already busy working his fields.

He waved us off with an enthusiastic "Adios" as he sprinkled feed to his crowing roosters.

For several hours, we followed the remains of an ancient Inca highway as we navigated around a glacier and climbed steeply towards the Yanama Pass. Rising levels of heat and humidity were making the going difficult and we made slow and laboured progress. Gradually, our surroundings started to evolve from cloud forest and exuberantly coloured flowers to high Andean puna covered with clumpy ichu grass.

Approaching Minas Victoria, we started to see brightly glinting stones lying scattered all around the path, confirming high concentrations of minerals and metals in the ground. We arrived breathlessly at the pass at 4,500 metres, from where we gained a superb view over a range of icy summits dominated by the huge bulk of Salcantay. We rested at the pass to regain our breath before we cautiously entered the cramped, darkened entrance to one of the many abandoned shafts of disused mines, in which workers hacked out silver until the 1960s.

Starting the descent from the pass, we could see way below us our goal for the day: the ancient village of Yanama. Perched picturesquely on the edge of a canyon, Yanama lies in the shadow of the magnificent 6,000-metre Pumasillo (whose towering rock spires resemble the upturned claws of a puma, hence its name), and is surrounded by a crooked patchwork of green fields.

Dwarfed by lofty ice peaks, we descended a precipitous trail carved into the cliff wall towards the canyon below. We emerged once again into cloud forest as we approached Yanama village. All around us, the glacial summits of Pumasillo, Choquetacarpo and other nearby peaks glowed in the afternoon sun. We set up camp in the village schoolyard, which enjoys an impressive setting overlooking the settlement and valley.

After another peaceful night, we awoke and breakfasted next morning to gradually increasing levels of chatter as curious but friendly children began arriving for school. During morning assembly outside the red and cream-painted school building, children practised singing the national anthem in both Spanish and Quechua.

Yanama lies at the crossroads of several important Inca roads that once linked the empire. We set off along the remains of another of these paths that had been hacked through thick tropical vegetation. Our winding trail passed several clusters of old houses that date back to the days when the mines above us thrived. We passed small isolated farms where people still live much as did their Inca ancestors, planting potatoes with digging sticks and leading a harsh, high mountain existence made tolerable only by the relief of (plenty of) coca leaves and chicha.

Farming methods in the high Andes haven't evolved much since the days of the Incas. The native Indians have long loved to farm. Even those skilled as artists or silversmiths would happily drop their crafts to plant or harvest their fields. Peasants worked the land using primitive hand tools, driving long pointed poles into the ground, and levering them up to break the soil.

Farming in the Andes has traditionally been a communal activity in which teams of men broke the soil while women followed behind turning over the soil and planting seeds. The whole group would sing and chant to lighten the work. Harvesting was a similarly communal affair, with great celebrations erupting once the harvest was in.

Attracted by the bait of free-flowing quantities of chicha, friends and even entire settlements would come to help work a field, this communal farming often being regarded as cheerful recreation rather than hard labour.

August was the time for seeding the year's crops. The Sapa Inca officially began the farming year by symbolically tilling the soil in a sacred field in Cuzco using a gold-tipped plough.

The Incas offered prayers to the deities of the earth and sky to beseech their continued protection, and to ask for bountiful harvests and the continued flowing of their rivers for irrigation. Like Andean campesinos before and after them, Inca farmers revered Pachamama, Mother Earth. They placed a long stone in the middle of their fields where, after finishing sowing, they solemnly slit the throats of a great many llamas and guinea pigs. They burnt these as sacrifices to Pachamama, the Frost, the Wind and the Sun, and sprinkled generous quantities of chicha over the soil.

That afternoon, the landscape once again changed markedly. Agricultural fields, dry savannah, thick cloud forest, waterfalls and rich llama pastures again started to yield to stark, rocky, ice-covered peaks and glinting glaciers. In the late afternoon, we emerged from a hanging valley below two of its glaciers into the shadow of Pumasillo itself, where we set up camp for the night at the foot of the intimidating, claw-shaped ice massif.

We left camp early next morning and continued along a ridge with magnificent Andean ranges extending north. In the distance, we could see the mountains of the Apurimac canyon. We climbed steeply for several hours and entered a broad glacier-sculpted valley overhung by towering granite pinnacles – a little reminiscent of the Italian Dolomites.

Climbing a section of well-preserved, stone-paved Inca trail, we reached the chilly summit of the Choquetacarpo Pass at 4,720 metres. This pass marks the watershed between the Apurimac and Urubamba, the two great rivers of the Inca heartland.

We set up camp at a site called Colamachay ("Cave of the Drawings"), on a small plain at the edge of cloud forest. We were just an insignificant speck among huge granite boulders, dwarfed beneath the massive fluted glaciers of Pumasillo's snow-burdened rock claws. I marvelled at the latest of a series of magnificent campsites as I helped Omar with the more prosaic task of preparing supper.

We spent a long time breakfasting the next morning, mostly due to my reluctance to move. I must have drunk five cups of coffee and hot chocolate as I took time gawping at the superb mountain views all around our camp.

After breakfast, Omar and I waved goodbye to Glicerio, who this morning began the long journey back to Cachora with his mules. As I drank the remnants of my last cup of coffee, I could hear Glicerio's hisses and occasional slaps on his mules' quarters echoing around the mountains, before all became still and silent again.

When Omar and I finally loaded our packs and hit the trail, it was pleasantly downhill all the way, as we descended steadily towards Omar's home village of Huancacalle. By early afternoon, the old trail was becoming more distinct and we started to see small groups of farmers working fields of potatoes and corn, and increasing numbers of horses grazing on lush meadows. By the middle of the afternoon, as we approached the outskirts of Huancacalle, chickens and pigs had become the predominant trail users.

CHAPTER TWENTY

VITCOS AND THE SUN FESTIVAL OF INTI RAYMI

The sun was setting by the time we arrived at Huancacalle and the Hostal Sixpac Manco, home of Omar's family – the famous Cobos explorers and guides of the Vilcabamba forests. The three senior brothers of the family – Don Flavio, Don Juvenal and Don Vicente – together ran the hostel. Their father had guided the legendary American explorer Hiram Bingham (discoverer of several major Inca sites, including Machu Picchu) through the darkened forests to a site called Espiritu Pampa (Plain of Ghosts). There, buried beneath centuries of forest growth, lay the ruins of Vilcabamba the Old – the final stronghold of the Incas.

The Cobos clan was out in force today. Don Flavio and Don Juvenal were directing not only preparations for our journey into Vilcabamba but also, far more importantly, the Inti Raymi celebrations that would take place tomorrow at nearby Rosaspata.

For centuries, the winter solstice has marked a critical reference point on the southern hemisphere calendar for planting and harvesting. Since pre-Hispanic times, Inti Raymi has been the greatest Andean festival to pay homage to the sun at the winter solstice. The re-enacted Inti Raymi festival at Rosaspata maintains the tradition and evokes the splendid Inca ritual (Rosaspata is believed to be the site of Vitcos, Manco Inca's post-Conquest capital).

The hostel's few rooms were crammed full of people visiting Huancacalle for tomorrow's festival. A light-hearted carnival atmosphere was already pervading the grassy courtyard behind the single row of simple accommodation with its covered veranda. A family from the nearby town of Quillabamba occupied the next-door room. We chatted to the friendly parents whilst their three children played on the veranda.

Inside the Cobos kitchen, a fleshy mound of skinned guinea pigs lay piled up in a large bowl and a gutted piglet occupied an even larger container, both in preparation for tomorrow when they would be served from the family's food stall at the festival. With all the contagious excitement and the anticipation of both the festival and our journey into Vilcabamba, I was almost – but not quite – too excited to eat supper.

The morning of Inti Raymi dawned bright and sunny, although Huancacalle had been humming with bustle since long before sunrise. Omar and I set off early and followed many villagers and visitors as they headed up the hill towards Rosaspata for the festival. We passed peaceful fields and gently sloping terraces. Densely forested valley sides surrounded a cascading stream. Well fed horses and cows with shiny, healthy coats grazed contentedly throughout the tranquil pastoral scene.

Leaving the main path, I followed Omar on a detour to a lonely pasture where stands one of the holiest shrines in Inca Vilcabamba – Yurac-rumi or the White Rock. This huge outcrop of white granite measures some 16 metres long, 9 metres wide and 8 metres high. Its surfaces are covered in complex and enigmatic Inca carvings, flights of steps, seats and square projections.

The Incas carved a channel on the flattened top of the rock. Various scholars have connected the channel with diverse theories about this being a run-off conduit for offerings of chicha or the blood of sacrificial llamas. Some believe that the channel might even have been used to direct the urine of the Inca or his princesses over the heads of people below, although there has been little consensus about who was doing the urinating or who was being urinated on.

Facing the front of the rock was once a swamp and pool of dark water (now silted up), which reflected the white surface of the rock, and in whose mirror surface Inca priests used to invoke images of demons.

The Incas venerated the devil, more in fear of the consequences of not so doing, rather than because they regarded him as a deity. Inca priests summoned the devil by fire as a method of divination in grave matters, such as when they suspected uprisings in distant provinces or plots against the Inca. They always accompanied this summoning of spirits with great sacrifices of children, llamas, gold, silver and other valuable items. The children were buried alive and the other sacrifices were burned.

The White Rock is nowadays dark due to a covering of lichen. Surrounding the rock lie the ruins of tumbled walls and a flowing spring. Called Yurac-rumi in early colonial times, the rock was discovered by Hiram Bingham at this site that is nowadays called Ñusta Ispanan (meaning the "Place Where the Princess Urinates"). A 17th century report had described the existence of a great rock rising above a spring of water, surrounded by the ruins of a Sun temple, not far from Vitcos, where Manco had established his first post-Conquest capital after abandoning Ollantaytambo. Bingham's discovery of this rock clinched the case for the ruins of Rosaspata being those of Manco's Vitcos.

Leaving behind the mysterious White Rock, we descended some broad, gently sloping terraces that eventually rejoined the path to Rosaspata. From far off, we could see the remains of the Vitcos ruins perched on a low hill.

Although Vitcos was difficult to reach from Cuzco, the city's position was neither remote enough nor sufficiently defendable. The Spanish captured Vitcos three times during its occupation by the Vilcabamba Incas. Gazing up at its isolated but highly visible position, and the moderate surrounding slopes, it wasn't difficult to understand why.

Entering the Rosaspata site, we passed a string of food stalls where countless guinea pigs were being prepared, skewered and grilled over crackling open fires. Smoke rose from a line of barbecues and the air was thick with the aroma of roasting meat. We found the Cobos stall, where we waved to several family members frantically finishing preparations for the forthcoming feast.

Reaching the main plaza, we found a spot shaded from the fierce sun by a remnant wall of Manco's city. It was in this square that Manco Inca is believed to have been stabbed to death by his Spanish guests during a game of quoits.

We waited for the Inti Raymi festivities to commence. Endless speeches of introduction and thanks by the event organisers provided me with an opportunity to examine our surroundings. Rising all around us were angular peaks covered in thick cloud forest. I asked Omar how long it might take to climb to the nearest of these summits. "Completamente imposible!" came the unequivocal reply.

Beyond the nearby wooded peaks soared the snow-covered rock towers of Pumasillo, whose upturned puma claws form we had passed beneath during our descent to Huancacalle.

When the Inti Raymi ceremony finally commenced, first to enter the parade ground were the ñustas (virgin princesses). These young girls wore striped dark red and purple dresses and expansive headdresses made of fine textile that reached down to their backs. Each carried a small ceremonial offering in a bowl.

Next ran on battle-dressed armies from the four suyos (quarters) of the empire. Each soldier was clad in a knee-length tunic of dark red or vibrant yellow and a gold diadem, and wielded a club or hand axe. Watching the displays of the native armies reminded me that notwithstanding their glittering achievements in so many areas, the Incas were militarily still firmly lodged in the Bronze Age, fighting with clubs, axes and spears. Despite their overwhelming numerical advantage, the Incas had little chance of resisting the guns, cannons, horses and medieval warfare technology brought to the battlefield by the Conquistadores.

Next to come running in were the Inca messengers or chasquis. Running chasquis provided the main means of communication around the Inca empire, relaying information and objects at high speed over vast distances (although one of today's chasquis didn't look as if he could run much further than onto and off the parade ground). The ñustas then prepared a path with sprinkled flowers, over which the Inca was borne into the plaza aboard the royal litter.

The Inca invoked Pachamama (Mother Earth) and issued various commands to his governors and people. The ceremony then called for the sacrifice of two llamas, one black and one white. The llamas' entrails and burning fat were handed to a pair of high priests. The first examined the intestines to predict what sort of year lay ahead. The second made his predictions based on the nature of the smoke that wafted up from the burning fat. The priests' predictions were then interpreted by Villac Umu, the Lord High Priest, who bore the news to the Inca. Chicha was then offered to the Inca, who drank from a ceremonial goblet and issued various further commands to his people.

Taking a break from the Inti Raymi festivities, I retreated to the Cobos footstall, where I had earlier promised I would eat my first cuy (roasted guinea pig). Having owned two guinea pigs as pets, I was steeling myself for a challenging transition from regarding the cuddly rodents as pets to now a barbecued delicacy. I had earlier seen a headless cuy cut in half along its spine, which hadn't looked too off-putting. To my horror, however, mine was carved in half at the waist, and I was handed the chest and head section, complete with eyes that were still staring at me!

As I pondered how best to tackle this meal, a pair of health inspectors suddenly turned up at the Cobos stall. They asked several abrupt questions and demanded to examine various utensils and some of the prepared food. Might this inspection provide an unexpected last-minute reprieve from the cuy? Sadly not, as the Cobos stall received a clean bill of health.

I struggled but was unable to finish my half cuy. I had expected the meat to taste a little like duck, perhaps with slightly more of a gamey flavour. The reality was a much stronger taste – more like gamey offal – that I was totally unprepared for. I munched and crunched on as much guinea pig as I could, but there always remained much more meat on the bones than I had managed to consume. Looking around me, other diners had cleaned up every last morsel of cuy, leaving just clean skeletons on their plates. I like to think that I am an eclectic eater, but a guinea pig portion complete with head and eyes was perhaps asking too much for a first-time experience of this dish.

I had been told that the piglet I had seen being prepared in the Cobos kitchen the previous evening was going to be roasted and served as lechón, one of my favourite Andean dishes. I was very much looking forward to diluting the taste of the cuy with that of the lechón. To my continued culinary disappointment, however, I learned that the Cobos's swine had been burnt in the communal oven and couldn't be served at all.

The obvious solution to the lingering taste of cuy then struck me: copious amounts of chicha. However, to my even greater horror, there was no chicha to be found in the whole of Rosaspata. I searched all of the stalls but couldn't find the royal drink of the Incas anywhere in the former capital of the Incas during the re-enactment of the most important Sun festival of the Incas! I had to make do instead with a large bag of limas (yellow-coloured citrus fruit, similar to oranges, but with a distinct aromatic flavour).

After the unexpectedly challenging lunch, Omar and I returned to the plaza to watch demonstrations of various regional dances, and take a closer look at the Vitcos ruins. Omar explained that these ruins have largely been reconstructed during the last few years over original Inca foundations and low walls. They are believed to give a good impression of how Manco's palace might have been laid out. As befitting a ceremony celebrating the sun, bright sunshine shone all day.

As the sun started to set, I headed back to Huancacalle to resume my search for chicha. To my dismay, there was none to be found in the whole of the village and I returned dispirited to the hostel.

Several more members of the Cobos clan had arrived at the hostel during the day, including Doña Christina (a cousin of Don Flavio), who was today celebrating her 72nd birthday. Chicha might have been the royal drink of the Incas but birthday celebrations in this part of the world call for beer – and lots of it. A small family gathering, including Don Flavio and Doña Christina, sat around a table in the courtyard, on which already clustered a large number of beer bottles. They invited me to join them, at which point more bottles were immediately produced.

In true Andean style, this was not an occasion for non-drinkers. Every time one of the party took a drink, which was frequently, they would raise their glass with a flourish and a communal "Salud!" to which everyone else was invited to clink glasses and of course take a drink too. In a jovial, though not drunken, group of eight, it didn't take many cries of "Salud!" before yet more bottles were called for. In this manner, afternoon turned to evening and the reality of beer firmly replaced all dreams of chicha.

An inner chill ran through me after all the beer and I once again sought the warmth of the Cobos kitchen. Dinner was being prepared over the wood stove: fried potatoes and delicious savoury pancakes served on a fried egg base. The scorched piglet carcass once again lay forlornly in its bucket, now covered by a shroud. As I huddled over the fire, I received several pre-dinner potato snacks straight from the pan as I finally warmed up enough to rejoin the others outside.

We enjoyed a final dinner on the Cobos veranda with the gregarious family from Quillabamba, after which we turned our thoughts to preparing for the following morning and the start of our journey through the darkened forests to Espiritu Pampa (Plain of Ghosts), the site of Vilcabamba the Old.

I was honoured to learn that Don Juvenal, one of the senior brothers, would accompany us on our Vilcabamba expedition. From the next Cobos generation, Omar's parents Leoncio and Agueda would also accompany us, Leoncio as an arriero and Agueda as our cook. Omar would continue to guide, working under the experienced direction of Don Juvenal. Completing our team would be Juan Bautista, another arriero from Huancacalle, and a large number of horses and mules.

CHAPTER TWENTY-ONE

PLAIN OF GHOSTS

The next morning dawned leisurely with little hint that we were about to set off on a major expedition. Omar and I breakfasted on the sunny veranda and said our goodbyes to our charming friends from Quillabamba. Waving them off as they drove away cheerfully in their jeep, I wondered where the rest of our team had got to. After the festivities of yesterday, Huancacalle had this morning been restored to peace and calm. Nobody seemed to be around.

Don Juvenal and Leoncio eventually arrived outside the hostel leading a large team of horses and a couple of mules. After brief discussions to determine what would be carried by which animals, the arrieros loaded our mountain of equipment and supplies surprisingly quickly, helped by Agueda and Juan Bautista, who had by then appeared out of nearby buildings.

With little ceremony, we were on our way climbing up a narrow track through a deep valley carved by a boisterous river. Parched cornfields covered the steep valley sides. We rode past isolated houses where we were greeted by snorting pigs and barking dogs. We exchanged greetings with occasional friendly campesinos. Riding at the head of our group, Leoncio pointed out various medicinal plants. Achankara contains a lemon-flavoured liquid that natives use for refreshment when they don't have any water. Locals use muña plants in tea (just as Paulino had shown me in Apolobamba) and rub its leaves to release an invigorating fragrance.

Halfway up the opposite side of the valley, another Inca trail (leading to Rosaspata and an impressive, recently discovered Inca ruin at Incahuasi) shadowed our progress. We passed several wooden crosses draped with white sashes, some of which, Leoncio explained, had been carved by Alex, one of Omar's brothers whom we hadn't met.

At midday, we reached the settlement of Vilcabamba the New, a tiny village of adobe houses, many thatched, set around a ruined colonial church. In the heart of the village was a compact but bustling market. We took this last opportunity to stock up on fresh oranges and limas for the next few days of wilderness.

A short distance beyond the village, we paused in a hollow beside a tiny creek, where we ate a delicious lunch of asparagus soup, chicken salad and coca tea. Our horses grazed quietly all around, mingling happily with the horses of local people.

After lunch, we climbed to the relatively tame Colpacasa Pass at 3,000 metres, marked by a strategically placed usno lookout platform that commands sweeping views over all sides of the pass. Lying beyond the head of the Vilcabamba River, Colpacasa marks the final pass before the jungle. It is also Pachacuti's "Salty Pass", which the great conquering Inca traversed on his first mission to subjugate the tribes of Vilcabamba.

Those all-vanquishing Incas could surely never have imagined that within less than a century of those first victorious expeditions, the remnants of their empire would once again summit the Salty Pass, except this time in full retreat fleeing from a force of even more terrifyingly powerful Spanish invaders.

As we admired the view from the usno platform, a cooling mist streamed up from the valley below and the temperature plummeted. We hurriedly remounted our horses and started downwards towards the forest. Beyond the pass, we descended gently to the head of the Pampaconas River, through a green valley and eventually onto a narrow road carved out of bright red sandstone.

We traversed a section of trail along one side of which plunged horrendously steep drop-offs over an unprotected edge. This extreme geography was particularly disconcerting given we were still getting to know our new horses. Mine was a sweet-natured bay named Almico who, like most of the other local horses, had an incredibly soft coat, particularly on his forehead. Almico seemed sure-footed and intelligent enough, but had a frightening habit of veering towards the edge of the precipice on the already very narrow path. More often than was comfortable, my outside boot dangled over nothing but thin air and a hundred-metre drop down the cliff face. Several times, I felt certain we were about to go over the side. My only comfort was the thought that Almico probably didn't want to die either.

Sections of the original paved Inca road to Espiritu Pampa came into view at intervals, although this had unaccountably been mostly destroyed during the construction of the new road over which we were now travelling. This new road continued its course to Chalcha and Pampaconas but we dismounted and descended steeply down the face of the lush valley. A small stream descended noisily beside us as we passed many more healthy looking cattle and horses.

By late afternoon, we reached our campsite at 2,700 metres: a deserted, misty pasture at Chankara. All around us were moss-draped trees, lichen-covered rocks and high, forested mountains. Large stacks of wooden branches and logs lay scattered around the pasture and we soon built a huge fire inside the low walls of a ruined house. After an excellent supper, we retired to our tents and I drifted off to sleep to the sound of the rushing river and some horses munching enthusiastically around my tent.

A bitingly cold wind whipping through my tent accompanied by the dripping of light rain woke me in the middle of the night, after which I slept only briefly. As I tried to curl up inside my sleeping bag, I couldn't believe that I was so cold at such a relatively low altitude. By daybreak, I desperately needed the roaring fire that Don Juvenal had rekindled within the ruins of the house using hefty logs from the forest. The added warmth of a delicious sweet drink made from oats, milk, sugar and raisins, and some tasty cheese fried in wonton wrappers, helped control the shivering, but I remained very cold.

Having camped in a deep bowl, the sun appeared only belatedly over the soaring peaks that closed in all around us. It took an agonisingly long time for its rays (which we could see warming the wooded slopes high above us) to reach our camp. As we hurried across the pasture to meet the first solar rays inching towards our tents, it immediately became clear why the Incas were such sun worshippers. It is the most natural reaction in such bitter morning temperatures to build structures that face the rising sun and capture its first rays as soon as possible, and to pay homage to those blessed, first warming rays.

Just as we were basking in the warming sunlight, Don Juvenal explained that one of the horses – mine! – and a mule ally had escaped in the night. Juan Bautista, one of the arrieros, had discovered the escape attempt at around 4am and had set off in the dark to apprehend the offending animals.

We drank more coffee and warmed ourselves in the sun as we awaited news of the escapers. The morning sun was high in the clear blue sky by the time Juan Bautista was spotted in the distance returning with the two animals. He had caught up with them grazing by a bridge we had crossed in the middle of the previous afternoon.

Finally able to load up the cargo and get on our way, we continued beside the trout-filled river, crossing it several times by precarious looking, wobbly bridges – definitely branch rather than log bridges. At other times, we criss-crossed the rushing stream over stepping stones. Our river was joined by another, after which we crossed the larger combined waterway by at last a more secure bridge. We descended a bumpy rocky path into the dense forest, which provided pleasant cooling from the now fierce sun.

We rode through a wonderfully tranquil world of beautiful, verdant meadows set beneath thick cloud forest that soared high above us on all sides. All around were trees and rocks draped with mosses and lichen. Below us rushed the boulder-strewn river. We met only one other person all day.

We passed occasional moccomocco trees, the leaves of which local people use (by rubbing together and adding water) to treat bruising and injuries to both people and animals. Once again, all the grazing horses and cattle we saw had the shiniest and softest coats and looked in prime health.

As the day progressed, the forest became denser and denser – so dense that it obscured most of the view of our side of the valley. On the other side of the valley, we could barely make out any patches of grass or other ground features beneath the now thick carpet of trees that resembled a gigantic broccoli. This increasing forestation shouldn't have come as a surprise after I noticed that Omar was today brandishing his machete.

We rode and walked along a narrow, undulating and twisting path as it snaked around the mountainside, once again protected on one edge by alarmingly steep and life-threatening drop-offs. Leoncio explained that we were probably following the same route taken by the massive Spanish force sent through Vilcabamba in 1572 to end the Inca "problem" once and for all.

One of the Incas' favourite defensive tactics was to lure Spanish troops onto a narrow valley path such as this, and roll massive boulders onto them from above, either killing them immediately or sweeping them away to die in the valley or torrential river below. Once again, I pondered how easy it would be for Almico and me to stumble over the edge and plunge into the abyss, even without having massive boulders rolled onto us from above.

We passed small, gnarled trees dripping with moss, tight vegetation and creepers clinging to impossibly steep slopes. The dark undergrowth crawled with many snakes. The prevailing atmosphere was becoming shadowy, mysterious and sombre.

The valley sides were now so steep that many trees looked as if they were growing on top of each other, with some root balls appearing suspended in mid-air. We passed numerous tumbling waterfalls. Distance and the thick, muffling carpet of trees smothered the sound of the fast-flowing river way below us. A lone eagle soared above this homogenous world of tangled green.

We stopped for lunch at a tiny clearing beside the path. The spot was so cramped the horses had to graze amongst the trees and regularly tangled their lead ropes on branches and thorns.

Don Juvenal explained that high above us on the opposite side of the river lay hidden the silent ruins of the church of La Mesada at Huarancalla. Its Christian priest Friar Diego Ortiz suffered a gruesome death at the hands of the Incas – who blamed him for the death of Titu Cusi – in one of their final acts of defiance.

By late afternoon, we were nearing the village of Vista Alegre. Seemingly out of nowhere, two granadilla sellers suddenly appeared out of the gloom of the forest at the side of the path. Omar had earlier explained that Vista Alegre was renowned for its fruit. Without hesitation or any thought as to how I might carry them, I immediately bought ten granadillas without even dismounting. I struggled for the rest of the afternoon, trying to ride whilst clutching my precious bag of delicious fruit.

Standing motionless on the last bridge before Vista Alegre were a young girl and two even younger boys. The young girl carried a baby on her back. All the children seemed entranced by our presence; particularly mine, as if they had never before seen an idiot riding towards their village desperately juggling a bag of granadillas. After a lengthy period of being stared at, I waved at the children to come down from the bridge. They finally hurried down onto the path, barefoot and filthy. We exchanged greetings of "Hola" and shook hands before continuing on the trail towards their settlement.

Thatched wooden huts appearing at occasional clearings in the forest seemed to be the extent of the "village", although even such an amorphous settlement had its all-important football pitch, set on a plateau above the river and bordered by dense bushes and trees.

We set up camp beneath the far set of goalposts. As night fell, fireflies lit up the valley banks like magical Christmas lights. The clouds lifted and stars appeared in the sky. Almico and his accomplice mule were tonight tied up while the other animals grazed freely around the meadow.

We woke to another surprisingly chilly morning and another by now not surprisingly delicious breakfast of hot chocolate, pancakes and scrambled eggs with chopped sausages. All horses and mules were present and correct this morning after last night's tightened anti-escape precautions.

Exploring our surroundings as the day dawned, we discovered that the small tin shack we had passed to reach the football pitch was in fact the local school. The single schoolroom was furnished with crude benches; pieces of artwork were stuck up on the walls. At 8am, just as we were finishing breakfast and starting to pack away our camp, the pupils started arriving. With little warning, several games of football erupted all around us and we were suddenly kicking balls around our camp, with two of our tents marking an oversize goal.

Shortly afterwards, the young female teacher arrived. She explained that she had 23 pupils from the surrounding area. Classes at the school started relatively late at 8:30am as some pupils travelled long distances across the school's large catchment area to reach here. At 8:30am, the teacher duly blew her whistle. Football ended as abruptly as it had begun, and the children filed obediently into class. We paid a small contribution towards school funds and began loading up the horses and mules.

We continued following the narrow, undulating path beside the Rio Vista Alegre, through dense vegetation that shaded the bright sun. To our left, a high bank of trees climbed steeply to much more elevated ground than we could see. To our right, through occasional openings in the vegetation, we could glimpse ranges of high wooded peaks rising beyond ranges of high wooded peaks, each successive range paling into the distant haze.

Gigantic banks of trees on the opposite side of the river gave an indication of how high the trees must have towered above us. We encountered very colourful flowers, birds and large butterflies. We briefly sighted a Gallito de las Rocas (Cock of the Rocks), Peru's national bird.

At a rare opening in the forest, we dismounted and cautiously traversed a path across a steep, crumbling escarpment. The path was so narrow – constrained by a near-vertical wall on one side and an unprotected drop-off on the other – that we took it in turns to edge our way across. I wondered how the pack animals carrying their wide loads could possibly negotiate this safely. We soon found out that they couldn't.

Following close behind me, and just as we feared, disaster nearly struck one of our team of packhorses. The white (almost albino) horse – carrying my bags! – swayed into the wall and momentarily lost its balance as it "bounced" off. The horse lost its footing on the gravelled path and to our horror started to slip down the steep slope. The terrified animal frantically clutched for grip on the crumbly surface as it threw its head about wildly. It was only saved by the quick thinking of one of the arrieros, Juan Bautista, who grabbed its lead rope and helped haul it to safety. The horse was fortunately not hurt by the experience (physically or seemingly psychologically) and suffered only minor bruising, although this could so easily have ended in tragedy.

We encountered wooden shacks so isolated in the dense forest I wondered how much their owners knew of the world beyond the immediate woodland that engulfed them. Still shaken by the incident with the packhorse, we stopped for an early lunch at one such shack, which perched on a ledge commanding magnificent sweeping views down into the forested valley.

The family living in this forest outpost comprised a woman, her daughter and a young boy wearing shorts with the fly wide open. Several pigs lazed in the sun whilst inside the darkened hut, a number of tiny chicks and guinea pigs scuttled around the dirt floor. The animals here appeared to live in at least as much comfort as the owners: the pigs resided in tidy thatched huts and the hens showed their appreciation for their spacious accommodation by depositing several large eggs around the thick carpet of straw of the henhouse. Next to the family's hut stood a large wooden hand press used for producing cane sugar and milling maize.

To our amazed delight, just as we were preparing lunch, the woman emerged from the dark of her home carrying a kettle of chicha. Maybe she knew that travellers reaching her had to survive that scary embankment and that most would probably need a fortifying chicha or four. Taking shade from the burning midday sun under the thatched eaves of the hut, few drinks could have tasted more refreshing.

Revitalised by lunch and several glasses of chicha, we rode down a ridge on an undulating path through dense vegetation, to the peculiar sensation of rivers rushing by on both sides. Pausing briefly, I looked back up at our lunch spot peeking out of dense trees now quite some distance above us – a tiny speck in an overwhelmingly thick forest.

For much of the next few hours, I rode with my face pressed hard against Almico's neck, but still ended up getting regularly snagged by the tangled growth. Thorns repeatedly ripped off my hat and I banged my head several times against hard branches in an experience I can only describe as, literally, being dragged through a very prickly bush. Eventually reaching the river, we faced a difficult choice between a dangerous looking high log bridge and a series of challenging stepping-stones. I opted for, and just survived, the stones although some braver members of the party chose the wobbly high logs.

The forest was becoming denser and denser. We passed huge fern leaves and even huger palm leaves. We briefly glimpsed a monkey as it swung away through high branches, and startled a snake that hurriedly slithered into the darkened undergrowth. Omar assured me that this was a lucky sign. Given the increasing regularity of getting entangled in bush, having my hat pulled off by barbed thorns and bumping my head painfully against branches, I was glad we hadn't disturbed an unlucky omen.

Omar did his best to clear a path in front of us, energetically thwacking away at protruding and dangling branches and pushing larger stumps off the path into the abyss below. Through rare breaks in the trees, we glimpsed the soaring forest forging up rugged mountain peaks on the opposite side of the valley. Most trees were of similar height although occasionally, a single massive tree soared high above the surrounding canopy, greedily snatching at the sunlight.

For the rest of the day, our trail continued its beautiful course along an undulating stony track that squelched muddily every time we passed one of the numerous cascading waterfalls. Even in the thick of the forest, the narrow, twisting, undulating path had many steep drop-offs. If any of us had fallen down one of these banks, I wondered how (assuming we hadn't been killed) we would ever have managed to climb back up again without mountaineering equipment.

The fast running river was never far away. We dismounted to cross several bridges constructed of not-so-solid branches tied together with vines. These invariably rocked scarily each time somebody dared to take a step. We edged our way carefully beneath three enormous tree trunks that lay at a crazy angle across our path having fallen from above, and which looked ready to slide further at any moment.

At one river crossing, we let a heavily laden horse train pass by in the opposite direction, its horses audible from a long way away from the ringing bells of the lead animals. We had reached the tropical zone and now started to see coffee plants and towering, sturdy canes of bamboo. Before long, we started to see many banana trees.

The extensive range of vegetation offered by the Vilcabamba forests provided the Inca survivors with most of the plants they wanted – from potatoes, quinoa and maize on high hills to coca and tropical fruits in the low canyons. Less palatable to them were the lower altitudes than they had grown accustomed to, and Vilcabamba's long rainy season, violent electrical storms, biting flies, fierce Amazonian heat and tropical humidity.

With people and animals starting to tire, Leoncio announced that there was only about an hour to go to camp. My spirits revived and I celebrated with a couple of juicy granadillas. One and a half hours later, however, he announced that there was still half an hour to go! I had earlier been warned to double any time estimate I was given, but always thought we were moving fast enough that I would never need to do this in practice.

Almost an hour later, we trudged into the tiny settlement of Consevidayoc, a cluster of simple wooden shacks with sugar cane growing all around. We set up camp at the top of a quiet, inclined field, next to the old schoolhouse. The field sloped away gently past an uneven football pitch to the new schoolhouse, around which we let the animals graze.

The schoolteacher who arrived early next morning was another young woman, who shared the 47 pupils at the school with a second teacher. I wondered whether breakfast this morning would spontaneously erupt into another game of football. However, the pupils arriving this morning were mostly young girls, several clad in traditional costumes and charming, shy smiles.

We climbed out of Consevidayoc on a bright, red clay path, and still had to force our way through dense foliage that was now enlivened by bright purple hawincha flowers. We paused for a snack at a pre-Inca lookout platform before continuing down a flight of broad clay steps to the tiny village of Espiritu Pampa.

All around the village were lots of freely roaming chickens and turkeys, some with very young chicks in tow. A young boy herded a flock of surprisingly skinny sheep back to the village from the river. All the dwellings were wooden huts with thatched roofs. Several of our unruliest horses immediately started to peck at the roof thatches of one such hut. Grazing had admittedly been a little thin during the past couple of days.

Outside the white-painted community building, local growers had spread coffee beans over a large sheet to dry in the bright sun. Another man was harvesting coffee from a nearby bush.

We set up camp on a small pasture bounded by bushes in front of the community building. Free roaming poultry continued to waddle all around Espiritu Pampa and we continually had to shoo chickens and turkeys away from our cooking area. In a state of some excitement at where I was, I hurried a quick lunch and followed Omar to the ruins of Vilcabamba the Old, the final stronghold of the last Incas.

From the village, we walked up a narrow trail past small coffee plantations bounded by thick foliage and some brightly coloured flowers. We crossed an area of open countryside and emerged through more woodland into a clearing in the forest that was scattered with low stone walls and foundations.

We had reached the history-laden stage where the Incas played out the final scenes of their empire. By the time they retreated here for the last time, the Incas were a small, demoralised force, a pathetic shadow of their once great empire. Despite knowing that they were living on borrowed time, these last Inca survivors still tried determinedly to maintain their traditions, religion, festivals and architecture.

We walked around the ruins in a respectful hush, almost stupefied by a heavy atmosphere coursing with poignant memories and the palpable presence of Inca ghosts. We cautiously entered through monumental doorways into densely overgrown chambers carpeted with long thick grass, in which we knew slithered numerous snakes. As we started to find our bearings around the site, we could make out that buried beneath this undergrowth hid the ruins of many Inca buildings, temples and palaces, most completely covered with unruly vines and lush tropical growth, all beneath a towering canopy of trees.

Some researchers estimate that Espiritu Pampa might once have housed 10,000 people, with possibly more surviving in the surrounding valleys. Expeditions occasionally discover new areas of the settlement buried beneath the dense growth, but it is a painstaking if not impossible task to find let alone clear the ruins of Manco's final capital. The exuberant jungle growth reclaims all excavations within a couple of years, once more covering the ruins of the great city in thick foliage and returning the site to a heavily overgrown "Plain of Ghosts".

Where sections of ruins peek above areas of cleared forest, the pervading sense is one of overwhelming sadness. Massive trees tear through crumbling Inca stonework – such as a broad trunk growing through the remains of the Sun temple – much as the Conquistadores tore through the Inca empire.

Some stonework bears unmistakable Inca characteristics such as trapezoidal forms and wall niches, but even the Inca's palace and the great halls and plazas of the city would probably have been relatively humble, even at their finest. With limited manpower, Vilcabamba could afford only soldiers to protect the city and farmers to feed its citizens. This Inca state could spare few skilled artisans to produce elaborate masonry or metalworking.

When Spanish forces marched into Vilcabamba the Old on 24th June 1572, they found the city deserted. The Incas had fled into the jungle taking with them whatever they could carry and abandoning everything else. They had set light to the Sun temple and the remaining provisions in their food stores, and these fires were still smoking. As Manco had done in 1537 and 1539, the elusive Vilcabamba Incas had once again disappeared into the jungle ahead of their Spanish pursuers. This time, however, the determined Spanish would not give up the chase.

I tried as hard as I could to imagine, but couldn't, the terror these final Inca survivors must have felt as they realised the battle to defend their Vilcabamba stronghold was lost. How does one feel fleeing into a dark and inhospitable jungle ahead of a highly equipped enemy determined to eliminate you at all costs? Such questions filled our heads as we retraced our steps out of the silent ruins, although we had no answers.

Returning to the village of Espiritu Pampa, I edged my way past several of our horses grazing along the narrow path that led down to a shallow creek. It had been a long and dusty day. I stripped off and jumped in to bathe in the cool, refreshing water.

That night, as we sat in the darkened pasture eating supper, the clouds in the sky parted and we were able to spend several hours spotting constellations. Having seen so many waddling around the village, it didn't come as any surprise when the cockerels began their raucous crowing at 2:30am next morning. The deafening racket was almost immediately followed by the loud barking of an aggressive pack of dogs, possibly, like us, furious at having been disturbed from their slumber.

We left Espiritu Pampa along a descending path through more thick, darkened forest. Where occasional clearings were able to catch sunlight, people grew maize, bananas, oranges and papaya, their wooden huts isolated in the middle of luxuriant, densely packed plantations. We encountered scattered tiny settlements, where we exchanged enthusiastic greetings and handshakes with campesinos.

We stopped for lunch beside a small adobe house cum shop in a tiny hamlet called Pajonal, named after the abundant paja brava grass growing on the hills above. Parched from the dry heat, we bought several large bottles of drink (sadly, there was no chicha here). I bought some bottles of Coke for 6 Soles but only had a 10 Soles note. The lady who owned the shop had no change and instead gave me eight packets of biscuits, which we took several days to munch our way through.

As the afternoon sun started to dip towards the westerly mountains, we reached Chuanquiri, where we rode across a scrubby village square under many inquisitive stares. The setting star cast rich tones over the brickwork of the pink church and blue school. Misty, cloud-wrapped mountains rose above the square in a smothering backdrop.

Almost by obligation, the square doubles as a football pitch. Don Juvenal pointed to a cow tethered to one of the goalposts. Motioning a cutting movement across his throat, he explained that it would be slaughtered the next day in preparation for the regular weekend market.

Curiously, none of the team looked in any hurry to put up their tents or indeed make any camp preparations. This was strange since the crew was usually expert at setting up camp and starting to boil the kettle within minutes of arriving anywhere. I started to suspect they didn't want to spend the night here. I too didn't feel very comfortable camping in the heart of a village, albeit not a large one. My suspicions were strengthened when Don Juvenal urged me several times to ensure I placed all my belongings inside my tent. Our horses and mules were usually allowed to roam freely, but tonight all were tethered around a single tree – a discomfort they thankfully endured surprisingly well.

It indeed transpired that nobody wanted to stay here, particularly as there was little grazing for the horses and mules, which had already endured several days of inadequate nourishment. However, there was no transport out of Chuanquiri for Omar and me, who would return to Cuzco while the rest of the team trekked back to Huancacalle.

Omar spent the evening making phone calls to increasingly distant transport companies, but to no avail. Not only was there no transport that evening, but prospects also looked grim for the following morning. Omar had managed to ascertain that there was a truck in Chuanquiri that night, but it seemed that nobody in the village could locate the driver.

It was dark and still nobody had even begun to put up a tent. The Coboses were clearly concerned about transport and the lack of grazing. Through the gloom, I re-crossed the square in the direction of the "Hoy Chicha" sign I had inevitably been drawn to on arrival. Despite the encouraging notice, the shop was firmly closed and a local man informed me that it wouldn't be re-opening this evening. The nearby public bathroom was unlit and had no water. Matters were getting worse.

Another local man eventually directed me to a dingy eating house on the square that was seemingly run by a family of young children, and which had several dogs and chickens roaming freely amongst its few rickety wooden tables. I managed to buy two small bottles of chicha. I wanted to buy more but couldn't, as the shop had no more bottles in which to sell me more.

Resigned to spending the night here, we eventually set up our kitchen in one corner of the square, outside a house with an earthen floor. The house doubled as a small eating house judging by the menu board offering roast chicken ("Hoy pollo al horno") that leant against the bare stone wall inside. Tonight, however, there seemed to be more people visiting to watch television than to eat.

In any case, I much preferred our dining facilities. The Coboses had been planning some celebratory wine this evening, but, stuck in this dreary place and concerned about the horses and our belongings, we were not really in the mood.

With the expedition in danger of finishing on a low note, Venus and Jupiter lit up the night sky to help brighten our mood. Before long, the heavens once again filled with stars. Our spirits revived, we decided to open the wine after all. I threw in the chicha and a bottle of Talisker I had been saving. Agueda fried up more of her speciality cheese parcels in wonton wrappers and boiled up a thick vegetable broth. Seated along the wall of the television house, we devoured a delicious supper to the heady cocktail of chicha, Scotch whisky and a star-filled sky. From things looking as if they couldn't get much worse, things suddenly couldn't get much better, despite our transport headaches.

Later that night, Omar eventually tracked down the truck driver and we were delighted to pay him 120 Soles to drive us through Yumeni to the steamy riverside town of Kiteni, from where we could catch transport to Quillabamba and eventually back to Cuzco.

After an early morning of sad farewells to the friendly Cobos team and their fine horses and mules, Omar and I jumped onto the back of the open truck and drove through a forest of fruit trees. I was very tempted to grab handfuls of limas, granadillas and oranges as we weaved our bumpy path, but they sadly stayed just out of reach. Several machete-wielding campesinos with puffed out, coca-filled cheeks stared at us disturbingly. We passed the houses of friendlier campesinos in various stages of undress, who smiled and waved. Above the forest hovered several buzzards.

The lengthy open truck journey provided me with a chance to contemplate the long voyage that was now approaching its end, and those mesmerising Incas, whose rise and fall I had traced through the expedition.

Despite the violence, oppression, disease and cultural upheaval that followed the Conquest and ensuing centuries of colonial rule, the Incas left a legacy that retains a powerful influence over the people of the Andes, even five hundred years after their overthrow.

Andean people still follow time-honoured lifestyles, ensuring that many ancient traditions survive to this day. People are still linked by strong ties of kinship. They live with a deep respect for the land, the heavens and nature, and align their activities with the course of the stars and seasons. Pre-Hispanic beliefs, rituals and ceremonies survive, even though they are now often intertwined with the festivals of the Catholic Church. Campesinos look out for one another with a sense of mutual support. Communal ownership of resources remains common in agriculture and herding.

Travellers continue to lay stones at shrines on the summit of every mountain pass. Houses have their own domestic deities, often displayed in wall niches that are so evocative of Inca dwellings. Many campesinos hang dried llama foetuses from internal roof beams for good luck. People perform challas for good fortune by sprinkling chicha or coca leaves at sacred sites. Householders consecrate new buildings by sacrificing and burying llamas, alcohol, sweets and a whole range of other offerings in the foundations. Some even claim that live, albeit stupefied by alcohol, humans are sometimes also buried in the foundations of large constructions where generous helpings of good fortune are particularly important. Many Andean people won't sip a drink of alcohol until they have first sprinkled some drops onto the ground for Pachamama, Mother Earth.

In Peru, the national currency is the Sol (Spanish for Sun) and the national soft drink is Inca Kola.

Never mind Inca Kola, I thought. After several hours of being bumped around in the back of the dusty truck, I needed a proper drink.

Why is there never a partying Bolivian around when you need one?

GLOSSARY

Achachila	Protector spirits of revered ancestors that inhabit – and are – the high mountains (Aymara)
Adobe	Bricks made of mud and straw
Aguayo	Brightly striped cloths that indigenous women fold into carrying sacks they wear on their backs
Alpaca	Andean camelid prized for its wool
Altiplano	High plateau covering areas of Bolivia, Peru, Chile and Ecuador
Apacheta	Mountain pass; pile of stones (like a cairn) laid on the summit of a pass by travellers
Apu	Quechua equivalent of achachila
Arriero	Horse or mule handler
Aymara	Andean tribe that lives mostly around Lake Titicaca
Bofedales	Boggy marshland interspersed with small lakes and streams
Campesino	Country person / peasant
Cerro	Mountain
Challa	Ritual blessing, toasting or offering to the gods
Chasqui	Inca runner or messenger
Chicha	Maize beer
Cholita	Woman dressed in traditional Andean costume
Chuño	Frozen and dehydrated potato
Coca	Mildly narcotic leaf chewed as a stimulant, anaesthetic or medicine, and used in rituals

Condor	Large Andean vulture
Conquistador	16th century Spanish invader of Latin America
Cordillera	Mountain range
Huaca	Shrine within the Incas' sacred geography, comprising natural landscape features and manmade features
Ichu	Short, clumpy grass
Inca	Quechua-speaking tribe located around Cuzco; the empire; the emperor
Inti	Sun or the Sun God
Kallawaya	Medicine men and fortune-tellers from Curva in the Cordillera Apolobamba
Llama	Andean camelid generally used as a beast of burden
Mallku	Elected community leader
Mamacona	Chosen, cloistered women who attended the Inca and Inca gods
Muchacho	Boy or young man
Neblina	Mist or fog
Oca	A form of sweet potato
Pachamama	Mother Earth, creator of everything
Paja brava	Clumpy grass found at high altitude (longer than ichu)
Pampa	Plain
Pueblo	Town or village

Puma	American mountain lion
Puna	High, treeless savannah
Quechua	Andean tribe that developed from the Aymaras; language of the Incas and many modern Indians
Quinoa	Andean grain staple
Rio	River
Suyo	One of the four regions into which the Inca empire was divided
Tawantinsuyo	The four parts (suyos) together, representing the Inca empire
Titi	Andean feline found around Lake Titicaca
Totora	Reed found around Lake Titicaca
Uros	Early Andean tribes who developed floating reed islands
Vicuña	Small, nimble mammals related to the alpaca and llama, but with even more highly prized wool
Viracocha	Creator god
Voceador	(Usually) young boy or girl shouting a bus's route from its window

BIBLIOGRAPHY

Betanzos, Juan de: *Narrative of the Incas* (translated by Roland Hamilton and Dana Buchanan, University of Texas Press, 1996)

Cobo, Father Bernabe: *Inca Religion & Customs* (translated by Roland Hamilton, University of Texas Press, 1990)

D'Altroy, Terence N.: *The Incas* (Blackwell Publishing, 2002)

Frost, Peter: *Exploring Cusco* (Nuevas Imágenes, 1999)

Hemming, John: *The Conquest of the Incas* (Papermac, 1995)

Lee, Vincent R.: *Forgotten Vilcabamba* (Sixpac Manco Publications, 2000)

Stanish, Charles and Bauer, Brian S.: *Archaeological Research on the Islands of the Sun and Moon, Lake Titicaca, Bolivia: Final Results of the Proyecto Tiksi Kjarka* (Cotsen Institute of Archaeology, University of California, Los Angeles, Monograph 52, 2004)

Ministerio de Desarrollo Sostenible y Planificación Servicio Nacional de Áreas Protegidas: *Sisteme Nacional de Áreas Protegidas de Bolivia* (2001)

Araucaria: *Manejo Sostenible de la Vicuña en Apolobamba* (2004)

RECEIVE NEWS AND UPDATES

To receive news and updates from the Andes, advance notice of lectures, book events and other opportunities to meet the author, and information on future journeys and expeditions (including details of how you can get involved in expeditions and development projects), sign up at the following website:

www.Inca-Trails.org

Printed in the United Kingdom
by Lightning Source UK Ltd.
125022UK00002B/241/A